From the wintry peaks of Chamonix to the remote villages of the Gasteinertal Valley, the Alpine regions of Europe are all-season wonderlands offering outdoor adventure alongside hearty cuisine and intriguing characters. In *Alpine Cooking*, you'll follow food writer Meredith Erickson as she travels through Italy, Austria, Switzerland, and France—by car, on foot, and via funicular—collecting more than seventy-five recipes and countless stories from legendary mountain huts, chalets, *stubes*, and *refugios*.

On the menu is an eclectic mix of elegant, rustic dishes: Fondue Brioche, the very best Wiener Schnitzel, Herdsman Macaroni, Venison Ragout, Bread Soup with Chicory and Egg, and decadent strudels and confections (*Salzburger Nockerl*, anyone?). Infuse your own Pine Schnapps or prepare A Proper Bullshot, warm up with a bracing Bombardino, and peruse the detailed Alpine wine guide.

Packed with spectacular scenic and food photography, this gorgeous cookbook and travelogue also includes foldout maps, travel tips, profiles of beloved local personalities, and Meredith's coveted recommendations for bars and restaurants, places to stay, and can't-miss attractions. Whether you love to cook, hike, ski, or armchair travel, this romantic ode to life in the mountains is a perfect way to gratify your yearning for the peaks.

MEREDITH ERICKSON

Photographs by Christina Holmes
Maps by Samuel Bucheli

Alpine Cooking

**Recipes and Stories
from Europe's
Grand Mountaintops**

TEN SPEED PRESS
California | New York

CONTENTS

1 **Introduction**

15 ALPINE WORDS OF ADVICE

ITALY

21 **The Italian Alps and the Dolomites: An Overview**

32 BREAKFAST ON THE MOUNTAIN

35 **Muesli**
SAN LUIS, AVELENGO

36 **Meranerwürstel**
MERANO

41 **Sofie's Goulash with Speck Dumplings**
SOFIE HÜTTE, ORTISEI

45 **Radicchio Dumplings**
FICHTENHOF, CAURIA

46 **Smoked Char, Col Alt–Style**
RIFUGIO COL ALT, CORVARA

48 **Beet Gnocchi**
HOTEL & SPA ROSA ALPINA, SAN CASSIANO

50 PUMPKIN SEED OIL SUNDAE

52 **Wine Cave Fonduta**
CIASA SALARES, SAN CASSIANO

53 JAN CLEMENS'S WINE
RECOMMENDATIONS FOR FONDUTA

57 **Bread Soup with Chicory and Egg**
EL BRITE DE LARIETO, CORTINA D'AMPEZZO

60 **Spinach and Cheese Mezzaluna**
SESTO

64 **Beet and Poppy-Seed Casunziei**
LAITE, SAPPADA

65 **Bombardino**
LIVIGNO

66 **Honey Semifreddo with Bee Pollen**
HOTEL MONTEROSA, ALAGNA VALSESIA

71 **Gobbi in Broth**
CHALET IL CAPRICORNO, SAUZE D'OULX

75 **Vitello Tonnato**
TORINO

76 **Piedmontese-Style Agnolotti**
DEL CAMBIO, TORINO

80 **Torinese Bonèt**
HOTEL LA TORRE, SAUZE D'OULX

84 **Veal Carbonnade with Polenta**
AUBERGE DE LA MAISON, ENTRÈVES

87 **Valpelline Soup**
CHATEAU BRANLANT, COURMAYEUR

91 **Cogne-Style Soup**
LOU RESSIGNON, COGNE

92 **Ditalini with Fava Beans**
BELLEVUE HOTEL & SPA, COGNE

95 **Aosta Preserves Trolley**
LES NEIGES D'ANTAN, CERVINIA

AUSTRIA

**101 The Austrian Alps:
An Overview**

107 VIENNA: THE PEAK OF
PASTRIES AND CAKE

108 Weisswurst, aka The Münchener
MUNICH, GERMANY, VIA TYROL

113 THE WURST CART

114 Huckleberry Dumplings
DÖLLERER, GOLLING

115 Tafelspitz
HOTEL SACHER, SALZBURG

118 Salzburger Nockerl
BÄRENWIRT TAVERN, SALZBURG

120 A NOTE ON ANDREAS DÖLLERER

122 Venison Ragout
VALERIEHAUS, SPORTGASTEIN

125 Pine Schnapps
KÖTSCHACH-MAUTHEN, CARINTHIA

126 Tyrolean Liver Salad
SIGWART'S TIROLER WEINSTUBEN, BRIXLEGG

129 Spring Rhubarb Cocktail
ALPBACH

133 THE ALMABTRIEB CATTLE
PROCESSION

135 Tyrolean Cake on a Spit
CAFÉ HACKER, RATTENBERG

**139 Hangover Soup with
Cheese Dumplings**
RESTERHÖHE BERGGASTHAUS & LODGE,
KITZBÜHEL ALPS

140 Spiced Cheese Spread
KITZBÜHEL

143 Sweet Bread Rolls with Jam
MAYRHOFEN

144 Wiener Schnitzel
GROSSGLOCKNER

145 THE SCHNITZEL PLAYBOOK

146 HOW TO CLARIFY BUTTER

148 Tyrolean Hash
WEISSES RÖSSL, INNSBRUCK

151 Quark Cake with Peaches
JAGDSCHLOSS, KÜHTAI

155 Poppy-Seed and Currant Roll
ICE Q, SÖLDEN

159 BOND IN THE ALPS

161 Kaiserschmarrn
GAMPE THAYA, SÖLDEN

166 Apricot Dumplings
ALMHOF SCHNEIDER, LECH

171 Cheese Spaetzle
ALTER GOLDENER BERG, LECH

175 Apple Strudel
KLÖSTERLE INN, ZUG

181 Mountain Juice: Alpine Wines

183 WHERE TO DRINK (GOOD) WINE
IN THE ALPS

189 MAIN ALPINE VARIETALS TO KNOW

190 PRODUCERS TO LOOK FOR

SWITZERLAND

195	**The Swiss Alps: An Overview**
196	**AUTOVERLAD!**
202	**THE SWISS ALPINE CHEESE HIT LIST**
204	**THE ALPINE EXPRESS**
207	**Fondue** NEUCHÂTEL
209	**HOT TIPS FOR FONDUE**
211	**Hot Chocolate with Alpine Herbs** LES DIABLERETS
212	**Veal Strips in Cream Sauce, Zürich-Style** ZÜRICH VIA BELLEVUE HOTEL, GSTAAD
215	**Salsify Soup** GSTAAD PALACE, GSTAAD
218	**GRAND HOTELS AND BASEMENT WORKSHOPS**
220	**Chamois Pie** FURKA PASS VIA CHESERY, GSTAAD
227	**Rosettes with Berries** CHESERY, GSTAAD
228	**Herdsman Macaroni** HOTEL ALPENLAND, LAUENEN
231	**Hazelnut Croissants** GÄSSLI-BECK, HABKERN
235	**Smoked Trout with Cabbage and Beet Tagliatelle** SALZANO, INTERLAKEN
239	**Pan-Fried Calf Liver** ZUM SEE, ZERMATT
240	**Raclette** CHÂTEAU DE VILLA, SIERRE
245	**A Proper Bullshot** ST. MORITZ TOBOGGANING CLUB, CRESTA RUN
246	**BISCHOFBERGER AND ALPINE ART**
248	**Vittorio's Paccheri** DA VITTORIO, ST. MORITZ
250	**Toggi-Schnitzel with Apple-Chive Slaw** GASTHAUS EBENALP, TOGGENBURG
253	**Rösti** BERGGASTHAUS AESCHER-WILDKIRCHLI, APPENZELLER
254	**Fitness Salad** WILDHAUS, ST. GALLEN
256	**Blue Trout** BERGGASTHAUS FORELLE AM SEEALPSEE
259	**Grape and Walnut Pizokel** HOTEL WYNEGG, KLOSTERS
261	**Ricola Ice Cream** ANDERMATT

FRANCE

267 **The French Alps: An Overview**

269 **THE FRENCH ALPINE CHEESE HIT LIST**

272 **ROUTE DES GRANDES ALPES**

274 **CHEESEMAKING IN THE ALPAGE DU MOUET**

276 **Abondance Salad**
LES CORNETTES,
LA CHAPELLE D'ABONDANCE

280 **Norwegian Omelet**
LES CORNETTES DE BISE, ABONDANCE

284 **Crayfish with Tarragon Mayonnaise**
KAMOURASKA, ANNECY

284 **OTHER SAVOIE TREATS**

287 **Cabbage Tart with Smoked Whitefish**
LE CLOS DES SENS, ANNECY-LE-VIEUX

291 **Cured Beef with Génépy**
GRENOBLE

292 **Tartiflette**
THÔNES

295 **Savoie Cake**
AVORIAZ

296 **Farçon Savoyard**
LES ÉCURIES DE CHARAMILLON, CHAMONIX

300 **Mont-Blanc Tart**
MONT-BLANC MASSIF

304 **Duck Magret with Pont-Neuf Polenta**
CHAMONIX

307 **Roussette-Poached Trout**
COURCHEVEL

308 **Fondue Brioche**
VAL D'ISÈRE

311 **Popcorn Bread**
LA BOUITTE, HAMEAU DE ST MARCEL,
SAINT-MARTIN-DE-BELLEVILLE

315 **Tomme Tartine**
CHALET FORESTIER DE ROCHEBRUNE,
MEGÈVE

317 **A LITTLE POETIC ALPINE SALAD**

318 **Savoie-Style Mushrooms**
FLUMET

319 **HOW DO YOU LIKE YOUR EGGS?**

321 **Chartreuse Soufflé**
CHARTREUSE MOUNTAINS,
VIA JEAN SULPICE, TALLOIRES

323 **Polka Dot Paris-Brest**
ALPE D'HUEZ

329 **Maps**

334 **Further Alpine Reading**

335 **Address Book**

338 **Acknowledgments**

340 **Index**

INTRODUCTION

I was told by a station agent that the ski from Plan Maison station in Cervinia, Italy, to the Riffelalp hamlet above Zermatt, Switzerland, would take "about two hours, if that." But what I should have paid attention to was the sign posted outside the lift ticket booth. "Weather conditions can change rapidly," it said. "Please be particularly careful in event of wind, rain, fog, hail, or snowfall."

And so, for the following hours as I made my way across the Italian border at an elevation of nearly 3,900 meters (13,000 feet), the winds increased, the sky turned black, and I couldn't see my ski poles in front of me. I felt I was in the Upside Down, with little ability to orient myself. As I inched along, I encountered few people, which eventually turned into no people. The last person I saw was the Klein Matterhorn lift operator, who told me he was shutting down the lifts due to wind and even if I wanted to go back, I couldn't.

I told myself to keep calm as I started the descent. What would normally take twenty minutes for an average skier like me took a lot longer, but I can't tell you the specifics because I was scared, but also angry. Angry at the weather, angry because of the lifts, but mostly angry at myself for doing this—all for the purpose of eating *Zürcher Geschnetzeltes* (see page 212).

Alpine Cooking will take you from the Olympic glory of Italy's Cortina d'Ampezzo, through the towering Dolomites to the northern Italian province of Alto Adige/South Tyrol, past Ötzi the Iceman's place of discovery in Tyrol, Austria, down the slopes of Zermatt, Switzerland, and over to Mont-Blanc, ending in the twenty-one hairpin turns of the Alpe d'Huez in France. This book took six years to research, write, and travel . . . more if you count the incubating stages when I was trying to wrap my head around how to capture the enormity of these Alpine mountains and the food served within, alongside, and atop them. After completing a handful of Alpine trips myself, I wanted to share the experiences with my family and friends, who were inspired by the stories—often about food—I brought back home to Montreal. I yearned to buy books, or even *a* book, that combined the narrative of my past Alpine experiences with actual how-to tips and on-the-ground knowledge. I wanted a book about *everything* Alpine: from the best *rifugios* (mountain huts) to kitsch mountain films (it's a genre!), Swiss folk art, mountain literature, hotels and the families who run them, history, and ghost stories. And, oh yes, recipes too. And maps. Lots of maps. Except that book didn't exist.

Sure, there are Frommer's and Lonely Planet and "just the facts" guidebooks. There are also haute cuisine cookbooks written by Alpine chefs. But that wasn't my speed nor my vision. So, I decided to write this book; partly because no one else had done it yet—fit all of this skiable feast under one roof—and partly because I couldn't resist the adventure of what lay ahead.

I remember early in my travels taking the chairlift in Alta Badia, Italy. As I ascended toward the church of La Crusc, with the alpenglow of the Dolomites behind it, I looked down, around, and behind me at the rifugios and huts all scattered in the snow like roasted chestnuts, and wondered what set one apart from another? Who served what? Could I ski to all of them? Were they open in the summer, and then could I *hike* to them? There was so much good eating in just one view.

I have skied and hiked mountains in Canada a few times, but rarely in the United States. The Alps are my first love, and they are all I *really* know. Upon seeing a photograph of my ski-day lunch, say, a *Tiroler Gröstl* (golden potato hash with local speck, and maybe cabbage and egg) with esoteric Alsatian bottles of wine sprouting out of the hills of snow behind me, my North American friends would comment about the lack of a Chef Boyardee facsimile served on a red plastic tray with a bag of Lay's and a soda. As they recalibrated their idea of what mountain lunch could be, I realized how much of a story there is to tell. And so, I started keeping a journal of the people (chefs, hoteliers, helicopter pilots, winemakers, cheesemakers) I met, the best things I ate, the cultural observations, and the mistakes I made. (So many mistakes.) In trying to see, but moreover, eat as much of the Alpine range (200,000 square kilometers/77,000 square miles) as I could, I sometimes overlooked a detail. It usually included overestimating what is physically possible to do in one day without *really* considering weather conditions; for example, skiing to a hotel over a country boundary with my sleepover bag (and my laptop—how do you think I wrote this?) on my back through a blizzard. (And yes, those *Zürcher Geschnetzeltes* were worth it.) Or underestimating the amount of time it would take to drive from place to place, not counting the multiple stops for anything that looked remotely delicious.

Even after so much Alpine traveling time, this book is still only an Alpine primer—a two-dimensional account designed to inspire you. I came back from the Alps with approximately 175 recipes stuffed in my mind and proverbial snowsuit. Of those, I whittled down this collection to more than 75 must-haves, either because they are valuable and unique additions to any arsenal, or because the story of them was intrinsic to my Alpine trip. On the foldout pages, you will also find four country maps identifying the mountain-hut locations that inspired the corresponding recipes of my Alpine tour. And I feel I've barely scratched the surface here; indeed, I can imagine traveling the rest of my life, writing books of this size, and I still wouldn't come close to capturing the magic of the mountains. Perhaps I'm just getting started.

I hope you cook from this book, sure, but the delicious and authentic recipes are just an excuse, really—a trail of little crumbs, and okay, fine, maybe some Reblochon too—to lure you into the mountains and to follow my journey, to encourage you to breathe in the mountain air. Many of these recipes are classics of mountain cuisine—dishes

WALKING THROUGH ITALY'S PARCO NATURALE DELL'ALTA VALSESIA

you'll find in almost every inn of an area. Others reflect the talent and individual creativity of chefs I've met along the way. Still others were created at home, away from the Alps, and dedicated to the regions that inspired them. But all are rooted firmly in the Alps.

·ᕽ·

As I reviewed these years of Alpine eating and traveling and attempted to capture my experiences, there were a few points that I returned to again and again.

The Alps are for everybody.

You may think of the Alps—Gstaad, Verbier, St. Moritz, Courmayeur— as all high-end glitz and glamour (and yes, you *can* sleep in high-thread-count sheets under feather-filled duvets). But I've slept in bunk beds, in "panic room"–style cells with padded floors, in hostels that sleep forty, in *pensions* (boarding houses), in family-run inns, in my car, and in other people's cars. This book is neither a guide to luxury nor to a backpacker's dream ski vacation. It's about how to eat well in the Alps, and how to eat great Alpine food at home.

Mountains are not permanent. They are alive.

Mountains are ever-changing. And that's the beauty of them. The creation of the Alps is often referred to in guidebooks as a "badly made lasagna that buckled in the cooking" (an especially apt metaphor for a cookbook). Around the time of the extinction of the dinosaurs, the Eurasian and African tectonic plates collided and the folding and compression began. The old seafloor around Africa was lifted up over the top of Europe and then twisted (over millions of years) like a giant tsunami across the continent. In the early 1900s and onward, scientists found fossils of sea creatures embedded in the limestone of the Pennine Alps. Another way to say this: The top of the Matterhorn is actually the bottom bed of the African seafloor.

Here, the proven theory of continental drift is exemplified by heights both literal and physical.

One apt location to actually *see* and *feel* this is Ticino's village of Lavertezzo, a rocky chasm of a valley where the Verzasca runs down from Alps thousands of miles in the north. Famously, it is very nearby where the Eurasian and African plates actually met. One afternoon while having a simple lunch on the rocky bank of Verzasca, I followed the river as far west as my eyes could see. I imagined the rupture fast-forwarded, ending with a little fish from the Tyrrhenian Sea, flip-flopping at the peak of the Matterhorn.

THE ALPINE ARCH

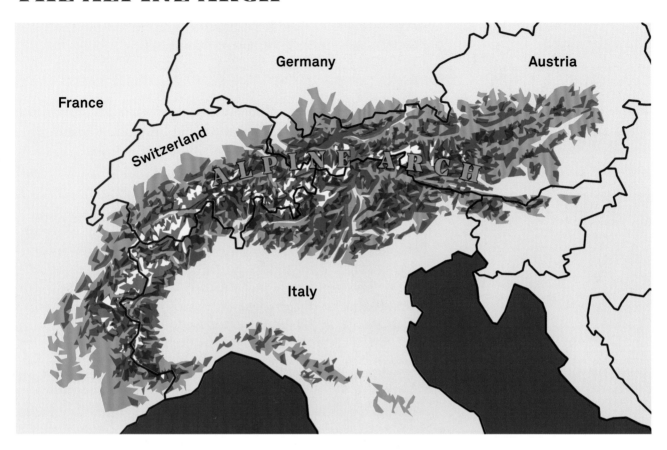

France

Germany

Austria

Switzerland

ALPINE ARCH

Italy

ALTITUDINAL ZONES

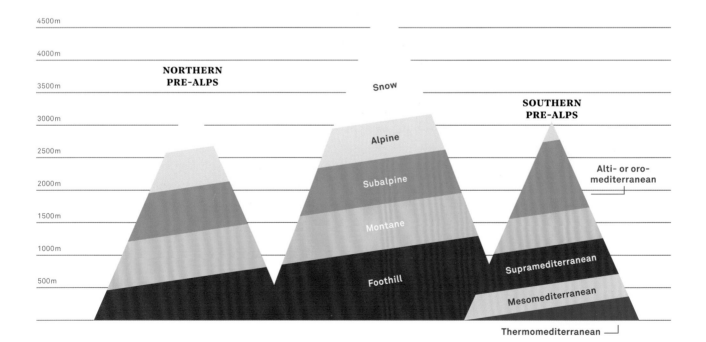

CENTRAL
ALPS

4500m

4000m

NORTHERN
PRE-ALPS

3500m

Snow

3000m

SOUTHERN
PRE-ALPS

2500m

Alpine

2000m

Subalpine

Alti- or oro-
mediterranean

1500m

Montane

1000m

Supramediterranean

500m

Foothill

Mesomediterranean

Thermomediterranean

These Alps have a beginning and an end.

In this book, I aim to cover the entire mountain region, also known as the "Alpine Arch" or "Alpine Crescent" (see facing page), that stretches from Grenoble, France, in the west up through the Savoie, across Switzerland and northern Italy, and as far east as the Austrian region of Carinthia. The Dolomites are considered part of the range but the Carnic and Julian Alps of the Friuli region in Italy, and Slovenia and Austria, are not; these are considered pre-Alps. Though Neuschwanstein Castle in Germany's Bavaria region marks a dramatic beginning to the Alps, the German mountain stake is small, and so I did not devote a full chapter to the German Alps.

My apologies to France and some of the world's best wine, but neither the Jura Alps nor the Haute-Alpes rolling down through Provence to Nice are included, as they also fall in the pre-Alps, or sub-Alps, category. Basically, they're smaller ripples from the spectacular clash of continents that generated the highest Alpine peaks. (I would have loved to be as inclusive as possible, but I had to keep this book to a size you could carry in your suitcase, rather than make it as large as the suitcase.)

No, it's not all about cheese!

Yes, of course, Alpine cuisine encompasses some incredible cheeses due to the common practice of transhumance, or moving cows up and down mountain pastures and creating some incredibly diverse dairy in the process. But that's only the tip of the Matterhorn. Alpine cooking is a showcase for ingenuity and grit in the face of remote living. Cooking in the mountains means you don't have access to much fresh produce during the winter, and you may need to make your provisions last a week between deliveries—while running an inn that serves 50 to 250 skiers and guests a day. Alpine culture is about survival, self-reliance, and independence. Even with a healthy tourism industry, no one is coming to shovel your snow or to help you out when your food delivery is delayed because the roads are snowed in.

Hard cheeses, canned goods, cured meats, and fresh dairy products— these are your resources. What some might regard as oppressive working conditions can actually work in your favor in the kitchen; from a creative perspective, limitations can lead to purity and clarity of thought (and this also goes for writing, painting, and everything else). The food in the Alps can be simple but it's not one-dimensional. The story of the Alps is one of isolation, language, and elevation. All three of these elements are obstacles to reaching the Alps, and yet all three also define the Alps. Tenacity is the trait that's shared between the person who attempts to climb the Eiger and the cook who builds a hut beside it. There's no easy route in either case.

Restaurants, hotels, and inns are almost entirely family-run, privately owned, and multigenerational.

In the following pages, you'll see that I use the words *custodian* or *maître de maison* to refer to the owner of an establishment. Though I would like to, I don't focus on individual chefs or cooks who are not owners, as they frequently hop from one place to the next and that would date this book quickly. The Alps are about family businesses passed down from generation to generation, and of cooks coming back to run the family farm after spending time in more cosmopolitan places. Skeptics may point to the ever-growing resort towns, places such as Verbier and Courchevel that have a more generic feel, and claim that authenticity in mountain culture is dying. But the Alps span far and wide and upward, and even in the most remote places there are interesting people creating wines, running restaurants, making cheeses and cured meats, making art, and producing events—more than one book could contain.

The food I've showcased here is traditional—not trendy. For the most part, these dishes have existed for hundreds of years and will continue to do so. Families such as the Schneiders (see page 168), the Döllerers

STUBE: A WOOD-PANELED DINING ROOM THAT SERVES AS THE HEARTH AND HEART OF A TYPICAL TYROLEAN/ SOUTH TYROLEAN HOME.

ALPINE COOKING

(see page 120), and the Trincazs (see page 268) all run independent, thriving family businesses. Why do they thrive? Because they adapt to the mountain. They work *with* it, in rhythm with the Alps, without pushing nature too hard. If you know the mountain, you know the mountain can push back. Piero Gros (see page 72), an Italian downhill skiing champion, knows a lot about that. As does Reinhold Messner (see page 35), the first person to climb all of the world's eight-thousanders (mountains higher than 8,000 meters [26,000 feet]) without bottled oxygen. I was so inspired by the wide breadth of Alpine legends—from cyclists to architects to Olympic climbers and beyond—that I included little snapshots of Alpine personalities throughout the book. With an avalanche of achievements among them, these folks represent only a light dusting of what's waiting for you in the mountains, if you choose to adventure.

A Note on the Recipes

In the Alps (and the rest of Europe), *pistes* (trails/ski runs) are classified by a color-coded system on all piste maps. Slopes marked blue are the easy runs, similar to the North American green circle; they are groomed and the slope (steepness level) is low. Those marked red are medium, or intermediate, difficulty, similar to the North American blue square; the slope gradient is about 20 percent steeper (on average) than an easy blue run. A black piste is an expert slope, similar to a black diamond or double black diamond in North America. In this spirit, I have given each recipe in the book a matching degree of difficulty.

For example, Bombardino (page 65), an egg and booze mixture, is a groomer of a recipe. The medium-level recipes are dishes such as fresh pasta or Tafelspitz (page 115) or a stew. This is the kind of recipe that might take you a couple of hours on cruise control. And then there are the black piste recipes. Stay alert! Whether due to a longer ingredient list, an involved technique, or a lengthy process (or all of the above; see Meranerwürstel, page 36), these recipes require you to (in the famous last words of a few ski instructors of mine): *Follow directions carefully and you'll be fine.* But seriously, you can trust me, I promise.

Oh, and unless otherwise stated, I rely on these rules for the recipes:

Butter is unsalted.

Cream is heavy.

Eggs are large.

Herbs are fresh.

Milk is whole.

Olive oil is mainly extra-virgin; unless I'm frying, in which case I use plain olive oil or grapeseed oil.

Stock is made from bones, mirepoix, and aromatics simmered in unsalted water, and should be used wherever possible. Broth is the store-bought low-sodium equivalent.

Sugar is granulated.

ALPINE WORDS OF ADVICE

In the course of my travels all over the Alps, I experienced many, many fails. With the following advice, you don't have to.

- Always rent a car with all-wheel or four-wheel drive. Don't let the rental-car desk clerk in Venice tell you "you'll be fine" with snow chains, because there is a good chance you won't be (see page 21).

- Each one of the countries featured in this book has an Alpine club: Club Alpino Italiano (CAI), Swiss Alpine Club (SAC), Austrian Alpine Club (AAC), and Fédération Française des Clubs Alpins et de Montagne (FFCAM). They are all great resources for local maps and mountain refuges and shelters.

- Copy the following link into your phone: www.piste-maps.co.uk. It's your access to all the piste maps of the best ski areas in the world. Chances are you're more protective of your phone than a folded-paper piste map from a hotel lobby.

- Most restaurants and hotels close for four to six weeks during the in-between seasons of fall and spring.

- www.refuges.info/nav is one of the first navigational sites where users take photos and add point-locations of rifugios throughout Italy, France, and Switzerland (sorry, no Austria). It's like the first-ever Reddit for Alpine addicts, or *House Hunters International* for extremists who want to live in subzero caves. You open the map and scroll through the highest peaks to find unguarded, guarded, or water points (meaning, empty shelters versus ones with a supervisor, and those with a working well for water) in the most remote locations. Even if you don't use this resource, it will give you hours of entertainment. No joke.

- Eat a schnitzel (see page 145) at almost every stop. It builds character.

- If at any point you would like help building an Alpine trip, please check out www.meredithuerickson.com.

ALPINE TERMINOLOGY

ENGLISH	GERMAN	FRENCH	ITALIAN
Alp (seasonal mountain pasture)	Alm	Alpage	Alpeggio
Mount	Berg, Stock	Mont	Monte
Mountain hut	Hütte	Refuge	Rifugio, Bàita
Pass	Pass, Joch	Col, Pas	Passo
Peak	Spitze	Pointe, Pic	Piz, Pizzo
Ridge	Grat	Crêt	Cresta
Summit	Gipfel	Sommet, Cime	Cima
Tower	Turm	Tour	Torre
Track, trail, run	Spur	Piste	Pista
Valley	Tal	Val	Valle, Val

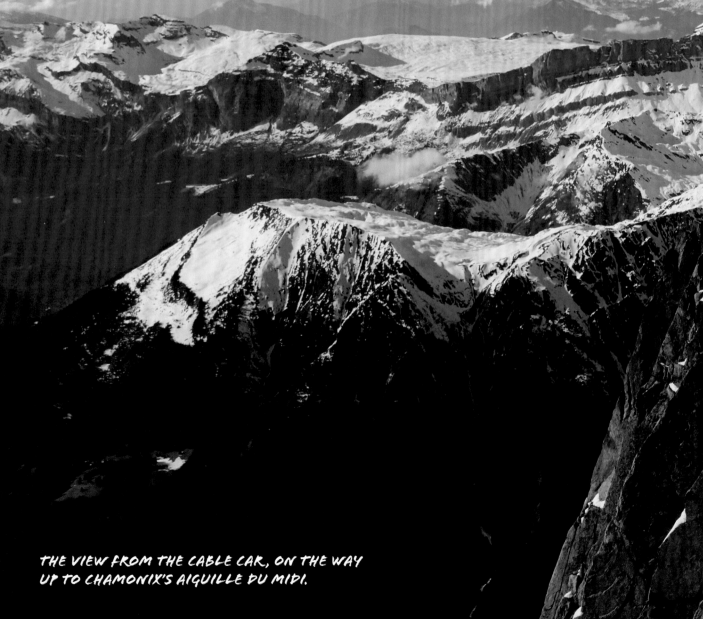

THE VIEW FROM THE CABLE CAR, ON THE WAY UP TO CHAMONIX'S AIGUILLE DU MIDI.

ITALY

The Italian Alps and the Dolomites: An Overview

The first time I ate dinner at El Brite near Cortina D'Ampezzo, it was a frigid January night. I grabbed my crinkled road map as I left my room at the Franceschi Park Hotel, confirming with the front desk that it would be about a fifteen-minute drive. "Yes, up through the forest," the receptionist said, waving her hands with that all-too-recognizable "far away" or "keep going" gesture.

Fast forward to twenty minutes later, my car was sliding uncontrollably backward on a narrow driveway, with what had seemed to be a manageable slope, lined tightly with larch trees many feet deep in snow. When I finally hit a snow bank, I was relieved and slowly took the keys out of the ignition. I opened the door, just barely, and squeezed out onto the ice. The moon was out and I could see the jagged peaks of Monte Cristallo and vaguely make out smoke rising from a chimney beyond the trees.

Just then, a glare of lights and a tractor came toward me. A tall Italian man with a mechanic's one-piece jumpsuit picked me up with one hand and put me in the passenger side of the tractor. Five minutes later, past a large barn, we arrived at the front door of the restaurant. He smiled and, in my broken Italian, I understood I was to leave the car, have a good meal, and take a taxi home; we would fix the car tomorrow. My rescuer was Mr. Gaspari, the owner of the farm and father of the chef. Kicking the snow off my boots, I went in and sat down alone next to a table of twelve friendly Romans.

I can't remember who originally recommended that I eat at El Brite; I found the name scribbled on a napkin in my ski pants from earlier in the trip. But I owe that person a big thank-you. The meal, homemade cheese (from the cows next door) served with a soft bun, brown bread soup with chicory and egg (see page 57), and *casunziei* (fresh stuffed pasta) with beets and poppy seeds (see page 64), has to be one of my best moments in all of the Alps. The place is small, authentic, and off the beaten path. It typifies the Alps; there will be well-to-do Milanese sporting furs at one table and local farmers from Tyrol at the next. Everyone is eating well, and after a day's lunch, it's off to the terrace to take in a bit of sun and an espresso.

Of all the Alpine countries, Italy offers the softest landing. The people are warm, the ski pistes seem to be managed better than anywhere else, and the food is, as you will see, delicious and varied.

There are two distinct areas of the Italian Alps—the west and the east—which share just a few similarities, such as stuffed *mezzaluna* (pasta shaped like half moons), incredible suntans, and a love of veal.

The western Alps encompass the regions of Aosta and Piedmont. Aosta sits between Piedmont and France and has historically been the connecting force between the Savoy Kingdom (the feudal territory of France, Switzerland, and northwest Italy) and the rest of Italy. In Italy's northwest corner is the Mont-Blanc massif, a benchmark point of orientation for the Alps, because if you look at a terrain map, or say,

BOLZANO

switch to "terrain" on Google, you will see that this area is where the Alpine Arch (see page 8) takes a sharp right turn coming up from France. It is here where three countries—France, Italy, and Switzerland—intersect and where, directly on the border of Aosta and the Valais region of Switzerland, some of the highest peaks in all of the Alps lay.

These are the Pennine Alps, the land of the four-thousanders (Alpine peaks of at least 4,000 meters, or more than 13,000 feet). Six of the ten highest mountains in the Alps, including the Monte Rosa massif, the Weisshorn, and Monte Cervino (aka the Matterhorn) all border Aosta, which has—for all the geographical reasons I've just pointed out—its own microclimate. It is the smallest region of Italy and, like the wine-growing region of Friuli–Venezia Giulia in the northeast Dolomites, Aosta's wine region is one of the most intriguing and least discovered (see "Mountain Juice: Alpine Wines," page 181). And just as Friuli is the gateway to the east, with Austria and Slovenia as its neighbors, Aosta is the gateway to France. It even has its own language. In the sixteenth century, the Savoy family ruled the region from Chambéry and decided to change the language from Latin to a neo–Latin French, or a Franco-Provençale patois. And so, for almost 300 years, this language was spoken in the Valais and Aosta, meaning that until 1861, when Italy was unified, Italian was considered a foreign language in Aosta. Imagine that!

Today, there are great things to be had in Aosta—the wine alone is one—and it feels, at least for the moment, like you can have them all to yourself. With the exception of two ski towns, Courmayeur and Cervinia, Aosta is sparsely populated and heavily agricultural. One of my favorite finds is the village of Cogne (population 1,500) wedged against the Gran Paradiso Park. This is a cross-country ski paradise, and a hiking nirvana as well. I stayed here a couple of times; the first occasion at Lou Ressignon, a fantastic roadside inn for hikers and climbers, and the second instance at Bellevue Hotel, a family-run beauty, which has one of the best wine lists in Italy. Aosta is the land of Fontina cheese, ergo, the land of eating soup with a fork. One of the specialties is a thick *Vapelenentse* soup made of Fontina, cabbage, and brown bread (see page 87).

And if Nebbiolo, truffles, and bagna cauda weren't enough, Piedmont also did well in the Alpine lottery with the altitudinal regions of Valsesia and Via Lattea. Valsesia is a group of small valleys along the Sesia River, ending in Alagna, the biggest of the valleys. Alagna is the end of the line, which is to say it's blocked to the north by the Pennine wall and Monte Rosa (just like Cervinia in Aosta butts up against the steep climb to Monte Cervino, the Matterhorn). You can't drive over these mountains, but you can (via cable-car routes) *ski* over them. The Monte Rosa ski system/resort connects Piedmont with Aosta, specifically at the top of the Pianalunga-Cimalegna at the Passo die Salati.

You can lunch at great heights here, in places such as Rifugio Gabiet, Rifugio Carestia (named after Alpine botanist Antonio Carestia), and, of course, at the highest rifugio in all of the Alps: Rifugio Margherita (named after Queen Margaret of Savoy who overnighted there in 1893). All of the huts serve Piedmontese cuisine, which is not Alpine per se;

MARKUS VALENTINI, OWNER OF RIFUGIO BIOCH HÜTTE.

ALPINE COOKING

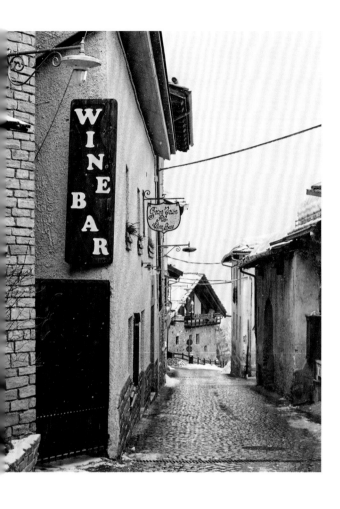

LUNCH ON THE TERRACE AT COL ALT

it's Alpine with the added bonus of Piedmont specialties such as truffles, fonduta, agnolotti, bolliti misti, bagna càuda, vitello tonnato, and Torinese chocolate with hazelnut. (For an easy day trip, hike into the Parco Alta Valsesia to the Rifugio Pastore for polenta and local charcuterie.)

The Lavazza blue skies of the Via Lattea ("the Milky Way") drew me in, in a way I was not expecting. This area of Piedmont encompasses the resort towns of Claviere, Sansicario, Sauze d'Oulx, Pragelato, and Sestriere along with the French town of Mongenèvre. Altogether, there are more than 400 kilometers (250 miles) of skiable pistes or hiking at altitudes of 1,600 meters (5,250 feet) and higher. I stayed in Sauze d'Oulx, holed up to write in the sweet Hotel Splendid, and became so obsessed with the weird and brutalist Hotel La Torre that I made a cake about it (see page 80). The food is alarmingly delicious in these parts. I especially loved the lamb chop at Ciao Pais (between pistes, right after the Clotes chairlift) and the *gobbi* (see page 71) at Il Capricorno. These towns collectively have a sense of faded glamour (which I like), and they're very accessible (their infrastructure was updated in advance of the 2006 Torino Winter Olympics).

The city of Torino is not really an Alpine town, but it is a gateway to the Alps, and a drive of about 1 hour and 15 minutes from Via Lattea. Torino is a culinary launching pad to the Piedmont, culturally rich, and one of my favorite cities, regardless of its proximity to the Alps. Home to the unification of Italy, Fiat, chocolate, vitello tonnato (see page 75), and northern Italian sophistication, Torino has the underground rumblings of Berlin and a mix of young chefs and wine bars alongside older famed cafes and established restaurants. Choosing one recipe for Torino was difficult, as the city's food culture is a (lengthy) book in itself. I chose Del Cambio's Agnolotti (page 76) as the recipe, and I suggest you start your first night in Torino with it as well. If not, wear your best jacket to dinner in your own dining room, open a fitting Nebbiolo, and start weighing your options on which soccer team to support: Juventus or Torino FC?

To reach the Eastern Italian Alps, you head northeast, past Milano, Verona, and even slightly past the Riva del Garda to Trentino, a winding valley that runs from the auto routes to mountain roads, including the Strada del Vino, the Alto Adige wine route. There are more than 60,000 square kilometers (some 38,000 square miles) of vineyards in Trentino and Alto Adige. It was there, while trying to find the best *canederli* (see page 45) that I experienced the summer version of the El Brite car fiasco.

After a visit to the lovable Foradori family, I was driving up, up on a road of challenging switchbacks to a small restaurant inn called Fichtenhof when one of the tires of my rental car actually blew up. The car abruptly stopped and then began rolling back down the very steep mountain road. After bringing the car to a safe stop (no snowbanks to assist this time), I was able to call an Italian mechanic and then spent the afternoon sampling the entire menu at Fichtenhof before driving on to Bolzano, the provincial capital. I should note that nearby is the Brenta Dolomites, and it's there that the busy yet beautiful ski town of Madonna di Campiglio sits. Though it's not connected to Dolomiti Superski (see page 30), there are still 150 kilometers (93 miles) of skiing in the winter, and hiking in the summer.

Bolzano and the town of Merano are 30 minutes from each other. Whereas Alto Adige is a cultural and culinary combination of Italy and Austria, these two towns have an added Mediterranean flavor. I split a summer between the two, eating lunch at Cavallino Bianco Weisses in Bolzano's center and snacking from the local wurst carts. Bolzano, or Bozen to native German speakers, is a student town with a lot of surrounding industry, including a favorite Alpine original, the wafer cookie *Loacker*. Cycling is the best way to get around—it's even possible in winter—and I loved the daily routine of espresso in the morning followed by a visit to Feinkost Egger, a speciality charcuterie shop (yes, they have *Meranerwürstel*), then a stroll through the market. As the sun set in the valley, I enjoyed a glass of local *Südtiroler Weissburgunder* at one of the local cheap and cheerful bars or at Banco 11, a very busy wine bar.

In Merano, there are palm trees, the climate is genteel, and the town is known for its healing waters. Both Ezra Pound and Franz Kafka spent time here, writing and bathing in the town spas, though I doubt it was at Palace Henri Chenot, the Swiss doctor's sanatorium of sorts for the cleanse-enthused. The teas created by Henri's wife, Dominique, are incredibly medicinal and comforting. Although I didn't bathe in the healing waters, I did take up a weeklong residence at nearby Hotel Bavaria, which was home to Austrian Empress Elizabeth's brother, Karl Theodor, himself a doctor, who because of lung disease was ordered to spend more time in Merano due to its warm microclimate. The Austrian connection to Empress Elizabeth (who was nicknamed Sissi) is found often in Alto Adige, and I even dined at the established Restaurant Sissi; it's a classic Viennese-style dining room with incredible fresh pasta *primi*, such as gnocchi with Fontina and truffles, made by its very Piedmontese chef, Andrea Fenoglio. On the flip side, there is the esoteric Mateo, a small restaurant, housed in an ancient pavilion over a waterfall, run by young chefs. Archaic and interesting, the menu is a result of whatever is fresh from the market each day. Oh, and after a couple of days in Merano, you'll be hooked on the local beer, Forst, a brewer that is proud of its Alpine roots with *stubes* (dining rooms) and signage throughout the area.

Moving west past the tiny village of Barbiano and toward Bressanone is where the wonder of the Dolomites begins. Named after French geologist Déodat de Dolomieu, who was the first to distinguish these mountains as a unique combination of rich magnesium combined with limestone, the Dolomites look different from any other mountain or rock form in the world. The sun reflects off the rocks, making them appear copper one minute and dark granite the next. I could look at these towers endlessly, and in fact, I've spent the last four winters there to do just that.

THE HORSE-DRAWN CARRIAGE WITH PULL-ROPES AT THE BOTTOM OF THE ARMENTAROLA PISTE IN THE DOLOMITES.

SCOTONI HÜTTE
IN ALTA BADIA

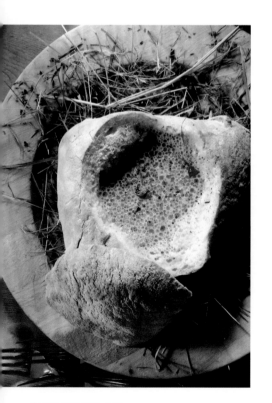

HAY SOUP AT
GOSTNER SCHWAIGE

Beyond their natural beauty, the Dolomites have a major advantage where food and skiing and hiking combine and that is the Dolomiti Superski region: 1,200 kilometers (745 miles) of slopes and twelve ski areas, each of which has one to two dozen rifugios at altitude. I'm talking about more than 120 huts at which to eat incredible food while still wearing your ski or hiking boots. That doesn't even consider the restaurants and hotels in the valleys. This area includes Cortina, Kronplatz, Alta Badia, Val Gardena, Alpe di Siusi, Carezza, Arraba/Marmolada, Passo Rolle, Valle Isarco, Civetta, and San Pellegrino.

And the food is *superlative.* At Gostner Schwaige in Alpe di Suisi, for example, Franz Mulser makes a much-celebrated hay soup in a bowl made of bread with edible flowers atop. The hay, herbs, and flowers are from the surrounding pasture. Franz trained under the Obauer brothers in Werfen (see snapshot, page 136) and flexes his technical cooking skills for dinner but keeps lunch more rustic and simple (and the room packed with hikers and skiers). Franz isn't an outlier; this level of culinary quality is the norm. There is smoked fish tartare with wine chilled in the snow at Rifugio Col Alt (see page 46), bread soup with chicory (see page 57) from my favorite restaurant adjacent to Cortina, gnocchi, Wine Cave Fonduta (page 52), and, of course, the best Bombardino (page 65).

The abundance of restaurants in the Dolomites is dizzying. It's as if each town used a slingshot to send their best cooks, nonnas, and bottles high up into the mountains, and when you arrive, they're all inside cooking and waiting for you.

I'll stop here and let the food in the coming pages speak for itself.
Ciao, Italia!

ALPINE COOKING

BREAKFAST ON THE MOUNTAIN

Waking up, opening the shutters to the first light, and seeing the Alps is a morning ritual of which I will never tire. If the weather is clear, I'm off to the mountains. If not, I'll head to the desk for writing, to the village to explore, or (worst/best case) to bed with newspapers to read and daydream about the scenery. Either way, I have a liaison with breakfast, and this is an appointment I never miss.

Breakfast in the mountains is plentiful and an expression of the local products. Similar to breakfast on a farm, we win here because of the proximity to local dairy and livestock. Across our Alpine countries, breakfast includes at least some of the following: fresh eggs, yogurt from an Alpine dairy, local (and usually rare) mountain cheeses (Edelweiss Camembert, Tyrolean grey cheese, Gruyère, Fontina, and so on), quark (the Alpine answer to sour cream), a homemade country loaf of brown bread or pumpernickel, a charcuterie plate of local smoked meats, smoked fish (especially in Alto Adige or Austria), fresh pastries (the best are, of course, in the Savoie region of France), and, if you're in Austria, little cakes that are a prelude to the afternoon kaffeeklatsch. If you're anywhere close to Bolzano, breakfast might even include Kohl juice, a brand of monovarietal apple juice from orchards at 1,000 meters (3,280 feet).

SAN LUIS LODGES IN AVELENGO

Muesli

EASY

SERVES 4

1 cup (90g) rolled oats

1 tablespoon sunflower seeds

1 tablespoon pumpkin seeds

1 tablespoon flax seeds

1 tablespoon sugar

⅓ cup (80ml) milk

½ cup (100g) plain yogurt,
plus more for serving

1 apple, grated

½ banana, sliced

2 strawberries, sliced

Peach or plum slices for serving

Fresh berries for serving

Chopped almonds for serving

Honey for serving

On the Alpine road, muesli is a constant. My two faves are from San Luis and Hotel & Spa Rosa Alpina, the latter a luxe hotel in the Dolomites that *knows* how to do breakfast. As Hugo Pizzinini, the owner of Rosa Alpina, likes to remind me, "Life's a mountain, not a beach."

In a large bowl, combine the oats, all the seeds, and the sugar, using your hands to mix. Add the milk, yogurt, apple, banana, and strawberries and stir well with a wooden spoon or spatula. Transfer to a small bowl (or a glass jar with a top) and cover. Refrigerate for at least 6 hours, or up to 3 days, to allow the oats to soak up the liquid.

When ready to serve, divide the oat mixture among four bowls. Top with a generous dollop of plain yogurt, peach slices, fresh berries, almonds, and a drizzle of honey, as desired.

TRAVEL HACK

One of the best-kept secrets for breakfast in Alto Adige is the Ottmanngut Merano, a gem of an inn. Owner Martin Kirchlechner and his team do breakfast in the Mediterranean style on the gentle slopes of the pre-Alps, which are covered in oleanders, orchards, cypress, and palms. It's a sophisticated and relaxed must-visit mountain hideaway. Another favorite (for break-fast and anyone thirsting for sanctuary and seclusion) is the San Luis Hotel in Avelengo, a 20-minute drive directly up the mountain from Merano (near the Merano 2000 ski resort).

Reinhold Messner is an international mountaineering legend. Born in South Tyrol, he spent his foundational years climbing all over the Dolomites. By the time he was in his early twenties, he was already considered one of the best climbers in Europe. Long an advocate of Alpine-style climbing (light and unassisted) in the Himalayas, at the age of thirty-four, alongside Peter Habeler, he was the first to ascend Mount Everest without using supplemental oxygen. He was also the first person to climb, without bottled oxygen, all fourteen eight-thousanders (peaks of at least 8,000 meters, or more than 26,000 feet) in the world. Since 1983, Messner has spent his summers at medieval Juval Castle at the entrance to Schnalstal Valley, which serves as one of the five venues for his epic Dolomites-wide Messner Mountain Museum project.

SNAPSHOT

Meranerwürstel

■■■ DIFFICULT

MAKES TWELVE 12-INCH
(30CM) SAUSAGES

YOU WILL NEED

Meat grinder with ¼-inch (6mm)
die and ⅛-inch (3mm) die
(preferably a KitchenAid stand
mixer with grinder attachment)

Mortar and pestle

Sausage stuffer

Grill or smoker

2 large handfuls apple wood chips

1 large handful hickory
wood chips

9-pound (4kg) bag charcoal
(without added lighter fluid)

One 12-foot (3.6m) length,
¾-inch (2cm) lamb casing

1⅛ pounds (500g) beef chuck,
cut into 1-inch (2.5cm) cubes

1⅛ pounds (500g) veal chuck,
cut into 1-inch (2.5cm) cubes

1 pound (450g) fatback, cut into
½-inch (12mm) cubes

1½ teaspoons freshly ground
white pepper

¾ teaspoon dried marjoram

¾ teaspoon mustard powder

1 teaspoon chili powder

1 teaspoon sweet paprika

1 teaspoon ground coriander

1 tablespoon chopped garlic

2 cups (230g) ice cubes, crushed,
plus more for keeping the mixer
bowl chilled

1½ tablespoons fine sea salt

2 teaspoons sugar

½ teaspoon curing salt #1

½ cup (55g) milk powder

This dish is inspired by the many sausage carts of Merano, which I frequented often during a monthlong stay there. While touring around on my bike, I would eat a Meranerwürstel around 11 a.m., accompanied by a local Forst beer. It's hot in Merano in the summer, sometimes 86°F (30°C) by noon, so this was a stabilizing routine for me: a quick sausage break after a morning of writing. I've combined my sausage knowledge (learned from working with Olympia Provisions in Portland, Oregon) with what I tasted at the cart to develop this recipe. Meranerwürstel are not that easy to source, but on the Corso della Libertà in Merano, Pur Südtirol, a fantastic marketplace, sells the region's best meats, cheeses, wine, and produce.

This sausage is equal parts veal and pork—a ratio that gives the final product a slightly lighter color than a frankfurter (which often has more beef than veal). The addition of marjoram also sets it apart, resulting in a more nuanced and sophisticated flavor than the frankfurters you might be used to. But franks and Meranerwürstel are both emulsions (like bologna), which is to say, they're airy, with a texture that's almost whipped. This is why they're great as a postbreakfast or prelunch snack. It's a hit of protein to keeps you going, with a bit of fat for satiety. In order to reach that peak (get it?) emulsion, the recipe requires two things: the smallest grinder die you can find (⅛ inch/3mm) and keeping the equipment as cold as possible throughout the process so the emulsion doesn't break (which would result in a greasy sausage). Meranerwürstel are typically grilled and served with a Kaiser roll, which is more of an optional accompaniment than a vehicle to hold the sausage. Eat with a knife and fork while browsing the pages of *Corriere delle Sera* or *Der Standard*.

Rinse out the casing by placing one end under the water tap and filling it with about ½ cup (120ml) water. Run this water through the casing by pulling up on the end that you filled, until water comes out the other side of the casing. It will come out a bit cloudy. This is totally normal, as you are removing salt from the inside of the casing. Place the rinsed casing in a bowl of clean warm water to soak.

Place all the parts of your meat grinder (including the grinder head and blades) and stuffer, as well as the bowl of a stand mixer and paddle attachment, in the freezer to chill. Place the beef, veal, and fatback in the freezer and let chill

for 30 minutes, or until the meat reaches an internal temperature of 32°F (0°C).

Using a mortar and pestle, grind the white pepper, marjoram, mustard powder, chili powder, paprika, coriander, and garlic to a fine paste. Set aside.

In a large bowl, mix together the chilled meats and fatback and half of the crushed ice.

Set up the grinder with the largest die you have (I use a ¼-inch/6mm die). Fill another large bowl halfway with ice cubes and set it under the grinder. Nestle the chilled stand-mixer bowl in the ice and grind the meat mixture

continued

into it. Check the temperature of the ground meat to make sure it is below 35°F (2°C). If it isn't, place the meat in the freezer to bring down the temperature. Run the meat through the grinder a second time. Do not allow the temperature to exceed 39°F (4°C).

Change to the smallest die you have—a ⅛-inch (3mm) die is perfect. (If you do not have a smaller die, continue to use the ¼ inch [6mm] one.) Add the remaining crushed ice, then run the meat mixture through the grinder another two times. (If using the larger die, run the meat through four more times, for a grand total of six times.) Again, make sure your meat does not exceed 39°F (4°C). You are looking for a mass that is uniform in color and texture and that is as cold as possible.

Add the spice mixture, sea salt, sugar, curing salt, and milk powder to the mixing bowl. With the chilled paddle attachment, mix on low speed until all of the ingredients are fully incorporated, about 2 minutes.

If you are stuffing from your grinder, you will need to remove the blades and dies and place the horn on the end. Get all the surfaces that the casing will be touching (the horn and a baking sheet) really wet with water so that the casing will slide and not tear; you can pour about ¼ cup (60ml) of water directly into your tray. Remove the casing from the water and slide one end onto the horn, and keep sliding it onto the horn until you get to the other end of the casing. Tie a knot on that end. Using your hands, a spatula, or a wooden spoon, press the meat mixture into the hopper.

Work the stuffer, taking care to fill the casing enough but not so full that you won't have wiggle room to link the sausages. Once you have all the meat in the casing, tie the

end and cut off any excess casing. Examine the stuffed casing; if you see any air gaps, pierce the casing lightly with the tip of a sharp knife.

To form the links, start at whichever end of the casing you like. With your dominant hand, measure 12 inches (30cm) from the end of the casing and, using your index finger and your thumb, pinch the casing and twist this first sausage two full rotations. It should feel nice and tight. Measure another 12 inches (30cm) from the spot you just pinched and pinch again. This time, rotate the sausage two full rotations in the opposite direction from the last twist. As you twist the sausage in the opposite direction, you will feel the last sausage you twisted getting tighter. Repeat this process for the entire length of the casing: pinch and twist one way, then pinch and twist the other way. This technique ensures that you do not untwist the link that you just made.

Transfer the links to a dry baking sheet and refrigerate until your smoker is ready.

Soak two large handfuls of apple wood chips and one large handful of hickory wood chips in water to cover for 10 minutes. Start the grill or smoker at the lowest temperature you can; you'll want to start smoking at about 70°F (20°C).

Once the heat is nice and even, drain the wood chips and sprinkle a small handful in an even layer over the coals. Add the sausages and cover with the lid. You want to see a steady flow of white smoke coming out of your grill or smoker.

After 30 minutes, add another handful of wet chips, but if you see the smoke slowing down, add chips more frequently.

A WÜRST CART IN THE CENTER OF MERANO

After 1 hour, the sausages should have a tan look to them. This is proof that the smoke is starting to stick. Add more coals or turn up your smoker and add another small handful of wood chips. If you can check the temperature of your grill or smoker, for this second hour, you should try to hold the temperature at 150°F (65°C) with a nice flow of smoke the entire time. Keep sprinkling on wood chips as needed to ensure that you have a steady stream of smoke. (If you run out of soaked chips, soak more in water for 10 minutes before using.)

After 2 hours, your sausages should have a smoky brown color, and the internal temperature should be about 140°F (60°C). You may need to add a bit more charcoal or turn up the heat to get to your finish temperature of 150°F (65°C). If you're not there yet, bump up the smoker's heat to 200°F (95°C) and check the temperature again in 15 minutes.

When ready, carefully remove the smoked sausages and let them cool. Wrap tightly in plastic wrap and store in the refrigerator for up to 3 weeks.

Sofie's Goulash with Speck Dumplings

GULASCH DI SOFIE

MEDIUM
SERVES 4

2 pounds (900g) beef shoulder, cut into 1½-inch (4cm) cubes

Fine sea salt and freshly ground black pepper

2 tablespoons grapeseed oil

2 yellow onions, finely diced

2 tablespoons tomato paste

1 cup (240ml) dry red wine

1 tablespoon sweet paprika

4 cups (950ml) beef stock or low-sodium beef broth

1 red bell pepper, cut into 1-inch (2.5cm) pieces

Speck Dumplings (page 42), hot buttered egg noodles, or spaetzle (see page 171) to serve

TRAVEL HACK

Sofie Hütte sits close to the start of La Longia, a narrow, 10.5-kilometer (6-mile) intermediate (red) run that winds its way down into the valley and the town of Ortisei/St. Ulrich. It's the kind of run that seems to lead you high up into the clouds, only to drop you at the front door of your hotel. It's long but not arduous.

Note to nonskiers: You, too, can eat at Sofie Hütte! Call ahead to make a lunch reservation, then hop on the Seceda cable car from Ortisei. At the top, call Sofie Hütte and a staff member will pick you up on a snowmobile and drive you the short distance down to the hut.

Sofie Prinoth has been running Sofie Hütte, located in the popular Seceda ski area, for fifty years—long before there was cable-car access to the hut. Back then, it was "just" a cattle farm and Sofie's home with her husband and their two children, Markus and Barbara. Sofie Hütte is one of the busiest restaurants on Seceda, and with twenty-one huts to choose from, that's saying something.

Sofie began cooking this goulash at a very young age, always serving it with speck dumplings, a Süd-Tyrol specialty. She uses hyperlocal beef; the land around the hut, at 2,480 meters (8,025 feet), is the summer pasture for the family farm. Sofie uses red bell peppers, paprika, and tomato in this stew, a rustic dish that brings out the best in a humble cut of meat—a very Alpine attribute indeed. (For a spicier venison stew, see page 122.)

Although Sofie's son, Markus, has taken over the cooking, they still make gin together, collecting the herbs from their land in the summertime. They call the gin "8025," after the hut's elevation. In true entrepreneurial form, Markus maintains one of the best wine lists I've seen at a mountain restaurant. I can't imagine that it's easy to stabilize wine at such an altitude, much less ship it to the hut safely. Sofie still lives above the hut. In winter, regardless of weather, she takes her snowcat down to the village once a week to get her hair done. (Sofie is a badass.)

In a bowl, toss the beef with 2 teaspoons salt and ½ teaspoon pepper.

In a large heavy pot over medium-high heat, warm the grapeseed oil until it shimmers. Working in batches (so as to not crowd the pot), sauté the meat until browned on two sides, about 5 minutes total. Transfer the meat to a plate.

In the same pot, add the onions and fry until they start to color slightly, about 5 minutes, then stir in the tomato paste and continue to cook for 2 minutes more.

Pour in the red wine, stirring to deglaze the pan and scraping up any browned bits from the bottom. Turn the heat to high, bring the liquid to a vigorous boil, and cook to reduce until syrupy, about 5 minutes.

Return the beef to the pot and stir in the paprika and beef stock. Bring to a simmer, turn the heat to low, cover, and braise for 1½ hours. Add the bell pepper and continue to cook for another 5 minutes. The meat should be fork-tender. Adjust the seasoning with salt and pepper.

Serve alongside dumplings, or ladled over bowls of hot buttered egg noodles or spaetzle.

Speck Dumplings

SERVES 4
(MAKES 8 TO 10 DUMPLINGS)

1 pound (450g) stale white bread, crusts removed, cut or pulsed into coarse crumbs

5 ounces (140g) speck or cured ham, diced

3 tablespoons unsalted butter

½ yellow onion, finely diced

2 eggs

1 cup (240ml) milk

1 tablespoon minced chives

1 teaspoon fine sea salt

½ teaspoon freshly ground black pepper

¼ cup (30g) all-purpose flour

2 tablespoons grapeseed oil

SOFIE PRINOTH

Speck, bread, chives, and milk—all hand rolled. These dumplings are like a fifth food group in the Dolomites.

In a large bowl, combine the bread crumbs and speck. Set aside.

In a medium frying pan over medium heat, melt the butter. Add the onion and sauté until translucent, 3 to 5 minutes. Set aside.

Whisk the eggs with ½ cup (120ml) of the milk to combine well. Add the egg-milk mixture to the bowl with the bread and speck. Mix well, using a wooden spoon or your hands. Add the remaining ½ cup (120ml) milk, mixing to soften the bread. Stir in the onion, chives, salt, and pepper. Add the flour and grapeseed oil, mix well with your hands, cover the bowl with plastic wrap, and let sit for 30 minutes so the bread can soak up the liquid.

Bring a large pot of salted water to a boil.

Moisten your hands (keep a small bowl of water next to you) and divide the bread dough into eight to ten equal portions. Working with one piece at a time, roll the dough into a firm tight ball using your hands to confidently shape it.

Slip the rolled dumplings into the boiling water and simmer, uncovered, for 15 minutes, until heated through. Use a slotted spoon to remove the dumplings from the pot and serve.

Radicchio Dumplings

CANEDERLI AL RADICCHIO ROSSO DI TREVISO

EASY

SERVES 4 AS A MAIN,
OR 6 AS A SIDE
(MAKES 12 DUMPLINGS)

11 ounces (300g) stale white bread, crusts removed, diced

¾ cup plus 2 tablespoons (200ml) milk, warmed

2 tablespoons extra-virgin olive oil

1 shallot, minced

11 ounces (300g) Treviso radicchio, finely chopped

Fine sea salt and freshly ground black pepper

2 eggs, beaten

½ cup (50g) grated Grana Padano or Parmigiano-Reggiano cheese, plus ¼ cup (25g) grated Parmigiano-Reggiano

7 ounces (200g) speck, finely diced

Freshly grated nutmeg

1 tablespoon all-purpose flour

2 tablespoons fine dried bread crumbs

¼ cup (60ml) melted unsalted butter

INGRID PARDATSCHER

Fichtenhof is a restaurant for idealists. Located way up on the ridge of the Monte Corno Natural Park between Trento and Bolzano, it's a drive of about 30 minutes into the mountains from the wine route. In the summer, which is when you should go, it's surrounded by a magical garden that maître de maison Ingrid Pardatscher tends when she's not cooking for guests. Ingrid is famous for these *canederli*, the traditional dumplings of Alto Adige, which she makes with herbs and vegetables from her garden. They are sort of the Italian counterpart to Sofie Prinoth's Austrian dumplings (see page 42), but require less bread, have more oil, include Parmesan, and are meant to be the main event.

In a large bowl, combine the bread and warm milk and stir to moisten. Set aside for 30 minutes. Line a plate with a layer of paper towels.

In a large frying pan over medium heat, warm the olive oil. Add the shallot and cook until translucent, about 3 minutes. Stir in the radicchio, continue to cook until wilted, about 2 minutes, and then season with salt and pepper. Set aside.

Add the eggs, Grana Padano, and speck to the soaked bread mixture. Season with salt, pepper, and a good grating of nutmeg. Mix well (don't be tempted to add more milk). Then add the radicchio mixture, flour, and bread crumbs and mix well with your hands until homogenous. The dough should come together but feel slightly tacky.

Bring a large pot of salted water to a boil.

Moisten your hands (keep a small bowl of water next to you) and divide the dough into twelve even portions. Working with one piece at a time, roll the dough into a firm tight ball using your hands to confidently shape it.

Slide the balls into the boiling water and simmer for 8 to 12 minutes, until the dumplings are heated through. Remove with a slotted spoon to the prepared plate.

Transfer the dumplings to shallow serving bowls and spoon a little melted butter over them, followed by a spoonful or two of grated Parmigiano-Reggiano. Serve immediately.

Smoked Char, Col Alt–Style

SALMERINO AFFUMICATO ALLA COL ALT

━━━ MEDIUM
SERVES 4

YOU WILL NEED
Small roasting pan or cast-iron pan with a rack that fits inside

Large handful of wood chips

Mandoline

High-speed blender

2- to 3-inch (5 to 7.5cm) ring mold

3 carrots, peeled, halved lengthwise

1 sprig thyme, leaves picked

Fine sea salt

CHAR
½ cup (150g) kosher salt

½ cup (100g) sugar

Grated zest from 1 orange

1 shallot, julienned

¼ cup (10g) coarsely chopped fresh dill

4 or 5 sprigs thyme, leaves picked

Coarsely chopped pink peppercorns

Four 4-ounce (115g) arctic char fillets, skin off, pin bones removed

MARINATED TURNIPS
1 multicolor baby turnip

1 yellow baby turnip

1 white baby turnip

1 tablespoon plus 1 teaspoon apple balsamic vinegar

1 tablespoon plus 1 teaspoon balsamic vinegar

¼ cup (60ml) water

Pinch of fine sea salt

Chicken stock or low-sodium chicken broth as needed (optional)

Fine sea salt

Extra-virgin olive oil for drizzling

Sesame seeds for sprinkling

Fresh dill and baby basil leaves for garnish

Col Alt is the name of the cable car (and the mountain) that takes you from Corvara—one of the prettiest villages in the Dolomites—up to Rifugio Col Alt at 2,000 meters (6,561 feet) in just 4 minutes. Back in the 1940s, it was the first chairlift system in all of Italy, and now its eight-seat yellow gondolas are the area's trademark.

Situated directly on the ski pistes, the hut is a meeting spot, a café, and a very, very good restaurant. When I arrived there on a fresh spring morning, chef Enrico Vespani made me a fish tartare with local arctic char. (The scientific name of arctic char is *Salvelinus alpinus*, because it's not just native to arctic and subarctic coastal waters, it's also native to Alpine lakes.) Vespani smoked the fish outside, next to the restaurant in the mountain air, and turned it into this little appetizer there and then. (The carrot cream and the vibrant marinated turnips can be prepared ahead of time.) This dish signals spring, and the end of a very busy winter season for the staff of the rifugio.

Preheat the oven to 325°F (165°C).

Lay the carrots on a large square of aluminum foil and then sprinkle with the thyme and sea salt. Wrap the foil into a neat package. Place on a small baking sheet and bake for 2½ hours, until completely soft.

To prepare the char: In the meantime, in a small bowl, combine the kosher salt, sugar, orange zest, shallot, dill, thyme, and peppercorns. Spread half of the mixture over the bottom of a small baking dish or pan. Lay the fillets in the dish, then spread the remaining mixture over the fish and refrigerate for 90 minutes.

When the fish is cured, line the bottom of a roasting pan or cast-iron pan with foil and place a large handful of wood chips on the foil. Oil a rack and set it in the pan. Place the pan on the stove top over high heat. The wood chips will self-ignite and start to smoke in 8 to 10 minutes.

While the wood chips are warming up, rinse each fillet well under running water, then completely pat dry with paper towels.

When the smoking starts to truly happen, turn on your kitchen fan

(maybe crack open a window or two) and lay the fish pieces on the prepared rack. Cover the pan tightly with foil. Turn off the heat. After 30 minutes, pour a cup of water onto the chips to extinguish the smoking.

To prepare the turnips: Using a mandoline, slice very thin rounds of each turnip into a bowl. Pour both vinegars and the water over the turnips, sprinkle with the sea salt, and let sit for 10 minutes. Drain and set aside.

Cut the roasted carrots into small pieces, place in a blender, and blend at high speed to make a fluid cream, adding a splash of chicken stock as needed. Season with sea salt.

Cut the char into small cubes and drizzle with a little olive oil.

Using a ring mold, portion the char onto each of four plates. Spoon a few dots of carrot cream around the fish and sprinkle sesame seeds atop the carrot cream. Arrange the marinated turnip rounds artfully on top of the fish, alternating colors. Garnish with dill fronds and tiny basil leaves on the top of the char. Serve immediately.

Beet Gnocchi

GNOCCHI DI BARBABIETOLA

DIFFICULT

SERVES 6 TO 8

YOU WILL NEED
24-hole half-sphere silicone mold (1⅓-inch [3cm] cavities)

Potato ricer

High-speed blender

2½-inch (6.5cm) ring mold or cookie cutter

HORSERADISH FILLING
2 cups (480 ml) heavy cream

½ cup (140 g) creamy horseradish

3 tablespoons agar powder

2¼ pounds (1kg) russet potatoes

⅞ cup (200ml) concentrated beet juice

2 egg yolks

2½ cups (300g) 00 flour, plus more as needed

1 teaspoon fine sea salt

DAIKON CREAM
4 ounces (115g) daikon radish, peeled and cubed

2 cups (480ml) heavy cream

BEER "SOIL"
4 ounces (115g) Puccia Bread (page 58), cut into cubes and staled

½ teaspoon activated charcoal

¼ cup (60ml) lager or pale ale

Beet microgreens for garnish

Think of the Hotel & Spa Rosa Alpina as the gateway drug to luxury in the Alps. Situated in the small pedestrian town of San Cassiano in Alto Adige's Alta Badia region, Rosa Alpina appears to be located in a normal Ladin-speaking mountain community, until you see the black sedans lining the road. Diplomats, dignitaries, artists, gallerists, and great chefs all gather in the hotel's restaurant, St. Hubertus, *the* five-star dining room of the Alps.

The formula for Rosa Alpina's success is equal parts owner Hugo Pizzinini and his wife Ursula's hospitality and work ethic (see snapshot), and equal parts the kitchen.

This recipe is the brainchild of Norbert Niederkofler, one of the most influential chefs in the Alps and the man behind the "Cook the Mountain" philosophy, which could be defined as a sort of Alpine locavorism. Niederkofler has been running the St. Hubertus restaurant since 1994. Many accolades and Michelin stars later, he is one of the two leaders, along with Andreas Döllerer (see page 120), of Alpine cuisine.

These little gnocchi look like tiny, shiny beets that you might have just plucked from the garden, but rather than being raw and inedible, they are in fact potato gnocchi filled with horseradish cream in beet-colored coats that just pop in your mouth! Indicative of Michelin-star cooking, this is a difficult recipe, but we tinkered with it to be sure it's accessible for home cooks. Rosa Alpina and Chef Niederkofler are part of the vernacular of mountain cooking, and for those of you who can't visit Alta Badia, this dish represents the genuine flavor of the Dolomites.

Notes: This recipe makes about seventy gnocchi, which is more than you need to feed eight people. However, if you go to the trouble of making these, why not make enough to freeze for future meals? Increase the cooking time to 3 minutes.

If you have a juicer, juice your own beets. Start with 2 cups (480ml) of juice, then reduce the juice over medium heat to a scant 1 cup (about 200ml) to concentrate it. Alternatively, purchase beet juice in a health food store, then reduce it as described.

Agar powder is available in most supermarkets and health food stores—look for the Eden brand. 00 flour can be found in Italian grocery stores/delis or ordered online. Unbleached all-purpose flour can be used as a substitute. Activated charcoal powder can be found in a health food store or ordered online.

To prepare the horseradish filling: In a medium saucepan over medium heat, bring 1¼ cups (300ml) of the heavy cream to a boil. Remove from the heat and stir in the horseradish. Set aside to infuse for about 1 hour. Strain through a fine-mesh sieve; discard the solids. Pour the infused cream back into a saucepan.

In a small bowl, soak the agar powder in the remaining ¾ cup (180 ml) cream for 5 minutes.

Pour the agar cream into the horseradish-infused cream and bring to a boil over medium heat. Lower the heat and simmer for 10 minutes. Pour one-third of the cream into the half-sphere mold. Let cool to room temperature and then freeze for 1 hour. Unmold the frozen half-spheres, place in a ziptop bag, and return to the freezer. Repeat twice more with the remaining cream.

Preheat the oven to 400°F (200°C).

Place the potatoes on a baking sheet and bake until tender, 45 to 60 minutes.

Peel the potatoes while still hot (holding them with a kitchen towel). Then pass each potato through a ricer into a large bowl. Pour the beet juice into the potatoes, add the egg yolks, and stir gently to combine. Sprinkle the flour and salt over the warm potato mixture. Using your hands, work the mixture into a soft, smooth dough. If the dough feels sticky, you may need to add a little extra flour. Cover and set aside for 1 hour.

Line a baking sheet with parchment paper.

On a lightly floured counter, roll out the dough to a thickness of ⅛ inch (3mm). Using a 2½-inch (6.5cm) ring mold, cut out as many circles of dough as you can. Place a frozen half-sphere of horseradish cream, dome-side down, onto each circle. Close up the dough around the frozen cream, pinching gently to form a seal. Transfer, dome-side up, to the prepared baking sheet in a single layer. Refrigerate for 3 hours.

To make the daikon cream: In a heavy saucepan over medium-low heat, combine the daikon and heavy cream. Bring to a simmer and cook until the daikon is soft, 30 to 40 minutes. Drain the daikon, discarding the cream, transfer to a high-speed blender, and purée until completely smooth.

To make the "soil": In a food processor, combine the stale bread and charcoal and pulse until you have fine crumbs.

Bring a large pot of salted water to a boil. Cook the gnocchi in batches until they float, about 2 minutes—don't hesitate to try one for doneness. Using a slotted spoon, transfer the gnocchi to a shallow serving bowl or platter and keep in a warm place while you cook the rest. (To store cooked gnocchi, lay them on a parchment paper–lined baking sheet and freeze for 4 hours. Transfer the frozen gnocchi to a ziptop bag and freeze for up to 2 months.)

Sprinkle some lager onto the "soil" to moisten it slightly, mixing with your hands or a spoon. Make a line of soil through the middle of each plate. Place three or four gnocchi along each line. Using two tablespoons, form the daikon cream into quenelles and place two on each plate. Garnish with beet microgreens and serve.

TRAVEL HACK

In Kronplatz, at the Plan de Corones Mountain Station at 2,275 meters (7,464 feet), you'll find the Lumen Museum of Mountain Photography, a modern institution that you can hike to in the summer and ski to in the winter. The museum also holds AlpiNN, Norbert Niederkofler's outpost restaurant.

PUMPKIN SEED OIL SUNDAE

Pumpkin seed oil with pumpkin seeds and a drizzle of pine oil is the Alpine equivalent to hot fudge and sprinkles. This combination was served to me over ice cream for dessert one night at Rosa Alpina, and the pumpkin seed oil was sublime. To make your own sundae, just add about 4 teaspoons pumpkin seed oil and 2 tablespoons raw pumpkin seeds to 2 scoops of ice cream and add a drizzle of pine oil. Although pumpkin seed oil is Austrian, you can order it online in North America from Samenkoenig, and while you're creeping the website, I suggest ordering the walnut oil too. (I wanted to include a walnut oil ice cream in the book, as walnuts are big in the French Alps, but I ran out of room.) To all of you industrious readers, please try adding walnut oil to the base ice cream recipe on page 261, and let me know how you like it!

NORBERT NIEDERKOFLER

Wine Cave Fonduta

████ EASY

SERVES 2 OR 3

YOU WILL NEED

Traditional fondue set or an enameled cast-iron saucepan (such as Le Creuset's 6-cup [2L] saucier pan) with a camping stove

1 cup (240 ml) milk

¼ cup (60ml) heavy cream

1 pound (450g) thinly sliced or grated Fontina Val d'Aosta cheese

1 whole baguette or French country loaf, cut into 1-inch (2.5cm) cubes

2 eggs

Dried smoked ham (preferably aged 2 to 3 years) for serving (optional)

TRAVEL HACK

There is also a gourmet Michelin-starred restaurant at Ciasa Salares, La Siriola, run by the very talented Matteo Metullio. I suggest one night there and one evening in the cellar with charcuterie, cheese, and fonduta. Either way, you're drinking well.

I first tried this dish deep inside the wine cellar at Ciasa Salares in Badia and it knocked my socks off. Fonduta actually originates in Aosta, where it's called *Fonduta alla Valdostana*. The Piedmont cousin of the French *Fondue Savoyarde* and all of the Swiss fondues (see page 207), fonduta typically has just two ingredients—a local Fontina cheese and milk—and, unlike other fondues, no local wine or kirsch.

That one in the wine cellar, though? Picture a hunk of Fontina, some milk, a splash of cream, and then, when you're almost finished, crack two eggs into the pot to make the most unctuous scrambled eggs of your life. Top with some shavings of local speck and drink your choice of the twenty-four thousand or so bottles that line the cave walls.

Ciasa Salares is one of the top three wine caves in the Alps. Stefan Wieser, the owner and cellar master, is a wine obsessive, and his long wine list, printed on luxurious paper, is so well considered that you may want to take it upstairs and spend the night with it.

Stefan's son, Jan Clemens, is just as dedicated, and he was the one who thankfully disclosed the cave fonduta recipe, and insisted on a little orange wine to go with it. On that particular night, it was Josko Gravner's Ribolla. Finding an incredible wine bar hidden in the Dolomites is one thing. Realizing the establishment is filled with rare finds and the best Friulian list outside of Friuli is quite another. Ciasa Salares and the wine cave at La Perla Hotel (just down the road in Corvara) also operate as bottle shops with separate to-go list prices.

Though fonduta is not quite fondue, you are still sharing a pound of hot cheese with bread for dinner here, so fondue rules (see page 209) do apply.

Note: Fontina is a salty cheese, so don't be tempted to season the fonduta until the very end, if at all. This recipe is based on the flavor of Fontina Val d'Aosta, so if you cannot find it, please skip—this is completely Fontina-centric. Optional accompaniments include sweet pickled white onions, gherkins, boiled new potatoes, fried polenta, and South Tyrolean speck or smoked ham.

In a heavy saucepan or a fondue pot over medium heat, combine the milk, cream, and Fontina cheese, stirring continuously with a wooden spoon. The cheese will melt quickly, but don't worry if the mixture feels and looks too runny. At around the 7-minute mark, the magic starts to happen. Transfer your fondue pot to the table setup, if using, and enjoy with the baguette. (Alternatively, you can hover over the stove top, using a fork to dip your bread, while standing. I've done this and much, much worse.)

At the first inkling of "Wow, I've eaten a lot of cheese," the bottom of the pot should be coming into view. You may even encounter a circle of burnt cheese sticking to the center, known in French, for reasons lost to history, as *la religieuse*, "the nun." Now's the time to crack the eggs into the pot and stir away for about 30 seconds until a perfect scramble has formed. Remove from the heat. If desired, shave in some dried smoked ham, and enjoy.

JAN CLEMENS'S WINE RECOMMENDATIONS FOR FONDUTA

Verdicchio from Marche • Dry Malvasia from Sicily • Orange wines, such as Josko Gravner's Ribolla, from Friuli • Garganega by Gianfranco Masiero • Pinot Noir from South Tyrol, such as Ansitz Dornach's Tenuta • Nebbiolo from the Alpine area of Gattinara, such as Nervi's Gattinara

RINO BILLIA IN HIS WINE CAVE AT
BELLEVUE'S LE PETIT RESTAURANT

Bread Soup with Chicory and Egg

PANADA CON CICORIA E UOVA

■■■ EASY
SERVES 4

YOU WILL NEED
Food processor or high-speed blender

5 tablespoons extra-virgin olive oil, plus more for serving

1 yellow onion, diced

7 ounces (200g) pancetta, diced

1½ quarts (1.4L) low-sodium vegetable broth

1 bun Puccia Bread (recipe follows), cut into 2-inch (5cm) pieces, plus 1 cup (50g) Puccia Bread croutons (see variation)

Fine sea salt and freshly ground black pepper

1 bunch wild chicory, chopped into ribbons

4 eggs

1 tablespoon minced chives

1 teaspoon fennel seeds, toasted

The first time I walked into El Brite de Larieto outside of Cortina d'Ampezzo, I immediately felt as if I were in someone's loving home and not a restaurant. Chef Riccardo Gaspari and his wife, Ludovica, welcomed me and sat me at my own table, next to a group of twelve Romans (who, incidentally, took me to El Camineto the following night to introduce me to its famous spaghetti alla cipolla). At El Brite, I had a six-course meal that included a stuffed pasta (Casunziei all'Ampezzana; page 64) that made an impact, and this right here: bread soup made with *puccia* bread and served with wild chicory and an egg.

Since that first visit, Riccardo and Ludo have had two girls and opened a boutique dairy where they make their own yogurt, ricotta, and Tyrolean grey cheese—all using milk from their cows. These two understand comfort and simplicity, yet they cook creatively and freely. Choosing a recipe to share from El Brite was difficult, because they are all so good, but I decided to go with the first dish I had on that snowy night.

Notes: Allow 3 to 4 hours to make the puccia, a sandwich bread made from a simple pizza dough, that forms the base of this soup. The puccia recipe makes four buns, which allows you to stale two of them for the garnish you need, plus more for future use. Alternatively, substitute store-bought ciabatta bread or panini and make the croutons from a country-style loaf.

It may seem like overkill, seeing as this is a bread soup, but at El Brite this is served with a side of fresh baked brown bread and fresh butter, and I suggest you do the same.

If wild chicory proves hard to find, substitute dandelion leaves, escarole, or radicchio for that welcome hint of bitterness.

In a Dutch oven over medium heat, warm 3 tablespoons of the olive oil. Add the onion and pancetta and sauté until starting to brown lightly, 5 to 7 minutes. Add the vegetable broth and bring to a boil. Add the bread, lower the heat, and simmer for 45 minutes.

Ladle the soup into a food processor or blender and process on high speed until smooth and creamy. Adjust the seasoning with salt and pepper. Return to the Dutch oven and keep warm over very low heat.

While the soup simmers, bring a large pot of salted water to a boil and fill a bowl with ice water. Add the chicory to the boiling water and blanch until wilted, 1 to 2 minutes.

Lift out of the boiling water, plunge into the ice water to stop the cooking, and drain.

Place a wide saucepan filled with water over high heat. While the water is heating, line a plate with a layer of paper towels.

In a medium frying pan over medium heat, warm the remaining 2 tablespoons olive oil. Add the chicory and sauté until starting to brown, 4 to 5 minutes. Season with salt and pepper.

When the water has started boiling, turn the heat to a simmer. Crack one egg into a small bowl, then gently pour it into the hot water, swirling the water around it with a spatula

continued

or wooden spoon to encourage the egg to take a nice shape. Repeat with the remaining three eggs. When the water returns to a simmer, set a timer and poach the eggs for 2 minutes, until the whites have just set. Carefully transfer to the prepared plate.

Ladle the soup into bowls. Gently place one egg in the center of each bowl, then lay some wilted chicory next to it, add some croutons, then sprinkle each bowl with the minced chives and fennel seeds. Add a splash of olive oil to each soup and serve.

Puccia Bread

MAKES 4 BUNS

1½ teaspoons active dry yeast

1⅓ cups (315ml) warm (105° to 110°F/40° to 45°C) water

2 cups (240g) whole-wheat flour

2 cups (240g) rye flour

1½ teaspoons fine sea salt

2 tablespoons olive oil

2 tablespoons fennel seeds

Coarse semolina for sprinkling

Puccia is a kind of sandwich bread you will find all over Italy. It is similar to a pizza crust in consistency.

In a small bowl, stir the yeast into the warm water and let sit for 5 minutes until bubbles form.

In a stand mixer fitted with the dough hook, combine both flours, the salt, and olive oil. Pour in the water-yeast mixture. Mix at low speed for 2 minutes, then increase the speed to medium-high and continue to mix for 5 to 8 minutes, until the dough is smooth. Set the bowl with the dough in a warm place and cover with plastic wrap. Allow to proof for 2 hours.

Lightly flour a work surface. Cut the proofed dough into fourths. Sprinkle ½ tablespoon fennel seeds onto each piece of dough, and knead each of the dough pieces to incorporate,

until smooth. Place on the prepared surface, cover with a towel, and let the four balls of dough proof, until doubled in size, 45 to 60 minutes.

Preheat the oven as high as it will go: 475°F (245°C) or up to 500°F (260°C). Sprinkle a baking sheet with semolina.

Flatten each piece of dough gently into a disk shape, then sprinkle on both sides with semolina.

Place each disk onto the prepared baking sheet. Bake until the puccia have puffed up and turned golden brown, with some darkening around the edges, about 20 minutes. These will keep, tightly wrapped in plastic, for up to 2 days. Reheat gently before serving.

VARIATION

Croutons: Let the buns cool completely, then cut into small cubes and let sit at room temperature for about 2 hours to dry out.

RICCARDO AND LUDOVICA GASPARI

Spinach and Cheese Mezzaluna

SCHLUTZKRAPFEN

SERVES 4 TO 6

YOU WILL NEED

Pasta machine or stand mixer fitted with the pasta attachment

Fluted pastry wheel

FILLING

7 ounces (200g) spinach leaves

¼ cup (55g) unsalted butter

1 garlic clove, minced

½ cup (100g) quark cheese

½ cup (100g) ricotta cheese

2 tablespoons grated strong hard cheese (your choice of Bergkäse [mountain cheese]), such as Montasio, aged Gruyère, or Berner Alpkäse

2 tablespoons grated Parmigiano-Reggiano cheese

1 tablespoon minced fresh herbs (a mix of parsley, chives, and oregano)

Fine sea salt and freshly ground black pepper

MEZZALUNA DOUGH

2 cups (240g) all-purpose flour, plus more for dusting

2 cups (240g) semolina flour or rye flour, plus more for dusting

5 eggs

2 tablespoons olive oil

¼ cup (55g) unsalted butter

Fresh herb leaves (a mix of parsley, minced chives, and oregano) for garnish

Grated Parmigiano-Reggiano cheese for dusting

These slippery (*schlutz*) parcels (*krapfen*) originate in the Val Pusteria valley, which runs along the north of Alto Adige, bordering Italy and Austria. It's the last Italian stop before Austria and the valley's ski towns: Sesto (Sexten), San Candido, Dobbiaco, Villabassa, and Braies are all part of the Tre Cime ski area within the Dolomiti Superski (see page 30). These stuffed half-moons (*mezzaluna*) have been made in this area for centuries, and locals spoke to me of a 300-year-old recipe unearthed in Sesto.

The mix of soft and hard cheeses makes the filling unique; in the original, ricotta and quark with Tyrolean grey cheese. Montasio, aged Gruyère, or Berner Alpkäse would work as stand-ins for the grey cheese (which is hard to find outside of the region). Rye flour in the dough adds to the depth of flavor. There are only two rules for this dish: the mezzaluna are ready when they float on top of the water, and they should be served only with melted butter, Parmigiano-Reggiano, and fresh herbs.

To prepare the filling: Place the spinach in a colander and pour boiling water over to wilt it.

In a large frying pan over medium-low heat, melt the butter and then stir in the garlic, cooking until fragrant and beginning to color, about 1 minute. Stir in the wilted spinach and cook for 1 minute more. Transfer the spinach-garlic mixture to a plate and let cool.

In a bowl, combine the spinach with the quark, ricotta, strong cheese, Parmigiano, and minced herbs, stirring until a homogeneous mixture is obtained. Taste and adjust the seasoning with salt and pepper as needed. (The filling will keep in an airtight container, in the refrigerator, for up to 1 day.)

To make the mezzaluna dough: Spoon both flours onto a clean surface or into a large shallow bowl and make a wide well in the center. Crack the eggs and pour the olive oil into the well. Using a fork, swirl the eggs and oil, slowly incorporating the flour into the center of the well. When the flour is completely incorporated, gather and knead the mixture together to form one large ball. Knead for 5 to 10 minutes on

the counter. Wrap the ball in plastic and place in the refrigerator for 45 to 60 minutes to rest.

Heavily dust a baking sheet with semolina flour. Divide the rested dough into fourths. Keep the dough covered while working with one piece at a time.

Roll the dough through the widest roller setting of your pasta machine (or attachment, if you're using a stand mixer), dusting with all-purpose flour along the way to ensure the dough doesn't stick, but not too much as you don't want the dough to become dry. Fold the sheet of dough in half onto itself, and roll it through this initial setting ten to fifteen times, folding it again after each pass.

Change the machine setting to the next, narrower setting and roll the sheet through once. You'll notice your sheet will become longer and longer as you work it through each successive setting. Keep rolling until Setting 7 (on most pasta machines); you want the sheet to be thin enough to just see your hand through it. Lay the pasta sheet out on the prepared

continued

WAITERS AT HOTEL HERMITAGE
IN CERVINIA

baking sheet. Repeat the rolling procedure with the remaining three pieces of dough.

Dust a work surface with semolina flour and spread the sheets of rolled dough out on it. Place 1-tablespoon mounds of the filling along the center of each sheet, 1¼ to 1½ inches (3 to 4cm) apart. Using a small glass of water and a brush or your fingers, gently moisten the dough between the mounds of filling. Then fold the dough over, pressing down gently in between each mound.

Using a fluted pastry wheel, cut a clean half-moon shape around each of the mounds to separate each mezzaluna.

Bring a large pot of salted water to a boil. Oil a large baking sheet.

Add the mezzaluna to the boiling water and cook until they float up to the surface, 2 to 3 minutes. Using a slotted spoon, transfer the pasta to the prepared baking sheet. (At this point, the pasta can be covered with plastic wrap and refrigerated for up to 2 hours.)

In a large sauté pan over medium heat, melt the butter. Add the mezzaluna and then gently sauté until tender and just golden, about 3 minutes. Stir in the fresh herb leaves and serve with a dusting of Parmigiano.

Harald Gasser is a South Tyrolean farmer who experiments with old and rare vegetable breeds. He cultivates more than four hundred varieties on his Aspingerhof Farm, where he grew up. He prefers to spend time in his garden rather than on a piste or trail (though he admits that the 800-meter [2,625-foot] elevation difference between his hut and his garden is, in fact, a hike). His favorite dish is *Schlutzkrapfen* (page 60), which he enjoys often with his view of the Sciliar (Schlern) peak in Alpe de Siusi.

SNAPSHOT

Beet and Poppy-Seed Casunziei

CASUNZIEI ALL'AMPEZZANA

EASY

SERVES 4 TO 6

YOU WILL NEED

Potato ricer or vegetable mill

2-inch (5cm) ring mold or cookie cutter

FILLING

1 pound (450g) beets, unpeeled

12 ounces (340g) russet potatoes, unpeeled

¼ cup (55g) unsalted butter

½ cup (50g) grated Parmigiano-Reggiano or smoked ricotta cheese

Fine sea salt and freshly ground black pepper

Freshly grated fresh nutmeg

¼ cup (25g) dried bread crumbs

Semolina flour for dusting

1 recipe mezzaluna dough (see page 60), rolled out

½ cup (110g) unsalted butter

16 to 24 sage leaves

1 tablespoon poppy seeds

½ cup (50g) grated Parmigiano-Reggiano cheese

TRAVEL HACK

Wine nerd alert: Laite in Sappada, Friuli, has a fantastic wine list, so plan your transportation accordingly.

Casunziei means "filled fresh pasta" in the Ladin dialect, which is mainly spoken in the Dolomites. Not to be confused with the town of Canazei, a ski town in the area, these beet and potato half-moons are Bellunese in origin, in the Italian region of Veneto, just over an hour southeast of Cortina. (Close to the Carnic Alps, the mountains begin in Veneto and Friuli and spread east to Slovenia. They hold fascinating food and wine worlds in their grasp, but that's the story of another book!) I've had this dish in two restaurants and both times it was delicious. The first taste was at El Brite (see page 21), and the second was at Laite, an incredible family-run restaurant in the hamlet of Sappada, on the border of the Veneto and Friuli.

The use of poppy seeds in this dish feels very Austrian/Friulian. To underline the influence of flavor, think of the merchants of Venice trading spices from the East—nutmeg, pepper, cinnamon, and poppy seed. This is the Adriatic direction of this dish.

Now, on the plate, this may look like the mezzaluna presented in the previous recipe, but it is a potato filling, not ricotta, and the resulting dumpling has more in common flavorwise with pierogi than ravioli. The filling is what makes this dish interesting, as the use of Alpine roots such as turnips, beets, and/or celeriac combined with poppy seeds and potato isn't what we normally consider Italian flavor. But it is! Welcome to the mountains. Impressive but not difficult, this is the Tuesday night version of Rosa Alpina's Beet Gnocchi (page 48).

To prepare the filling: Set a steamer basket over a large pot of boiling water. Add the beets and potatoes and steam until tender (a knife can easily be inserted with no resistance), about 30 minutes. Peel while still hot (using some paper towel to protect your hands) and pass both through a potato ricer.

In a large sauté pan or Dutch oven over medium heat, melt the butter. Stir in the riced beets and potatoes and cook gently until well combined, 3 to 4 minutes. Stir in the cheese and season with salt, pepper, and nutmeg. Add the bread crumbs and stir until the filling is smooth and well combined. Set aside to cool.

After the filling has cooled, dust a work surface with semolina flour and spread the sheets of rolled dough

out on it. To form the typical crescent shape, use a 2-inch (5cm) ring mold to cut out circles of dough. Place 1 teaspoon of filling in the center of each circle, then gently close each casunziei by folding the dough over the filling and pressing on the edges of the half-circles to seal.

Bring a large pot of salted water to a boil. Add the pasta and simmer until al dente, about 5 minutes.

In the meantime, in a large sauté pan over medium heat, melt the butter. Add the sage leaves and, using a slotted spoon, transfer the stuffed pasta to the pan. Stir gently to coat.

Divide the pasta into shallow bowls, then sprinkle with the poppy seeds and Parmigiano and spoon the sage leaves and melted butter over top of each. Serve immediately.

Bombardino

YOU WILL NEED

Four tea cups, coupes,
or Irish coffee glasses

6 egg yolks
½ cup (100g) sugar
¾ cup (175ml) dry Marsala
½ cup (120ml) brandy
Whipped cream for topping
Ground cinnamon for garnish

My first time with a bombardino was during a dream morning of exploring Corvara and Colfosco on skis. At the foot of the Sassongher peak, I stopped in at Col Pradat, a hut that began as a tiny refuge back in 1920. It was late morning, and I was so elated to have a day of exploring ahead of me. With no definitive plans, I threw caution to the wind and tried this electric egg-yolk drink. If you love zabaglione (an egg-based custard)—and I do—this drink is delicious. It can also be described as an Irish coffee with the mouthfeel of Pepto-Bismol—it's thick, it's soothing, and, for 30 minutes after you down one, it gives you a nice warm kick.

The bombardino famously originated in the Alpine part of Lombardy, and more precisely in Livigno, at the Mottolino hut. According to lore, a young man from Genoa had moved to the mountains and, after many years working as an Alpine trooper, was assigned to run the Mottolino hut. On a cold winter day, four men came in from a blizzard, looking for a drink that would warm them up. The Genovese quickly threw together milk, whiskey, and zabaglione and heated the ingredients almost to boiling. When served the bubbling hot beverage, one of the men cried out, *"Accidenti! È una bomba!"* ("Damn! It's a bomb!")

Note: If you don't want to make zabaglione, you can use Zabov, the flavored egg liqueur, instead.

Bring a saucepan of water to a simmer.

In a glass or stainless-steel bowl, whisk the egg yolks and sugar until pale and thick, a good 2 to 3 minutes of vigorous whisking. Whisk the Marsala into the egg-sugar mixture and set the bowl over the simmering pot (make sure the water does not touch the bottom of the bowl). Whisk continuously and thoroughly until the custard becomes light and airy, starting to gain in volume. The key is to not have the eggs scramble, so remove the bowl from the heat from time to time and keep whisking, then return to the heat. The zabaglione is ready when it holds its shape, like a pudding, when spooned.

Pour 2 tablespoons of the brandy into each glass. Slowly spoon the zabaglione into each glass and stir. Top each drink with whipped cream, garnishing each with a sprinkle of cinnamon before serving.

VARIATIONS

Pirata Bombardino: For a hit of warmth (and more booze), add 1 tablespoon rum to each glass after you've stirred the brandy and zabaglione.

Monaco ("monk") Bombardino (This one doesn't have an official name, so I'm spit-balling here.): For an Alpine herbal kick, add 1 tablespoon génépy to each glass after you've stirred the brandy and zabaglione.

Do not be tempted to include both the rum and the génépy. Even if you're not on skis.

Honey Semifreddo with Bee Pollen

SEMIFREDDO AL MIELE CON PÒLLINE

■■■■ EASY

SERVES 4

YOU WILL NEED

Four 4-ounce (120ml) ramekins or one 2-cup (480ml) semifreddo mold

Digital instant-read thermometer

¾ cup (255g) acacia honey

1 cup (240ml) heavy cream

3 egg yolks, plus 1 egg

1 tablespoon rum

½ cup (60g) hazelnuts, grated

4 tablespoons (60g) organic bee pollen

TRAVEL HACK

The Monte Rosa lift system is similar to the Dolomiti Superski zone (see page 30) in that it connects many valleys, mountains, and pistes in the area. You may have to harness a bit of your inner MacGyver to sort out logistics, but once you do, the reward is a much-less-crowded terrain with some of the best hiking and skiing in the Alps. You're also only a 1½-hour drive from Milan-Malpensa airport, so this remote-feeling region is unusually accessible.

The main road to Alagna from the south is especially quaint; it's like a winding escalator toward the Monte Rosa massif, from which you can spot whitewater rafters shooting down the Sesia River. Along the river, there are pastel-colored bee boxes, where keepers harvest one of the area's best products: Alpine honey! Alagna, with its population of 400, feels like a very high and final pit stop before a wall of a mountain . . . because that's exactly what it is. The migrating Germanic Walser tribe knew this, too, having set up shop and homes here in the 1100s (many of which still stand today, including what is now a Walser museum).

I have been to Alagna in winter and summer, and in both seasons, the village feels like the best kind of Alpine secret with fresh local dairy products, authentic lunch huts, incredible skiing, and the base camp for the Margherita Hut—the highest rifugio in the Alps—which requires a two-day ascent, including a five-hour glacier walk, to reach. It is in this village that I found one of my favorite places: the Hotel Monterosa, a thirteen-room inn run by two formidable Swedes, Joakim and Tine Guth Linse, who were so charmed by the property, they left their life in Malmo behind to take it over. The semifreddo recipe of their chef, Salvatore Dimo, features cream from the local cows and honey from the beehives around the village, with bee pollen as garnish.

Note: The honey I used here is from local acacia blossoms. Use the best-quality honey you can find. Organic bee pollen can be found at health food stores.

Grease four ramekins or a semi-freddo mold with nonstick cooking spray.

In a small saucepan over medium heat, warm ½ cup (170 g) of the honey until it reaches 175°F (80°C) on an instant-read thermometer, about 5 minutes.

Using a stand mixer fitted with the whisk attachment, whip the heavy cream until stiff peaks form. Transfer to a medium bowl and place in the refrigerator.

In the cleaned mixer bowl, whisk the egg yolks and whole egg until well combined. With the mixer running on medium-low speed, slowly pour in the warmed honey, continuing to mix until the mixer bowl no longer feels hot but warm (room-temperature) to the touch. Whisk in the rum.

Transfer a third of the whipped cream to the egg-honey mixture and whisk gently until the mixture is lightened. Then, using a spatula, gently fold the remaining whipped cream into this semifreddo base. Sprinkle the grated nuts into the mix and whisk very gently to combine.

Fill the ramekins or the larger mold to the top with the semifreddo base. Place the molds on a small tray and freeze for 4 hours. (Long enough to be freddo but still semi . . . freddo!)

Carefully flip each ramekin upside down onto small plates. Garnish with a drizzle of the remaining ¼ cup (85g) honey and a generous sprinkle of the bee pollen. Serve immediately.

ALAGNA HONEY BOXES

Gobbi in Broth

SERVES 4 TO 6
(MAKES 1 GALLON [4L]
BROTH, 48 TO 54 RAVIOLI)

YOU WILL NEED

Pasta machine or stand mixer fitted with the pasta attachment

Fluted pastry wheel

BEEF BROTH

About 5 pounds (2kg) beef bones

2 carrots, peeled and cubed

1 yellow onion, peeled and cubed

3 celery stalks, cubed

5 sprigs thyme

5 sprigs flat-leaf parsley

3 garlic cloves, smashed

1 tablespoon black peppercorns

Water as needed

GOBBI FILLING

2 tablespoons olive oil

1 celery stalk, finely diced

1 carrot, finely diced

½ yellow onion, finely diced

2 teaspoons minced fresh rosemary

8 ounces (225g) ground veal

8 ounces (225g) ground beef

8 ounces (225g) sweet Italian pork sausage meat

1 teaspoon fine sea salt

½ teaspoon freshly ground black pepper

GOBBI DOUGH

1 pound 2 ounces (500g) all-purpose flour

3 eggs

7 tablespoons (100ml) water

1 cup (100g) grated Parmigiano-Reggiano cheese

Fine sea salt and freshly ground black pepper

Semolina and all-purpose flour for dusting

Gobbi, literally "hunchbacks," is a type of Piedmontese ravioli made by folding a sheet of pasta dough over a meat stuffing, then cutting out little individual pasta pockets. I'm not really sure if the name refers to how the pasta *looks* or to how you *feel* after making it. Either way it's worth it. Typically, gobbi is served raw along with a bowl of hot beef broth in which you warm the ravioli tableside (the stuffing is cooked prior to making the gobbi), in the belief that this allows you to really taste the nuances of the pasta dough. Gobbi can, of course, be cooked in a generous puddle of butter and sauced with veal jus instead.

This recipe is inspired by the gobbi I had at Chalet Il Capricorno, a twenty-seat restaurant and hotel owned by the Carezzana family of Torino, a few hundred meters from the Cloates cable-car station in Sauze d'Oulx. If you're not sleeping at the hotel but want to dine here (it's worth it!), you can. But as the hotel is located *on* the piste, you have to schedule a meeting time with their designated snowmobile driver, who will drive you up. You will be going uphill in subzero temperatures, so don't forget gloves and maybe thermal underwear at least for that night. A cozy stube awaits, lined with an eclectic collection of Torinese Alpine ceramics and (of course) gobbi!

Notes: It takes 12 to 16 hours to make the initial beef stock, and you'll need to cook the meat stuffing and refrigerate both the stock and stuffing overnight. The beef stock freezes well, and this makes a large batch, so you can have homemade stock on hand whenever you need it.

When making fresh pasta, the ambient humidity in your kitchen will affect how much flour you need. If it's humid (during the summertime, or you have lots of cooking happening), you may need to add a tablespoon or two of flour to the dough. The pasta dough can also be made a day ahead.

To make the beef broth: Preheat the oven to 425°F (220°C).

On an unlined baking sheet, spread out the bones in a single layer. Roast until the bones take on a dark golden color, 45 to 60 minutes.

Transfer the roasted bones to a stockpot and add the carrots, onion, celery, thyme, parsley, garlic, and peppercorns. Add cold water to cover. Bring to a simmer (not a boil) over medium-low heat, then cover, turn the heat to low, and simmer for 12 to 16 hours. (When you like the taste, it's ready.)

Remove and discard the larger bones, then strain the broth through a fine-mesh sieve into a pot or large jar. Refrigerate overnight; any fat will rise to the top and set. The next day, spoon off the fat cap and set the broth aside. (The broth will keep in an airtight container in the freezer for up to 3 months.)

To make the filling: In a large sauté pan over medium-high heat, warm the olive oil until it shimmers. Add the celery, carrot, onion, and rosemary; turn the heat to medium-low; and cook until the vegetables start to soften, 10 to 15 minutes. Stir in all the ground

continued

LENCI ARE ITALIAN CERAMICS, OFTEN WITH AN ALPINE TWIST.

I once had lunch with Olympic skier **Piero Gros** at Jimmy Hütte (a personal favorite) above Colfosco and then skied down the mountain with him afterward. It was very difficult to keep up, much less not just stop and admire his style. Born in Sauze d'Oulx, he won his first World Cup slalom race at the age of eighteen. From there, he went on to reach the World Cup podium thirty-five times, while also winning gold in the slalom at the 1976 Olympics in Innsbruck, Austria. In his mid-sixties now, Piero still skis as often as possible.

SNAPSHOT

meat, separating any large clumps of meat with a spoon or spatula to cook evenly. Sauté until cooked completely, 7 to 8 minutes. Season with the salt and pepper. Transfer the filling to an airtight container and let cool before refrigerating for at least 3 hours or preferably overnight.

To make the dough: Spoon the all-purpose flour onto a clean surface or into a large shallow bowl and make a large well in the center. Crack the eggs and pour the water into the well. Using a fork, begin to swirl the eggs, slowly incorporating the flour into the center of the well. When the flour is completely incorporated, gather and knead the mixture to form one large ball. Knead for 5 to 10 minutes on the counter. Wrap the ball tightly in plastic and rest in the refrigerator for at least 45 minutes or up to overnight.

In a bowl, combine the filling with the cheese, mixing until homogeneous. Adjust the seasoning with salt and pepper as needed.

Heavily dust a baking sheet with semolina flour. Divide the rested dough into fourths. Keep the dough covered while working with one piece at a time.

Roll the dough through the widest roller setting of your pasta machine (or attachment, if you're using a stand mixer), dusting with all-purpose flour along the way to ensure the dough doesn't stick, but not too much as you don't want the dough to become dry. Fold the sheet of dough in half onto itself, and roll it through this initial setting ten to fifteen times, folding it again after each pass.

Change the machine setting to the next, narrower setting and roll the sheet through once. You'll notice your sheet will become longer and longer as you work it through each successive setting. Keep rolling until Setting 7 (on most pasta machines); you want the sheet to be thin enough to just see your hand through it. Lay the pasta sheet out on the prepared baking sheet. Repeat the rolling procedure with the remaining three pieces of dough.

Dust a work surface with semolina flour and spread the sheets of rolled dough out on top. Place a row of 1-tablespoon mounds of filling just below the center of the sheet, 1¼ to 1½ inches (3 to 4cm) from each other. Using a small glass of water and a brush or your fingers, gently moisten the dough between the mounds. Then fold the pastry dough over the filling, pressing down gently in between each mound.

Using a pastry wheel, cut a clean line along the length of the pasta sheet. Then cut out the individual gobbi.

Heat 2 cups (480ml) of beef broth per person (or 1½ cups [360ml] if you're serving a smaller portion of gobbi as an appetizer) until steaming, then season with salt and pepper.

Portion the gobbi into bowls, then ladle a generous amount of hot broth over each. Serve immediately.

Vitello Tonnato

■■■■ MEDIUM
SERVES 4

YOU WILL NEED

Digital instant-read digital thermometer or meat thermometer with a probe

POACHED VEAL

1 pound (450g) veal eye round

½ yellow onion, chopped

1 celery stalk, thinly sliced

1 carrot, thinly sliced

1 garlic head, sliced horizontally in half

1 small bunch flat-leaf parsley

2 bay leaves

20 black peppercorns

Peel of 1 lemon, left whole

1 cup (240ml) white wine

TUNA SAUCE

3 egg yolks

2 teaspoons freshly squeezed lemon juice

Fine sea salt

1⅔ cups (395ml) extra-virgin olive oil

11 ounces (300g) high-quality tuna, canned in oil

3 salted anchovies, soaked, rinsed, and filleted, or 6 oil-packed anchovy fillets

2 ounces (55g) salted capers, rinsed, plus more to serve

Vitello tonnato—cold, pot-roasted veal slices bathed in a tuna mayonnaise sauce—is not typical mountain food (though, my *Oxford Companion to Italian Food* confirms that it originated in Torino, Piedmont). But this tonnato from mountain hotel Chalet Il Capricorno in Sauze d'Oulx is the best one I've had in my many travels to Italy. Somehow, the ratio of sliced veal to tuna sauce is just right; the veal isn't drowned in a lake of fish sauce.

Note: Il Capricorno uses girello *(a cut of veal from the hind leg, also known as veal top round or topside); however, veal loin is traditional and is much easier to slice thinly at home.*

To poach the veal: In a small stockpot or Dutch oven, combine the veal, onion, celery, carrot, garlic, parsley, bay leaves, peppercorns, lemon peel, and white wine and cover with water, enough for the meat to be submerged. Place over medium heat, bring to a simmer, and poach gently until pink on the inside (internal temperature of 140°F [60°C] on an instant-read thermometer), about 45 minutes. Remove the meat from the cooking water and set aside to cool. Wrap the meat and transfer to the freezer for 45 to 60 minutes—this will firm it up and help you attain restaurant-grade thin slices. Strain and reserve ½ cup (120ml) of the cooking liquid; discard the other solids.

To make the tuna sauce: In a medium bowl, combine the egg yolks, lemon juice, and a pinch of salt and whisk briefly to dissolve the salt. Whisking more rapidly, gradually add a few small drops of the olive oil, allowing the egg and oil to emulsify, until you've added about one-fourth of the oil. The mixture will start to look like mayonnaise, and you can whisk in the rest of the oil faster. Taste and adjust the seasoning with salt.

In a blender, combine the tuna and its oil, the anchovies, and capers and blend until smooth, using a bit of the cooking liquid to thin out the sauce as needed—I usually use about ¼ cup (60ml). Add the egg yolk mixture and blend until well incorporated—the tonnato sauce should have a slightly runny consistency.

Remove the poached veal from the freezer. Using a sharp knife, cut the meat into very thin slices.

Using the back of a spoon, spread a generous amount of tuna sauce over the center of the plate, then layer a handful of veal slices over the sauce. Top with a generous dollop of tuna sauce and sprinkle with capers. Serve immediately.

Piedmontese-Style Agnolotti

AGNOLOTTI ALLA PIEMONTESE

MEDIUM

SERVES 4

YOU WILL NEED

Meat grinder with ¼-inch
(6mm) die (optional)

Pasta machine or stand mixer
fitted with the pasta attachment

Fluted pastry wheel

AGNOLOTTI DOUGH

1 pound 2 ounces (500g)
all-purpose flour, plus more
for dusting

1⅓ cups (165g) semolina flour,
plus more for dusting

1½ teaspoons fine sea salt

3 eggs, plus 7 egg yolks

2 tablespoons extra-virgin
olive oil

2 tablespoons water

FILLING

5 ounces (140g) spinach leaves

¼ cup (60ml) olive oil

¾ cup (80g) celery, finely diced

½ cup (50g) carrots, finely diced

½ yellow onion, finely diced

2 pounds (900g) veal shoulder,
cut into 1½-inch (4cm) cubes

12 ounces (350g) pork belly, cubed

Fine sea salt

11 ounces (300g) sweet Italian
pork sausage meat

5 ounces (140g) grated
Parmigiano-Reggiano cheese

1 egg

Generous grating of nutmeg

½ cup (120ml) veal jus or
Venison Glaze (page 224)

1 cup (110g) panko bread crumbs,
toasted in 2 tablespoons unsalted
butter

If you're traveling to Italy's Piedmont Alps, it is likely you will find yourself passing through the gateway city of Torino. Here, in the former capital of Italy and still one of the most aristocratic cities of the Italian peninsula, you will find yourself completely seduced and overwhelmed by the restaurant options. Immigration to the city has caused an incredible burst of variety of dishes and available products in restaurants and markets. However, if you want to sample the old-world essence of northern Italian eating and elegance, then I suggest Del Cambio, a quintessential Torinese dining tradition. The chef, Matteo Baronetto, is a disciple of Gualtiero Marchesi, who is regarded as the founder of modern Italian cuisine (in a similar way to, say, Paul Bocuse in France). I was lucky enough to be given his agnolotti recipe, one of my favorites; so let's come down from the mountains—at least for the night—and indulge in the city.

To make the agnolotti dough: Spoon both flours and the salt onto a clean surface or into a large shallow bowl and make a large well in the center. Pour the eggs, egg yolks, olive oil, and water into the well and, using a fork, begin to swirl the eggs, slowly incorporating the flour into the center of the well. When the flour is completely incorporated, gather and knead the mixture together to form one large ball. Knead for 5 to 10 minutes on the counter. Wrap the ball tightly in plastic and let rest in the refrigerator for 1 to 2 hours, or up to overnight.

To prepare the filling: Put the spinach in a colander and pour boiling water over to wilt it. Let drain.

In a Dutch oven over medium-high heat, warm 2 tablespoons of the olive oil until it shimmers. Add the celery, carrots, and onion; turn the heat to medium-low; and cook until the vegetables start to soften, 10 to 15 minutes.

In a large frying pan over medium-high heat, warm the remaining 2 tablespoons olive oil. Add the veal and pork belly in batches and cook until nicely browned, 5 to 7 minutes per batch. Remove from the pan with a slotted spoon.

Drain any excess fat from the pan before transferring the meat to the Dutch oven. Sprinkle with 1 teaspoon salt. Add just enough water to cover the meat and vegetables, turn the heat to medium, and bring to a simmer. Turn the heat to low, cover, and braise for 4 hours, until the meat is exceedingly tender.

Stir the sausage meat and spinach into the Dutch oven and cook for another 10 minutes.

Drain the meats and vegetables, reserving the cooking liquid. Spread the meat and vegetables onto a chopping board to cool. Chop as finely as you can, using a large sharp knife or a few pulses in a food processor. Alternatively, embrace tradition and pass through a meat grinder.

Combine the chopped meats and vegetables in a bowl with the cheese, egg, and grated nutmeg. Stir to combine well, adding a splash or two of the cooking liquid as needed. Adjust

continued

the seasoning as needed with more salt and nutmeg. Set aside.

Heavily dust a baking sheet with semolina flour. Divide the rested dough into fourths. Keep the dough covered while working with one piece at a time.

Roll the dough through the widest roller setting of your pasta machine (or attachment, if you're using a stand mixer), dusting with all-purpose flour along the way to ensure the dough doesn't stick, but not too much as you don't want the dough to become dry. Fold the sheet of dough in half onto itself, and roll it through this initial setting ten to fifteen times, folding it again after each pass.

Change the machine setting to the next, narrower setting and roll the sheet through once. You'll notice your sheet will become longer and longer as you work it through each successive setting. Keep rolling until Setting 7 (on most pasta machines); you want the sheet to be thin enough to just see your hand through it. Lay the pasta sheet out on the prepared baking sheet. Repeat the rolling procedure with the remaining three pieces of dough.

Dust a work surface and baking sheet with semolina flour and spread the sheets of rolled dough out on the surface. Place a row of 1-tablespoon mounds of filling just below the center of the sheet, 1¼ to 1½ inches (3 to 4cm) apart. Using a small glass of water and a brush or your fingers, gently moisten the dough between the mounds. Then fold the pastry dough over the filling, pressing down gently in between each mound.

Using a pastry wheel, cut a clean line along the length of the pasta sheet, then cut out the individual agnolotto and transfer to the prepared baking sheet. Set aside in the refrigerator.

When you are ready to cook, bring a large pot of salted water to a boil. In a sauté pan over low heat, warm the veal jus.

Slip the agnolotti into the boiling water. Lower the heat to a simmer and cook for 2 to 3 minutes, until the edges are al dente (pick one out and bite into it). Drain, transfer to the pan with the warm veal jus, and turn gently to coat with the sauce.

Serve the agnolotti in a deep dish and sprinkle with the toasted bread crumbs.

CHEF MATTEO BARONETTO

Torinese Bonèt

BONÈT TORINESE

■■■ **DIFFICULT**

SERVES 10 TO 14
(MAKES ONE VERY TALL
6-INCH [15CM] TORTE)

YOU WILL NEED

High-speed blender or
food processor

Two 6-inch (15cm) round cake
pans or identical saucepans

Piping bag fitted with a plain tip

Rotating cake stand (optional)

Offset spatula

BONÈTS

7 ounces (200g) amaretti cookies

1 cup (200g) granulated sugar

1 cup (80g) unsweetened
cocoa powder

9 eggs

4 cups (950ml) milk

2 tablespoons amaretto liqueur

2 tablespoons brewed espresso

FROSTING

2 cups (480ml) heavy cream

Scant ½ cup (50g) confectioners'
sugar

48 amaretti cookies

From the moment I laid eyes on the Hotel La Torre in Sauze d'Oulx, a seductively French-sounding commune an hour from Torino, I thought: *I want to make a replica cake of that building and eat it.*

The building was first commissioned by Giovanni Agnelli, founder of Fabbrica Italiana di Automobili Torino (Fiat), to house the motor company's families on their Alpine holidays.

It's had a few different incarnations over time, including various attempts at upscale hotels—which it now definitely is not. However, I still recommend staying there for its authentic 1970s rotary-phone, sexed-up Italian faded glamour, and communal good fun. Besides, you can see the Torre from every chairlift in Sauze.

My idea was to build the Hotel Torre in dessert form, using only Piedmont products: hazelnuts, Torinese chocolate, amaretti cookies, and Alpine dairy for the frosting. I had the concept but neither the kitchen nor the skill for the final version, so I convinced insanely talented, Piedmont-born pastry chef Paolo Griffa to create it. He suggested that rather than make a cake, we make a Piedmontese *bonèt*, which is closer in texture to a flourless chocolate torte. Edible history.

Notes: You will need to refrigerate the two bonèts overnight before decorating, so plan accordingly. We used two narrow saucepans as molds to bake the two bonèts and then constructed them into one tall tower. Two 6-inch (15cm) cake pans that are 3 to 4 inches (8 to 10cm) tall will also work. (Do not be tempted to use springform pans because the liquid batter will leak right through them.)

If you have a favorite recipe, homemade amaretti taste superior here, but don't be afraid to purchase a bag of cookies to pulse into crumbs to adorn the finished tower.

To make the bonèts: Preheat the oven to 300°F (150°C). Bring a kettle or large pot of water to a boil. Coat two 6-inch (15cm) cake pans with nonstick cooking spray.

In a high-speed blender or a food processor, combine the 7 ounces (200g) amaretti cookies, granulated sugar, and cocoa powder and blend or pulse until the cookies turn to fine crumbs and the sugar and cocoa are evenly distributed throughout (about ten pulses). Add the eggs, milk, amaretto, and espresso and blend or process until smooth, about 30 seconds. Pour the batter through a sieve directly into each prepared cake pan, dividing it evenly. Transfer both pans to a 9 by 13-inch (23 by 33cm) baking dish and fill the dish with boiling water until the water level reaches halfway up the cake pans.

Bake until a cake tester inserted into the center of a bonèt comes out clean, 40 to 50 minutes. Set the cake pans on a rack and let cool before refrigerating overnight.

continued

To make the frosting: The next day, in a medium bowl, combine the heavy cream and confectioners' sugar and whip until firm peaks form. Transfer to a piping bag fitted with a medium plain tip, and refrigerate for up to 4 hours if you're not immediately starting to frost.

Because a bonèt has a wobbly, puddinglike texture, it's good to give it a good flat foundation, such as an upside-down plate. Very gently unmold the first bonèt onto the plate, then unmold the second one directly on top of the first. Place this plate on a rotating cake stand if you're using one.

Starting at the bottom, pipe the frosting around the bonèt, working in a circle, around and around. Don't worry about getting it perfect; that's what an offset spatula is for. Completely cover the top of the cake, then trade the piping bag for an offset spatula and gently smooth the cream over so there's no cake or cracks showing. (Pro tip: To achieve the smoothest frosting look, dip your offset spatula in a tall glass of hot water, then wipe it dry before each smoothing maneuver.) Garnish the bonèt to look like the Hotel Torre, placing the whole amaretti in even rows around the circumference, like little windows. Cut carefully, serve, and enjoy.

Veal Carbonnade with Polenta

CARBONADA DI VITELLO CON POLENTA

MEDIUM

SERVES 4

2 pounds (900g) veal rump, cut into 1-inch (2.5cm) cubes

½ cup (60g) all-purpose flour

Fine sea salt and freshly ground black pepper

1 cup (220g) unsalted butter

½ cup (100g) thick-sliced bacon lardons

2 yellow onions, halved and thinly sliced

Pinch of freshly grated nutmeg

½ teaspoon ground cinnamon

2 cups (480ml) dry white wine

Polenta (page 86) to serve

The village of Entrèves, about 10 minutes' drive from Courmayeur, is the last stop before the Mont-Blanc tunnel, which technically makes it the last Italian stop before France. There, you'll find the Auberge de La Maison, a small hotel and restaurant run by Léo Garin and his daughter, Alessandra. You could be on a plane flying from Montreal to Zurich, or maybe at your neighborhood bookshop looking for an Alpine map, and the person beside you will say, "Do you know Léo Garin?" He is that kind of guy. A history buff and collector of Alpine engravings, he wrote a book called *Voyage au Coeur des Alpes (Journey to the Heart of the Alps: Two Centuries of Engravings from the Mont Blanc to the Matterhorn)*, all about the eighteenth- and nineteenth-century explorers and their narrative through engravings and oil paintings. That the book was written in French shows how easily Italian and French are swapped in Entrèves.

It was Alessandra who welcomed me for lunch after I came down from 4,000 meters (13,125 feet). A fantastic hotelier and Alpine enthusiast, she and I sat for lunch facing out the window. In front of us, wooden slats supported freshly baked round loaves, and the beginning of the Mont-Blanc massif was our backdrop.

Note: The kitchen team served me a veal carbonnade in a copper pan alongside a dome of perfect polenta. Most carbonnades are reduced with beer. If not beer, at least red wine. But the hook here is that these thin pieces of veal were cooked in white wine, and the onions and bacon lardons melted into the creamy sauce dusted with nutmeg for a layer of depth. I could have eaten this for lunch, dinner, and the next morning's breakfast.

Preheat the oven to 300°F (150°C).

In a large bowl, toss the veal in the flour until coated. Season with salt and pepper.

In a large sauté pan or Dutch oven over medium-high heat, melt the butter. Working in two batches, shake any excess flour from the meat, then toss the veal into the pan and brown on all sides, 5 to 7 minutes per batch. Transfer the meat to a plate.

Add the bacon and onions to the butter and cook over medium heat until beginning to brown, 10 to 12 minutes. Stir in the nutmeg and cinnamon.

Return the browned meat to the pan and pour in ½ cup (120ml) of the wine, scraping the pan bottom with a wooden spoon to loosen the caramelized flour. Simmer gently, adding the rest of the wine in three ½-cup (120ml) batches over the next 15 minutes, until the braising liquid starts to thicken. Adjust the seasoning. Cover, transfer to the oven, and braise until the meat is completely tender, about 1 hour.

Serve the stew in shallow bowls with a side of polenta.

Polenta

SERVES 4

1 quart (950ml) water

1 teaspoon fine sea salt

1 cup (150g) organic polenta corn grits

2 tablespoons unsalted butter

This makes a "tight" polenta, with a tendency to set. For a looser polenta, increase the water to 1½ quarts (1.4L).

Fill a large heavy saucepan with the water and bring to a boil over medium-high heat. Lower the heat to a simmer, add the salt, and pour in the corn grits in a slow stream, whisking continuously to prevent clumping. Return the liquid to a simmer and keep whisking until the mixture starts to thicken.

Turn the heat to its lowest setting, cover, and cook for 45 to 50 minutes, stirring well around the sides and the bottom of the pot every 4 or 5 minutes. The polenta will become soft and tender, and start to come off the walls of the saucepan. Stir the butter into the polenta and adjust the seasoning as needed. Transfer to a round bowl, and let cool slightly and start to set.

Serve warm, using a large spoon.

Valpelline Soup

SEUPA À LA VAPELENENTSE

■■■■ EASY

SERVES 4

YOU WILL NEED
2-quart (1.9L) round casserole dish

1 tablespoon olive oil

½ cup (115g) bacon lardons

1 small savoy cabbage, coarsely chopped

1½ quarts (1.4L) beef or veal stock or low-sodium beef broth

Fine sea salt and freshly ground black pepper

1 pound (450g) rye bread, sliced and staled

14 ounces (400g) Fontina cheese, thinly sliced

⅔ cup (145g) unsalted butter, cubed

1 teaspoon ground cinnamon

In Courmayeur, Guido Riente at Chateau Branlant has been perfecting his version of this soup, which hails from the remote micro-village of Valpelline. That is, he makes this recipe when he's not running the Tour of Giants, a 330-kilometer (205-mile) foot race that is meant to be completed in less than 150 hours. (The "giants" are the mountains, naturally—the Matterhorn/Monte Cervino, Mont-Blanc, Monte Rosa, and Gran Paradiso—all connected by the famed Alta Via 1 and Alta Via 2 trails.) Maybe because there's nothing better than hot soup that doubles as a casserole when you finish a race like that? His spot, Branlant, is one of my favorites for Alpine lunches. It's always jammed with people in their ski gear (of course), and the food, like this soup, packs a hearty punch for high-altitude fare.

Preheat the oven to 400°F (200°C).

In a Dutch oven over medium-high heat, warm the olive oil until it shimmers. Add the bacon and sauté until it's released its fat and is starting to brown. Stir in the cabbage, turn the heat to medium, cover, and let it sweat, while stirring regularly, until it begins to wilt, 5 to 7 minutes.

Pour the beef stock into the Dutch oven, turn the heat to medium-high, and bring to a boil. Lower the heat and simmer until the cabbage is tender, about 5 minutes. Adjust the seasoning with salt and pepper, as needed. Strain the cabbage and bacon, reserving the broth.

Cover the bottom of an ovenproof casserole dish with a layer of the bread slices. Spread half the cabbage and bacon over the bread, followed by half the Fontina slices. Repeat the layers with another round of bread, cabbage with bacon, and cheese. Gently pour the warm broth into the dish, around the edges. Dot the top with the butter, then sprinkle the cinnamon all over.

Bake until the Fontina is golden brown and a crust is starting to form, 30 to 40 minutes.

Serve piping hot in big shallow bowls.

ALESSANDRA GARIN MAKING VIN BRULEÉ,
AUBERGE DE LA MAISON.

BREAD COOLING AT
AUBERGE DE LA MAISON

Cogne-Style Soup

SEUPETTA À LA COGNEINTZE

EASY

SERVES 4

YOU WILL NEED

2-quart (1.9L) round casserole dish

2 quarts (1.9L) beef stock or low-sodium beef broth

1 cup (220g) good-quality unsalted butter, plus melted butter for drizzling

11 ounces (300g) whole-wheat bread, sliced

1⅓ cups (260g) Baldo rice

¾ cup plus 2 tablespoons (200ml) dry white wine

Fine sea salt and freshly ground black pepper

7 ounces (200g) Fontina cheese, thinly sliced

Pinch of ground cinnamon

You've got to love a soup that's so cheesy, you have to eat it with a fork!

Its origin? Coping! Coping with snow. Coping with elemental Alpine life. Coping with a lack of bright, fresh produce during winter months. This soup was made at Lou Ressignon in the quiet village of Cogne and, per its namesake, it originated here and you won't find out outside of the Aosta Valley.

Siblings David and Elisabeth Allera run Lou Ressignon as their parents did before them. It is a little roadside hotel and restaurant where serious skiers or hikers will bunk upstairs, while locals (and some Milanese) enjoy the dining room. It's the kind of inn that I would want to write a novel in if I ever actually wanted to write a novel. The Cogneintze soup is an Alpine classic, as is the Valpelline variation (see page 87), which trades the rice for rye, cabbage, and bacon. Both are incarnations of a very hearty zuppa di Aosta.

Note: If you can't find Baldo rice (a Turkish short-grain hybrid of Arborio), use Arborio rice instead.

Line a plate with a layer of paper towels. In a saucepan, bring the beef stock to a simmer.

In a large frying pan over medium-high heat, melt one-third of the butter. Add the bread slices and fry on both sides, working in batches (and adding more butter as needed). Set aside on the prepared plate.

In a Dutch oven or large sauté pan over medium-high heat, melt the remaining two-thirds butter until foamy, then stir in the rice and keep stirring until the rice is completely coated and starts to toast, about 5 minutes. Now it's time to *sfumare*, to soften the rice with the white wine. Turn the heat to medium and pour the wine into the pan, stirring continuously all along the sides and the center to prevent the rice from sticking, until the wine evaporates.

Preheat the oven to 400°F (200°C). Butter an ovenproof casserole dish.

Add a ladleful of beef stock to the rice and stir until the stock is mostly absorbed. Repeat, one ladleful at a time, until all the stock has been incorporated and the rice is creamy but still fluid, 25 to 30 minutes. Season with salt and pepper.

Transfer one-third of the rice into a prepared casserole dish. Place one-third of the bread slices over the rice, followed by one-third of the cheese slices. Repeat another two times, then finish with a sprinkle of cinnamon on the last layer of Fontina. Add a small drizzle of warm butter.

Bake for 5 to 10 minutes, until the cheese has melted.

Serve very hot.

Ditalini with Fava Beans

LA FAVÒ VALDOSTANA

EASY

SERVES 4

1 cup (120g) shucked fava beans (about 2½ pounds [1.1kg] in the shell)

½ cup (110g) unsalted butter, plus 2 tablespoons

2 cups (120g) diced dark bread

Fine sea salt

2 cups (240g) ditalini pasta (or other small pasta tube shape)

1 shallot, thinly sliced

1 cup (240ml) tomato passata (or canned tomatoes passed through a food mill)

4 ripe tomatoes, cubed

Freshly ground black pepper

4 ounces (115g) Fontina cheese, thinly sliced

This recipe was given to me by Laura Roullet, the maître de maison at one of my all-time favorite hotels in Cogne: the Bellevue. A beautiful, Alpine-pink (yes, it's a thing: Wedgewood has a line of bone china that comes in Alpine pink) building, the Bellevue lies on a plateau surrounded by cross-country skiing trails, right near the main entrance to Gran Paradiso National Park, part of the Gran Paradiso massif in the Aosta Valley. *La favò* is packed with mountain ingredients: pasta, Fontina, black bread toasted in butter, sausage, bacon, and the delicious fava beans that give the dish its name. La favò is served at the Bellevue's wine and cheese bar—a more casual option than the main (and incredible) restaurant in the hotel.

Deep within the entrails of the hotel lies one of the best-kept secrets of the Alps, the hotel's wine cave. This is where you want to get snowed in! Start your snow day with a nice Italian breakfast, followed by a morning of cross-country skiing, a little time in the sauna, and an evening with sommelier Rino Billia and some of his favorites—from a 1980s Mouton Rothschild to an Emidio Pepe you can't find anywhere else. Rino loves Piedmont (who doesn't?) and the wines of Gaja, Clerico, Altare, Federico Graziani, Ottin, and Cuom. I can't think of a better wine cave to be trapped in (except *maybe* that of La Perla Hotel in Corvara or Ciasa Salares in Badia).

Fill a bowl with ice water for an ice bath. Line a plate with a layer of paper towels.

In a large pot of boiling water, blanch the fava beans for 1 minute. Remove the beans with a skimmer or large slotted spoon and plunge into the ice bath; reserve the cooking water. Drain the beans, then lay them on a tray and begin peeling, squeezing gently to slip off the skins. Set the peeled favas aside (this can be done a day ahead).

In a small saucepan over medium heat, melt the ½ cup (110g) butter and cook until it has stopped foaming and starts to take on a golden, hazelnut color. Add the bread and fry until crunchy, about 2 minutes. Transfer to the prepared plate.

Generously salt the fava bean water and return to a boil. Add the pasta and cook until al dente, 9 to 10 minutes.

While the pasta is cooking, in a large sauté pan over medium-low heat, melt the remaining 2 tablespoons butter. Add the shallot and sweat until softened, about 5 minutes. Stir in the tomato passata and cubed tomatoes. Season with salt and pepper.

Drain the pasta, return it to the pot, and add the tomato-shallot mixture, fava beans, and Fontina. Turn the heat to medium-high and stir vigorously until the cheese melts and the dish becomes creamy. Finally, add the fried bread.

Serve very hot.

Aosta Preserves Trolley

MEDIUM

SERVES A LARGE FAMILY
OF HUNGRY SKIERS

Duck liver pâté wrapped
in lardo (1)

Pickled Alpine trout (2)

Smoked herring with carrots,
onions, and bay leaves (3)

Fried zucchini with red onions,
vinegar, and sage (4)

Anchovies, garlic, chiles,
and oil (5)

Beef tongue in salsa verde (6)

Cannellini beans with onions
and oil (7)

Salignoùn ricotta with fennel,
cumin, parsley, and chiles (8)

Aosta fresh peppers with
red vinegar and sugar in
bagna càuda (9)

Tomini cheese in vinegar with
red chile and garlic (10)

The name Les Neiges d'Antan (Snowfalls of Yesteryear) gives away the spirit of this restaurant before you set foot inside. Though I have located it at Cervinia on our Italy map, it is actually ten minutes down the road, closer to the charming village of Valtournenche (see Travel Hack, page 96). Being farther from the reach of the Zermatt/Cervinia connection, the town is more low-key. The current custodian of Les Neiges d'Antan, Ludo Bich, is a generous host, and if you find yourself within 24 kilometers (15 miles) or so of here, I really suggest you drive over for the food and the company. The walls are lined with Alpine paintings by Ludo's grandfather, Maurizio Bich, a famed mountain guide and climber. Ludo's father built the hotel, and Ludo has kept many of the recipes his grandparents would cook for him when his father was away.

One mainstay is the charcuterie board, made from meats caught by local hunters; a second is this Aosta trolley, really a complete larder on wheels. It's the equivalent of an American all-you-can-eat salad bar, except . . . good. Almost everything is made in-house, all of the products are from Aosta, and everything on the trolley is shelf-stable.

The wine list here runs deep with French and Italian greats. And though it's tempting to wander from the Alps over to the wines of Burgundy or Loire, I suggest that you stay in Aosta with a Prié Blanc from local producer Ermes Pavese.

This dish isn't as much a recipe as it is a grocery suggestion, or perhaps a prescription for Alpine betterment through food!

Elisabetta Foradori took over her family's winery at the age of nineteen and has since become one of Italy's superstar winemakers. When she's not tending to her Teroldego grapes, you can find her dining at Krone in Aldino, where she enjoys the gnocchi di erbe, one of her favorite dishes. She loves to hike any stretch of the 1,000-kilometer (621-mile) Grande Traversata delle Alpi, and finds the best month in the Alps to be July, because of the mountain flowers. It was Elisabetta who suggested I go to Fichtenhof to try the canederli.

SNAPSHOT

TRAVEL HACK

On the Zermatt/Cervinia/
Valtourneche piste map,
red piste #1 begins at Cime
Bianche (White Summit)
and ends 1,500 meters
(about 5,000 feet) below in
Valtourneche. Where it actually
ends is a little restaurant, as
famous and old as the area,
called Foyer des Guides, or The
Guide's Hearth (pictured here).
The parents and grandparents
of the current owners were
Italian mountain guides back
to the era of Jean-Antoine
Carrel, the Italian guide who
competed for the ascent of
the Matterhorn/Mt. Cervinia
against Edward Whymper. This
restaurant isn't about the food;
it's about the reward of making
it down the run and taking in
the history of mountain guiding
presented on its walls.

AUSTRIA

The Austrian Alps: An Overview

For some, the catchy showtunes of Rodgers and Hammerstein's *The Sound of Music* are as sweet and traditional as *Apfelstrüdel* (see page 175). For others, they represent an overly sentimental piece of nostalgia that ignores the backdrop of one of the most evil regimes in history. For me, the 1965 film is all of these things, and while I can't remember *ever* sitting down to a full viewing, I can whistle the tune of the lyrics "How do you solve a problem like Maria?" These were my thoughts as I passed the town of Werfen in the Salzburger Alps, where, in the film, Julie Andrews spun around like a *Baumkuchen* (Tyrolean Cake on a Spit, page 135) in front of Hohenwerfen Castle. Considering this region's history, it struck me that the ancient myth of monsters in the Alps (avalanches and the sounds of ice cracking made villagers think the mountains were filled with dragons) evidently had some real-life resonance at one time.

Although some believe Austrian cuisine to be a handful of classics, it is in fact deeply rich. Perhaps one of the reasons for this misconception is because many of the dishes you find in the Austrian Alps originated from the capital, Vienna. This is one element that sets the Austrian Alps apart from their sisters in this book. The food of the Italian Alps bears little resemblance to the food of Rome. Nor do you often see Parisian classics such as escargot or steak frites on menus in the Savoie. Whereas many dishes—Kaiserschmarrn (page 161), Tafelspitz (page 115), *Backhendl* (fried chicken), and apple strudel—are Viennese at heart but thrive at altitude.

During the time of the Austro-Hungarian Empire, Vienna was a cultural and culinary crossroads, a melting pot for the ethnic minorities folded into the empire. And from empire to republic, Vienna's reputation was fortified as a hub of civility in art, music, coffee, and cuisine (of which pastry and cakes have their own summit; see sidebar on page 107). Vienna is located in a valley basin between two mountain chains: the Alps (to the west) and the Carpathians (to the east). It is its own city-state among a total of nine Austrian states, and its gastronomic arm stretches west to the four Alpine states of Salzburg, Carinthia, Tyrol, and Vorarlberg (with a minor reach into Styria). The distance is not far; it's only about three hours by car from Vienna to the slopes of the Salzburg Alps. That we see Viennese mainstays on mountain menus is (in my opinion) less about the short distance and more about the national heritage, the passing down of Austrian recipes; also many of these dishes aren't made from market-fresh ingredients.

Although Austria has its fruit belt in the Wachau Valley, this is not the land of avocados and kale (or whatever the new fad is); this is the Old World and it's refreshingly untrendy. That said, I do look forward to spring mountain menus when places such as Almhof Schneider in Lech offer special *Spargel* (asparagus) dishes in which the pale spears are served a dozen ways. The foodstuffs of the Austrian Alps are mainly boiled and cured meats (speck and wursts), offal, cured cheeses (Tyrolean grey cheese), sauerkrauts, breads and cakes, hearty root vegetables (especially horseradish), and the beautiful Alpine fish such as char and trout of the Bluntautal Valley. All of these items are relatively shelf-stable and can be easily stored in high-elevation kitchens and cellars.

You can eat very well and relatively inexpensively in the Austrian Alps. Many rural farmhouses open their doors to hiking guests for hearty meals in the summer; and in the Salzburg region alone, there are more than two hundred traditional huts from which to choose. Alternatively, when Austria goes high with restaurants, it goes very *high*. In Werfen (where I began with Fraulein Maria), the Obauer restaurant run by brothers Karl and Rudolf Obauer serves technical, luxurious nouvelle cuisine. Though they use local ingredients from the Salzburg Alps, Obauer is not what I would call cozy stube food. So many incredibly talented chefs have come from under the Obauers' wings, there should be a heritage plaque hanging outside its door. (Franz Mulser, owner of Gostner Schwaige in Alto Adige, Italy, is one; see page 30.) Döllerer in the town of Golling (see page 120) is another example of an Austrian Alpine heritage restaurant that should be on your Salzburger hit list, as is Sissy Sonnleitner in Kötschach-Mauthen, Carinthia (where you'll find Sissy behind the stove).

Salzburg is an Alpine city. Within one hour, you can be among the sheep and cows and ibex. If you eat one morsel here, it has to be Salzburger Nockerl (page 118), an iconic dessert of three eggy peaks meant to represent the baroque view of the mountains from Amadeus Mozart's birth city. I loved it (and the rest of the menu) at Bärenwirt restaurant, a little tavern beside the Salzach River. If you have a second dining opportunity in Salzburg, I suggest Vienna's outpost the Hotel Sacher Wien, which has the most wonderful Tafelspitz (page 115), complete with a serving setup so imperial that you will feel like Empress Sissi in the royal court of Hapsburg (before the whole assassination fiasco).

Surrounding Salzburg are many small Alpine towns that make for good eats and weekender trips: Lofer, Zell Am See, St. Johann im Pongau, Mittersill, and Kaprun (which includes the skiing region of Kitzsteinhorn at 10,509 meters [3,203 feet]). And I still haven't even touched on the Gasteinertal Valley, which includes Dorfgastein, Bad Gastein, Böckstein, and Sportgastein.

While researching this book, often on a plane or train or dining in a restaurant (I had many dinners alone, but no lonely dinners), someone would ask what I was writing in my journal. After providing my usual two-liner about the book and dodging the inevitable crack about it being only about cheese, people usually referenced the film *The Grand Budapest Hotel* and how they loved it. "Then you should go to Bad Gastein," I would say. I suggested this because in addition to the story (inspired by Viennese playwrite Stefan Zweig), I think people are reacting to the Belle Époque grandeur stylized by Wes Anderson, as well as the singularity of an independently run mountain hotel complete with quirks.

De l'Europe Gastein Rooms & Apartements in Bad Gastein is one such example. This is an analog space, meaning traditional stationery, push-button telephones, no screens for distraction; tactile and rich in story and silence with an Alpine-ness you can *feel*. It's in the air and especially in the water, as the Gasteiner Ache creek running throughout this valley is fed by radon-rich mineral springs and thought to cure gastric ailments, rheumatism, bronchitis, and even allergies. In German, *Bad* translates to "bath," as this is an Alpine town built on a ridge overtop thermal waters.

ANTON SIGWART AND HIS GRIFFON BLEU DE GASCOGNE

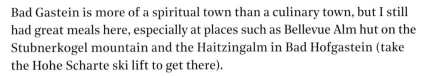

Bad Gastein is more of a spiritual town than a culinary town, but I still had great meals here, especially at places such as Bellevue Alm hut on the Stubnerkogel mountain and the Haitzingalm in Bad Hofgastein (take the Hohe Scharte ski lift to get there).

Go through an aquaduct tunnel and across a gorge from Bad Gastein and you're on the plateau of the Sportgastein ski area. The weather was too dicey to dine on the mountain when I was here, but I did have a memorable meal at the beloved Valeriehaus. Venison Ragout (see page 122), a remnant from the Hungarian side of the region, is the specialty here, made with venison from the in-house *Jägermeister* (hunt master). Paprika, fried onions, beef or game, and *plenty* of time are the main ingredients of this stew, which is a typical herdsman's supper in the Alps.

Eastward, over the spiraling Grossglockner, Austria's highest mountain, lies the state of Tyrol.

When we imagine the Austrian Alps, I think it is Tyrol that we picture. *Tiroler Gröstl* (page 148) is as Tyrolean as Austria's national costume: lederhosen and loden for the man, and a dirndl for women. *Gröstl* is a dish that helps you use up yesterday's leftovers of potatoes, speck, and onions. Served in a frying pan, it is the ultimate rustic lunch, something cooks in the region of Tyrol know everything about. This area is full of high peaks that maintain cold temperatures all year-round (although this used to be more true years ago than it is today) and a simplicity that is characteristic of old Alpine towns. There's the town square with a church as its centerpiece, the sound of bells tolling in competition only with the sound of cowbells from the *almen*, where the herd of cows graze in the Alpine pastures above.

Tyrol also has the pistes and glamour of Kitzbühel, and Austria's most famous downhill race, the Hahnenkamm; this hill and Switzerland's Lauberhorn (see page 195) are the most notorious runs in all the Alps. Families have been returning to Kitz (as they say) annually for generations, and you could spend months without hiking or skiing or eating on the same piece of mountain twice. Tyrol also has the authentic villages of the Kitzbüheler Alps: Alpbach, Brandenberg, and Brixlegg, which are smaller, more idyllic places where you can hear what is known as "undiluted" Tyrol local speak. There are the resorts of Mayrhofen and Ischgl (bordering Switzerland's Silvretta range, it's known mainly for its nightlife), and St. Anton in the Arlberg. You can also visit the glaciers of the famous saddle passes of Hintertux (where you can ski 365 days a year), Kühtai (see page 151), and Sölden, where Ötzi the Iceman (a five-thousand-year-old man preserved in the ice) was found in 1991. This area is a jackpot of *Jagdschloss*, a German word that means "hunting lodge" or "castle." Innsbruck, one of the biggest cities in the Alps, is in Tyrol. It's my preferred location to fly in to and out of because of its central location, but I admit that I also like the thrill of the steep takeoff (there isn't much wiggle room to climb over those Alps) and (somewhat scary) landing. Tyrol is also easily accessible via the Brenner Pass, which leads through the Zillertal Alps and South Tyrol's Stubai Alps on the way to Italy.

I have a soft spot for the marshmallowy mountaintops of the Vorarlberg, the most western region of Austria (and the tiniest aside from Vienna). As soon as I drive into the small town of Stuben, only 1½ hours or so from Zürich, with its quaint Après Post Hotel and spot skiers lunching on the terrace, my heart skips a beat. I know I've arrived and that the town of Lech is just around a few more well-engineered bends. Lech is one of my favorite spots to vacation in, and I've managed to make good friends there (from cooks to hoteliers to guides) over the years. Lech's Almhof Schneider is the gateway to luxury in the Austrian Alps (like Rosa Alpina is in Italy; see page 48). It has a simple but excellent restaurant where I had the best *Wiener Schnitzel* (yes, even compared to Vienna). The skiing and hiking is great here—I especially love to cross-country ski to the small huts of Zürs (try the Flexenpass hut for its speck and ribs) and Klösterle (for the afternoon cakes). The eating is at such a high level in this region, it is a complete joy. (There are too many examples to list here, but check out the Address Book on page 335 for my recommendations.)

And finally, the Alter Goldener Berg is a great introduction to Austrian Alpine cooking. The menu is democratic and so is the arrival; anyone can take the cable car from Lech to Oberlech to get here. *Knödels* in beef broth, mezzalune, speck, cheese boards, herb salads—this type of spread served in a century-old stube (complete with gingham curtains and low ceilings) embodies all that the Austrian Alpine classics can be.

ALPINE COOKING

VIENNA: THE PEAK OF PASTRIES AND CAKE

One of my favorite books on Austrian cuisine is Joseph Wechsberg's *The Cooking of Vienna's Empire*. On its cover (and in the pages) is the *Spanische Windtorte*, an elaborate vanilla cake that is a sort of haven for a baker's piping bag. Tall and commanding, it's covered, down to the last inch, with frosted meringue rosettes. Although it's rare to find a *Windtorte* in the Alps, you will find other Viennese pastries, like the *Gugelhupf, Burgtheater Torte, Linzertorte, Kaffeecreme Torte, Topfen-Obers-Torte* (see page 151), *Annatorte, Sachertorte,* and various strudels, stollens, and kuchens.

If you're in Vienna, check out one of the oldest confectionary shops, Demel. Around Christmastime in Tyrol, many confectionaries carve Alpine scenes into marzipan and serve specialty *krapfen* (cream- or jelly-filled donuts). The mountain bakeries may not have marbled counters or imperial silver trays, but it's what atop the serving vessel that counts.

Weisswurst, aka The Münchener

■■■■ DIFFICULT
MAKES 10 SAUSAGES

YOU WILL NEED

Meat grinder with ¼-inch (6mm) die and ⅛-inch (3mm) die (preferably a KitchenAid stand mixer with grinder attachment)

Sausage stuffer

Large bowl half-filled with ice, water, and salt, for an ice bath

Digital instant-read thermometer

1½ pounds (680g) pork skin

2 pounds (900g) pork shoulder

1 pound (450g) fatback

6 ounces (170g) skinless pork jowl

8 ounces (225g) crushed ice

2 tablespoons fine sea salt

2 tablespoons brandy

½ teaspoon grated lemon zest

2 teaspoons freshly ground white pepper

Pinch of ground cinnamon

½ teaspoon ground mace

½ teaspoon freshly grated nutmeg

3 feet (1m) of 1¼- to 1⅜-inch (3 to 3.5cm) hog casings, rinsed and flushed with cold water

Grain mustard or yellow mustard for dipping (optional)

This minced veal sausage is made in butcher shops across Bavaria, but it can also be found in the German-speaking parts of Switzerland and in Austria. Like Meranerwürstel (see page 36), or even a cappuccino, Weisswurst is intended to be enjoyed before lunch—mornings only. You have to love a culture that includes a midmorning sausage break!

This recipe includes two of the best tricks in all of sausage-making (which I learned from sausage-god Eli Cairo at Olympia Provisions in Portland, Oregon). First, this uses pork jowl as part of the fat content of the sausage (jowl is added to emulsified sausages when you want a heavenly, light texture similar to a frankfurter), and second, this includes boiled pork skin to add a unique mouthfeel.

Similar to mortadella or *Appenzeller Siedwurst* (see page 113), Weisswurst must be peeled before eating. I peel mine like a banana, then dip it directly into mustard. I've had a good Weisswurst in all sorts of situations, but my three favorites are at Dallmayr in Munich, Germany, Alter Goldener Berg in Oberlech (pictured here), and the Salzburger Würstelkönigin ("Sausage Queen") cart in Salzburg. During a meal, Weisswurst is best served with cheese spaetzle (see page 171).

Notes: Ask your butcher for the pork skin; it doesn't have to come in one piece. (You may, however, have to preorder the hog casings.) It will take about 5 hours to cook, cool, and purée the pork skin before you can make the sausage.

Keeping the meat cold at all times is imperative when making sausage. Adjust your refrigerator's thermostat to a cooler, near-freezing setting in preparation.

Place the pork skin in a large pot and cover with water. Bring to a simmer and adjust the heat so that it stays at a nice simmer. Cook for 1 hour, adding water as needed to keep the skin fully submerged. Using tongs, remove the skin from the water and place it, skin-side down, on a cutting board. Using the back of a large knife, scrape off and discard the fat from the skin. (You need to remove this fat *before* you put the skin into the sausage, otherwise the final product becomes greasy when fully cooked.) Return the skin in the simmering water and continue to cook until it is fall-apart tender; this could take up to another 2 hours. If in doubt, cook it longer. There no such thing as overcooked skin! (You will know it is done when you try to remove it from the pot and it will not be able to bear its own weight. Or, when you bite into it and find the texture mushy.) Remove it from the water, pat dry, and cool in the refrigerator for 1 hour.

While you're waiting for the skin to cool, cube the pork shoulder and fatback, and dice the pork jowl. Return to the refrigerator.

Place the cooled, cooked skin in a food processor and purée completely. Transfer to a bowl and return the bowl to the fridge for 1 hour.

When all of the meats are fully chilled (32°F/0°C), combine them with half of the crushed ice in a large bowl. Set up your meat grinder with the largest die you have, preferably a ¼ inch (6mm) die, so that the ground meat can land into a bowl resting in an ice bath.

Grind the meat and crushed ice mixture two times through. After the

continued

second time, be sure to check the meat temperature. If it's above 39°F (4°C), return it to the fridge for 15 minutes.

Change the die to the smallest you have, preferably a ⅛-inch (3mm) die. Add the rest of the ice to the bowl with the ground meats and run this mixture through two more times. (If you do not have a smaller die, you may have to run it through the ¼-inch [6mm] die four more times. So that would make it six times total). On the final pass on the small die, add the puréed skin.

Transfer the meat mixture into the bowl of a stand mixer fitted with the paddle attachment and add the salt, brandy, lemon zest, white pepper, cinnamon, mace, and nutmeg. Mix on medium speed for 3 minutes.

Shape the meat into two separate balls and, working manually, give each one a few good hits on your counter to get all of the air out. Set aside in the refrigerator.

Before setting up your stuffer, if possible, place the hopper (the part that the meat goes into) in the fridge or the freezer so that it's nice and cold. If you are stuffing from your grinder, you will need to remove the blades and dies and place the horn on the end. Get all of the surfaces that the casing will be touching (the horn and a baking sheet) really wet with water so that the casing will slide and not tear; you can pour about ¼ cup (60ml) of water directly into your tray. Remove the casing from the water and slide one end onto the horn, and keep sliding it onto the horn until you get to the other end of the casing. Tie a knot on that end. Using your hands, a spatula, or a wooden spoon, press the meat mixture into the hopper.

Try to fill the casing full without any gaps of air, but don't overfill it; you need enough space to "link" the sausages. If you do get a few air gaps, you should pierce the casing lightly with the tip of a small, sharp knife. Once you have all the meat in the casing, cut off any of the excess casing that you have and tie a knot in the end.

To link the sausage, start at whatever end you would like and, with your dominant hand, measure a hand length from the end of the casing. Using your index finger and your thumb, pinch the casing, then twist the sausage away from you two full rotations. Measure another hand length from the spot that you just pinched and pinch again. This time you will rotate the sausage toward you two full rotations in the opposite direction that you just did. The initial sausage should feel nice and tight. Repeat this for the entire length of the casing: pinch-twist one way, pinch-twist the other way.

Finally, the sausage just needs to be poached. And like the rest of the process, it's the cooling period that is really crucial to the final product and its telltale color. Bring a pot of water to simmer (not a boil) and add the sausages. Poach for 4 to 5 minutes, or until the internal temperature reaches 155°F (68°C). As you are poaching these heavenly gems, they may turn a bit gray: don't despair! When they finish poaching, just shock them in a large ice bath and, like meat magic, the wurst should turn as white as snow. When you heat them for serving, they will have the texture of a cloud.

HUS 8 IN LECH (GREAT WURSTS!)

THE WURST CART

Here are *some* of the sausage options available at various carts throughout Austria, Alto Adige, and, in fewer cases, Switzerland.

Appenzeller Siedwurst: A very pink Swiss cousin to Weisswurst. Small wooden skewers tied onto the casings bookend the sausage; this is the marking of a Siedwurst, and a calling card of Appenzeller. If niche sausage-making is your thing, visit Metzgerei Fassler in Appenzell for further investigation.

Debrecziner: Hungarian pork/beef/sheep saddle (loin) sausage with paprika.

Frische Blutwurst: Black pudding sausage.

Käsekrainer: Boiled pork and beef sausage stuffed with Emmental cheese.

Meranerwürstel: A South Tyrolean veal/beef cousin to the frankfurter (see page 36).

Puzsta: Debrecziner (see entry) with the addition of diced green and red bell peppers.

Waldviertler: Double-smoked beef/pork tenderloin sausage from Lower Austria's Waldviertel region.

Wurstsemmel: Smoked sausage in the form of smoked ham, with cucumber or pickle in a Kaiser roll.

Huckleberry Dumplings

HEIDELBEERE KNÖDEL

███ EASY

SERVES 4 (MAKES
8 DUMPLINGS)

2½ cups (400g) fresh
huckleberries or blueberries

¾ cup (100g) stone-ground
whole-wheat flour

¼ cup (60ml) whole milk

3 tablespoons unsalted butter

2 to 3 tablespoons
granulated sugar

Confectioners' sugar for sprinkling

½ cup sour cream (optional)

This kind of dumpling is a very traditional Austrian dish. It's just flour, milk, huckleberries, and sugar, pan-fried in butter. It's not what North Americans would consider a blueberry pancake; the ratio of fruit to flour is reversed (4 to 1), and it contains just enough flour to hold the berries together as a small and sweet dumpling.

The recipe originates from chef Andreas Döllerer's grandparents' farm in the Pinzgau region, where huckleberries grow extremely well in the woods nearby. Andreas loved to visit as a child, and in his book *Cuisine Alpine,* he tells the story of eating so many berries that his teeth turned blue (the book also includes the helpful remedy of fresh lemon juice to remove any stains!). This dish is all about feeling: use your hands to shape and size the dumplings. I find the perfect ratio to be about two generous tablespoons of batter per dumpling. At Döllerer (see page 120), the dumplings are served with a glass of fresh milk from cows that live just over a kilometer away. If you don't have the luxury of fresh local milk, try the dumplings with a dollop of sour cream and a sprinkle of confectioners' sugar.

Note: Sadly, huckleberries may be hard to find. Use blueberries instead.

In a large bowl, combine the berries with the flour and milk, stirring them and crushing about half the berries in the process to release their juices (a potato masher works well). Mix well.

In a large nonstick frying pan over medium heat, melt 2 tablespoons of the butter. When the foam subsides, drop in eight dumplings—¼ cup (60ml) of batter each. Fry the dumplings for about 3 minutes on the first side. Sprinkle with 1 tablespoon of the granulated sugar, add another 1 tablespoon butter to the pan, and then turn the dumplings. Sprinkle again with 1 tablespoon granulated sugar and fry for another 3 minutes. Transfer to a large serving plate and sprinkle with confectioners' sugar.

If desired, mix the sour cream with the remaining 1 tablespoon granulated sugar.

Serve immediately, with the sweetened sour cream on the side.

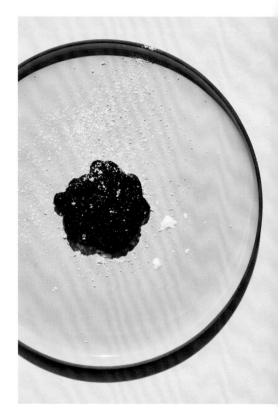

Tafelspitz

YOU WILL NEED
Food processor or high-speed blender

1⅔ pounds (750g) beef bones, including marrow bones

3½- to 4-pound (1.5 to 1.8kg) beef rump roast, fat cap on

1 large yellow carrot

1 large orange carrot

2 parsley roots

2 large leeks

4 lovage stalks, cut into 2-inch (5cm) pieces and leaves reserved for the garnish

½ medium celeriac

2 yellow onions, skin on, halved

10 black peppercorns

2 bay leaves

4 juniper berries

CHIVE CREAM
2 slices white bread, toasted, soaked in milk

2 hard-cooked egg yolks

2 uncooked egg yolks

½ teaspoon apple cider vinegar

¾ cup (175ml) grapeseed oil

Fine sea salt and freshly ground black pepper

1 tablespoon minced chives

APPLE HORSERADISH
2 cups (300g) peeled and diced tart apples

1 tablespoon freshly squeezed lemon juice

1 teaspoon sugar

½ teaspoon fine sea salt

1-inch (2.5cm) piece horseradish root

In my mind, tafelspitz, a simmered beef rump, is the dish that best exemplifies Austrian cookery. It features a humble cut of meat; a wonderful, carefully made broth; inexpensive ingredients; and traditional sides—all served in copper cookware atop family heirloom china with Hapsburg-era cutlery. It's a true estate-sale picker's delight.

For the best tafelspitz, you have two choices: Go to Hotel Sacher in Salzburg, sit in the parlor, and let yourself be spoiled by Michael Gahleitner and his team. Don't forget to try the *Backhendl* (spiced fried chicken) and Sacher Torte. Or, make this recipe, while listening to a Mozart greatest-hits playlist and basking in the Biedermeier glow of early-nineteenth-century Central European history.

Or do what I did and do both.

Note: If you feel the broth is lacking flavor, simmer a stalk of lovage in it for 2 minutes or so.

In a large heavy pot over medium-high heat, combine the beef bones and water to cover. Bring to a very gentle boil, then lower the heat and simmer gently for 30 minutes, skimming regularly.

Add the beef rump to the pot and return the cooking liquid to a gentle boil, then simmer for another 30 minutes, skimming regularly to remove any impurities from the surface.

Cut both carrots, the parsley roots, and leeks (white part only) on the bias ½ inch (12mm) thick. Be sure to reserve the trimmings, including the green part of the leek, and add them to the pot now. Refrigerate the cut vegetables until 30 minutes before the meat is cooked. Gently stir the lovage, celeriac, onions, peppercorns, bay leaves, and juniper berries into the pot. Continue to simmer for another 2 hours.

To make the chive cream: Squeeze the excess milk from the toast. Place in a food processor with all the egg yolks and pulse to make a paste. With the food processor running, add the vinegar, followed by a gentle, continuous drizzle of grapeseed oil until the sauce forms and all the oil has been incorporated. Season

with salt and pepper. Transfer to a serving bowl and top with the chives. Set aside.

To prepare the apple horseradish: In a high-speed blender, combine the apples, lemon juice, sugar, and salt and process to a sauce consistency. Adjust the seasoning to taste. Transfer to a serving bowl. (The horseradish is added right before serving.)

To make the creamed spinach: Bring a large pot of salted water to a boil. Plunge the spinach into the water and simmer for 30 seconds. Drain and pat dry.

In a large sauté pan over medium heat, warm the butter. When it starts to foam, add the onion and garlic and cook until translucent, about 2 minutes. Turn the heat to medium-low and stir in the flour, cooking for a minute or two. Pour in the milk and cook until the mixture starts to thicken, another 2 to 3 minutes. Stir in the spinach and season with salt and pepper. Cook for another minute or two to heat the spinach. Transfer to a blender or food processor and purée until smooth. Transfer to a serving dish.

continued

CREAMED SPINACH

1¾ pounds (800g) spinach

3 tablespoons unsalted butter

½ yellow onion, finely diced

½ cup (60g) all-purpose flour

½ cup (120ml) whole milk

1 garlic clove, minced

Fine sea salt and freshly ground black pepper

Fine sea salt

Freshly grated nutmeg

Minced chives for sprinkling

Rösti (page 253) for serving

About 30 minutes before the meat is fully braised, bring a large saucepan of salted water to a boil. Blanch the carrots and parsley roots until near tender, about 15 minutes, then add the leeks and continue to simmer for another 5 minutes. Remove from the heat, but keep in the hot water until you are ready to serve.

Once the meat is fork-tender, transfer the whole rump to a cutting board. Strain the cooking stock into a saucepan. Discard the aromatics, vegetables, and trimmings, but spoon out any marrow into the liquid before discarding the bones. Taste and adjust the seasoning with salt and a grating of nutmeg.

Reheat the creamed spinach as needed. For the applesauce, peel and grate the horseradish now. Sprinkle 1 tablespoon on top of the sauce.

Keeping the fat on the meat, cut the meat into ½-inch (12mm) thick slices and transfer to a large serving dish. Top with the blanched vegetables and the marrow. Sprinkle generously with minced chives. Moisten the meat with a generous amount of broth, then pour the remaining broth into a gravy boat. Serve tableside with rösti and all of the trimmings.

MICHAEL GAHLEITNER, CHEF AT HOTEL SACHER, SALZBURG.

Salzburger Nockerl

■■■■ MEDIUM
SERVES 8

YOU WILL NEED

Straight-sided oval baking dish (I used a Le Creuset 1¾-quart [1.7L] dish)

Flexible bench scraper

2 tablespoons unsalted butter, at room temperature

2 tablespoons granulated sugar

6 eggs, separated, plus 4 egg whites

½ cup (100g) superfine sugar

2 teaspoons vanilla sugar

½ teaspoon fine sea salt

⅓ cup (40g) all-purpose flour

⅔ cup (200g) cranberry jam

½ cup (120ml) whole milk

2 tablespoons confectioners' sugar

This dramatic soufflé, the Austrian cousin to French *îles flottantes* ("floating islands"), is a fluffy concoction shaped into three peaked mounds—said to represent three of the mountains that surround Salzburg: the Mönchsberg, the Kapuzinerberg, and, depending on to whom you talk, the Rainberg or the Gaisberg—all resting atop cranberry jam. Like a floating island, or the "Ziggy Pig" that Napoleon eats in *Bill & Ted's Excellent Adventure*, the Salzburger is a spectacle—half of the fun happens when it appears at the table and onlookers' mouths drop.

I was able to wrangle this recipe from the Bärenwirt Tavern, which is tucked away on a cobblestone street in Salzburg. Similar to Savoie Cake (see page 295) or a Kugelhopf, the feature that made this dessert a specialty in the Alps is the use of eggs, which was extravagant for a dish that predates advanced mountain transportation techniques.

Note: Vanilla sugar, a very common ingredient in European baking, can sometimes be found alongside superfine white sugar at specialty grocery stores. Or you can make your own by scraping and stirring the seeds from a vanilla bean into a jar of granulated sugar and letting it infuse for a few days. If you don't have a few days, simply stir the seeds from one vanilla bean into the amount of superfine sugar you need for the recipe.

Preheat the oven to 370°F (190°C). Generously grease the inside of an oval baking dish with the butter and then sprinkle evenly with the granulated sugar.

Using a stand mixer fitted with the whisk attachment, on medium speed, beat all the egg whites until foamy and starting to gain in volume, about 3 minutes. Increase the speed to medium-high, gradually sprinkle in the superfine sugar, and continue to work air into the egg whites, until thick and glossy and doubled in volume, about another 3 minutes. Shortly before the end, sprinkle in the vanilla sugar and salt and incorporate.

Place all the egg yolks in a bowl and stir with a fork to blend. Gently whisk the yolks into the egg whites. Switching to a spatula, fold the flour into the egg mixture until just combined.

Spoon the cranberry jam into the prepared baking dish and spread to cover the bottom of the dish. Pour the milk evenly over the jam.

Using a flexible bench scraper, scoop out one-third of the egg mixture, shaping it into a dome, using the inside of the mixing bowl as your guide, then lay it inside one end of the baking dish. Repeat twice with the remaining two-thirds whipped egg, laying them in the center and the other end of the dish respectively. Use the scraper to adjust the shapes and make them look like three distinct peaks, making sure the egg mixture is towering but contained within the edges of the baking dish. Transfer onto a baking sheet.

Bake for 11 to 14 minutes, until the souffléd meringue is browned and cooked to your liking. Slide a paring knife between two of the mounds to check for doneness.

Sprinkle with the confectioners' sugar and serve immediately.

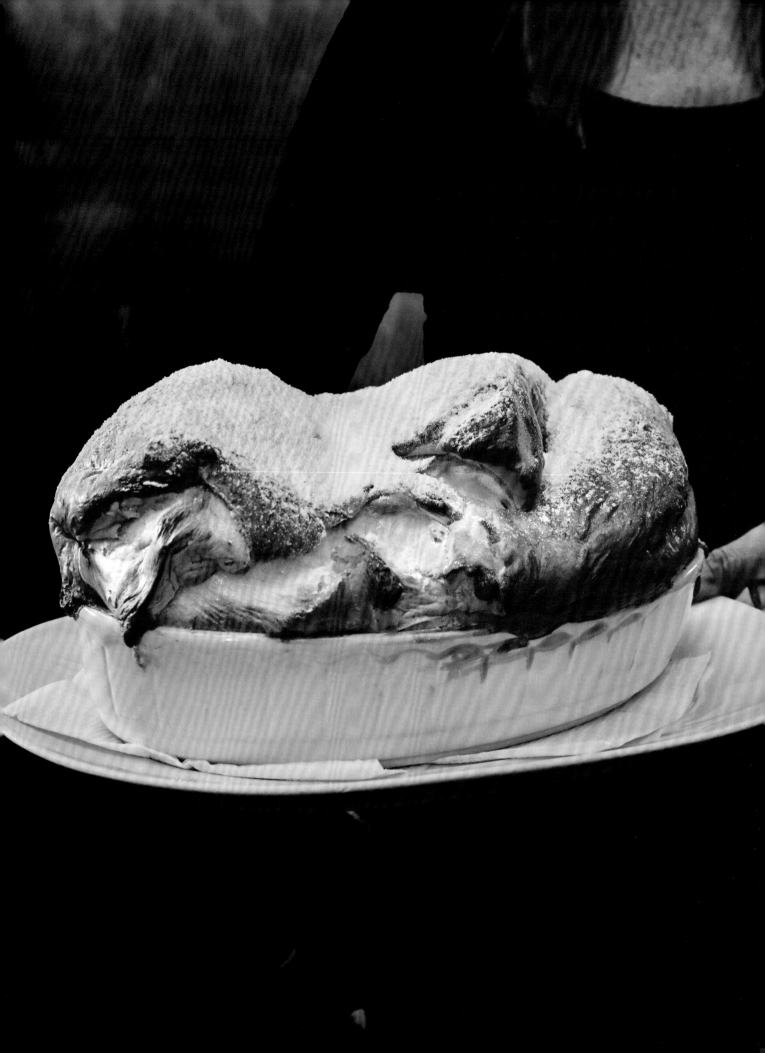

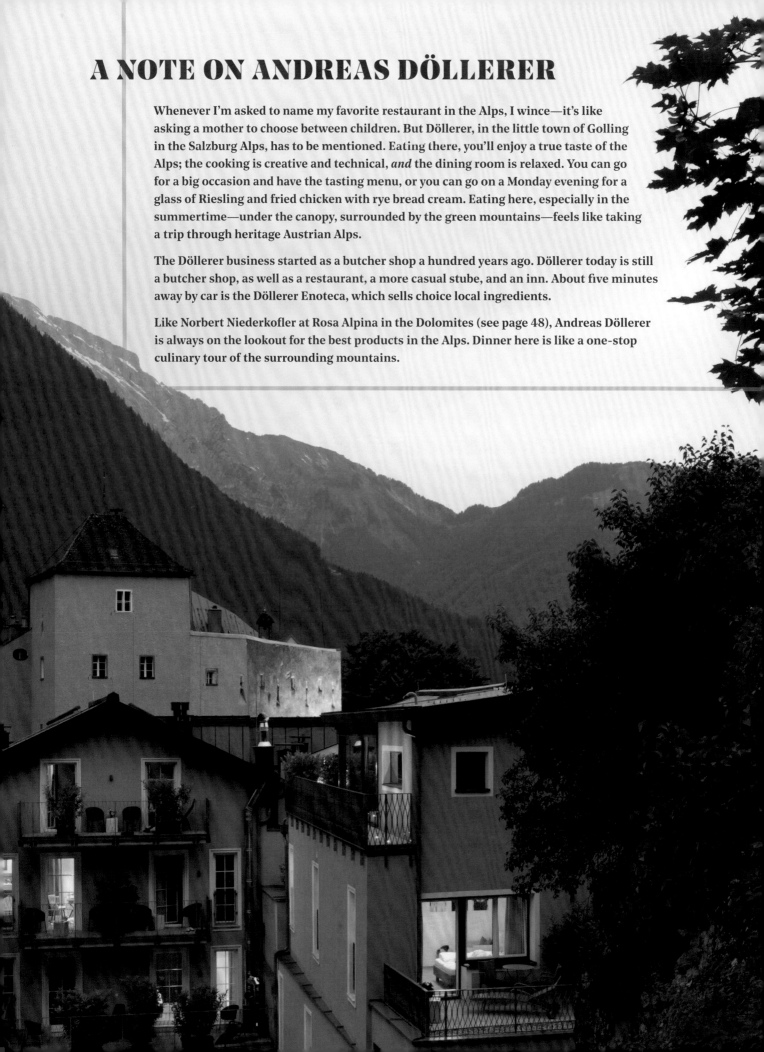

A NOTE ON ANDREAS DÖLLERER

Whenever I'm asked to name my favorite restaurant in the Alps, I wince—it's like asking a mother to choose between children. But Döllerer, in the little town of Golling in the Salzburg Alps, has to be mentioned. Eating there, you'll enjoy a true taste of the Alps; the cooking is creative and technical, *and* the dining room is relaxed. You can go for a big occasion and have the tasting menu, or you can go on a Monday evening for a glass of Riesling and fried chicken with rye bread cream. Eating here, especially in the summertime—under the canopy, surrounded by the green mountains—feels like taking a trip through heritage Austrian Alps.

The Döllerer business started as a butcher shop a hundred years ago. Döllerer today is still a butcher shop, as well as a restaurant, a more casual stube, and an inn. About five minutes away by car is the Döllerer Enoteca, which sells choice local ingredients.

Like Norbert Niederkofler at Rosa Alpina in the Dolomites (see page 48), Andreas Döllerer is always on the lookout for the best products in the Alps. Dinner here is like a one-stop culinary tour of the surrounding mountains.

Venison Ragout

HIRSCHRAGOUT

■■■□ MEDIUM

SERVES 4

2 pounds (900g) venison shoulder, cut into 1-inch (2.5cm) cubes

Fine sea salt and freshly ground black pepper

3 tablespoons grapeseed oil

3 cups (480g) finely diced yellow onion

½ cup (50g) finely diced celery

½ cup (55g) finely diced carrot

1 tablespoon tomato paste

1¾ cups (415ml) dry red wine

3 tablespoons balsamic vinegar

1½ quarts (1.4L) beef stock or low-sodium beef broth

10 juniper berries

2 whole cloves

3 bay leaves

½ cup (110g) cold unsalted butter, cubed

2 tablespoons minced flat-leaf parsley

1 cup (320g) cranberry jam

TRAVEL HACK

Sportgastein, even in good weather, is an intense mountain; do not let anyone tell you otherwise. On a clear day in February, I took the cable car to Kreuzkogel at 2,686 meters (8,812 feet). It's a long climb up, and at the top, you can see to the Carinthian Alps toward Slovenia. The piste keepers like to put the "sport" in Sportgastein with minimal upkeep—so this mountain is best for strong skiers. For good eaters, I can tell you that, food-wise, you're not missing much on the mountain, as the best awaits at the bottom.

Perhaps it was the terrible weather high above the clouds. Or the fact that I had even made it down Sportgastein (see Travel Hack) on skis, alive. Whatever the reason, arriving at Valeriehaus was pure relief. This little restaurant sits in a small valley with mountain ridges on all sides. The position is . . . vulnerable; the view is both stunning and imposing. (It's no coincidence that one of Austria's best avalanche training centers is here.) A little history: The original hut was taken over in 1889 by the German and Austrian Alpine Club as a refuge for mountaineers and hikers and as a starting point for the crossing of the main Alpine ridge to Carinthia. It was named in honor of Valerie, youngest daughter of imperial couple Franz Josef and Elisabeth.

Otto Klaffenböck runs Valeriehaus just as well as any hospitality professional I've met in New York or Paris. The Valeriehaus refuge was converted to a restaurant by Otto's father, who was a *Jagermeister* (master hunter) and was so accustomed to feeding the locals that he made a business out of it. Otto works with his wife, Liene; and their daughter, Estell Laura, works the bar, making coffee and hot chocolate when she's not in school. On the terrace, there are fifty-some yellow-and-white-striped loungers that prove difficult to stand up from after a morning of skiing, and maybe a few of Otto's *Zirbenschnapps* (Pine Schnapps; page 125).

In the tradition of his father, Otto and his team prepare venison to the highest standard. If you visit, you *have* to order it. In the meantime, here's the recipe.

Note: This stew is best served with dumplings; either cheese dumplings (see page 139) or speck dumplings (see page 42).

In a large bowl, toss the venison with 2 teaspoons salt and ½ teaspoon pepper.

In a large heavy pot over medium-high heat, warm the grapeseed oil until it shimmers. Add the meat and sauté until browned on all sides, about 5 minutes total. Using a slotted spoon, transfer the meat to a plate.

Add the onion, celery, and carrot to the pot and sauté until they start to color slightly, about 5 minutes, then stir in the tomato paste and continue to cook for 2 minutes more. Pour in the red wine and balsamic vinegar and deglaze the pan, stirring to scrape up any browned bits. Increase the heat to high and bring the liquid to a vigorous boil. Cook to reduce until syrupy, 10 to 15 minutes.

Return the meat to the pot and pour in the beef stock. Bring to a simmer, cover, and braise for 2 hours. Then, stir in the juniper berries, cloves, and bay leaves and continue to cook for another 30 minutes. The meat should be fork-tender.

Using a slotted spoon, transfer the meat to a plate. Strain the braising liquid, discarding the solids. Return the liquid to the pot and adjust the seasoning with salt and pepper. Return the meat to the pot, then stir in the butter until melted; the sauce will look enticingly glossy.

Serve in shallow bowls. Sprinkle with the parsley and spoon a generous amount of the cranberry jam on the side.

Pine Schnapps

ZIRBENSCHNAPPS

▬▬▬▬ EASY
MAKES 1 QUART (950ML)

1 cup (200g) sugar
16 pinecones (gathered in spring)
1 quart (950ml) grappa

Whenever I spy a demijohn of schnapps when entering a hut, I know I'm in the right place. Schnapps is the Alpine arbiter of quality and can be served after the meal, or perhaps, depending on your day, as soon as you walk in the room.

In order to make a true pine schnapps, you must gather pinecones in late spring (any time between late March and early June, depending on where you are). In terms of your schnapps receptacle, you need a glass container large enough at the mouth to fit a pinecone through. An emptied magnum bottle works.

Pour the sugar into a glass container. Insert the pinecones one by one, then top off with the grappa and swirl the container around to start dissolving the sugar. Seal with a cap and leave to infuse for 6 to 8 weeks. The schnapps keeps indefinitely at room temperature; strain before serving.

Growing up in the Carinthian Alps, **Sissy Sonnleitner** had no intention of taking over her parents' inn, called Landhaus-Kellerwand ("basement wall") because of its location at the foot of Kellerwand Mountain. But she did, and after changing the name to Sonnleitner, she began to win regional and international awards for her restaurant and hotel. Sissy loves eating at Zur Rose across the border in Alto Adige. At home, her cuisine is marked by its Italian influence (and sure enough, her favorite dish is a regional spin on ravioli, called *Kärntner Nudel*). When it comes to wine, she's Austrian at heart though, and if you're thirsty, she recommends Jamek, an iconic wine producer from Wachau.

SNAPSHOT

Tyrolean Liver Salad

TIROLER LEBERSALAT

■■■■ MEDIUM
SERVES 4

YOU WILL NEED

Digital instant-read or deep-frying thermometer

CRISPY ONIONS

2 cups (480ml) olive oil or grapeseed oil

½ cup (60g) all-purpose flour

1 teaspoon fine sea salt

½ teaspoon freshly ground black pepper

¼ teaspoon red pepper flakes

2 yellow onions, sliced into very thin rings

DRESSING

¼ cup (60ml) white balsamic vinegar

2 tablespoons apple cider vinegar

1 teaspoon fine sea salt

2 to 3 tablespoons sugar

⅓ cup (80ml) grapeseed oil

1 to 2 tablespoons extra-virgin olive oil

1 pound (450g) fresh deer or calf liver, cut into ⅜-inch (1cm) thick slices

Fine sea salt and freshly ground black pepper

3 tablespoons olive oil or grapeseed oil

1 teaspoon minced garlic

1 teaspoon minced fresh rosemary

1 teaspoon minced fresh thyme

⅔ cup (160ml) beef stock or low-sodium beef broth

Mixed salad greens (mesclun, baby gem, radicchio) for serving

On the way to the slopes of the Wiedersberger Horn in Alpbach, I passed through Brixlegg, one of the oldest settlements in Tyrol. I noticed a very old-looking tavern with signage that simply read in a black Bavarian font, *Sigwart's Tiroler Weinstuben.* You know those places where you just feel there is magic inside, that "oh, this is going to be *good*" feeling in your gut?

It was the first warm day of spring, and after weeks spent at higher elevations and lower temps, I was ready for some brightness. I sat down in one of the cozy parlors and talked with Anton Sigwart, the fourth-generation keeper of the stube. His hospitality and his dog's charm were only outdone by his wife, Traudi, who is also the chef. Beloved by her cooks, she runs a calm yet very warm kitchen (and, I learned, one of the best in the Alps, as they have been awarded two Gault & Millau toques). And so, while we talked, the kitchen team prepared this salad of sautéed slices of fresh liver tossed with local greens, fried onions, and a simple dressing.

To make the crispy onions: Line a baking sheet with a layer of paper towels.

In a heavy pot or a cast-iron frying pan over medium-high heat, warm the olive oil until it registers 320° to 340°F (160° to 170°C) on an instant-read thermometer.

In a shallow bowl, whisk together the flour, salt, black pepper, and red pepper flakes.

When the oil is at the correct temperature, dredge one-fourth of the onion rings in the flour mixture, shaking off any excess before transferring to the hot oil. Fry until golden brown, 1 to 2 minutes, then transfer to the prepared baking sheet. Repeat with the remaining onions, working in batches.

To make the dressing: In a small saucepan over medium-high heat, combine both vinegars, the salt, and sugar and bring to a boil. Stir well to dissolve the sugar. Remove from the heat and whisk in both oils. Set aside.

Generously season the liver with salt and pepper. In a cast-iron pan over high heat, warm the olive oil until it shimmers. Pan-fry the liver slices, turning them over only when you see a nice golden-brown crust forming on the bottom. Stir in the garlic and herbs, followed by the beef stock. Continue to cook over medium heat until the stock has reduced to a sauce consistency and the liver has softened, another minute or so.

Arrange the salad greens on four plates, topping each with a portion of liver. Spoon the warm dressing over each plate and top with crispy onions. Serve immediately.

TRAUDI SIGWART

Spring Rhubarb Cocktail

FRÜHLINGS RHABARBER ELIXIER

EASY

SERVES 1

Ice cubes

1½ ounces (45ml) gin

3 tablespoons Rhubarb Syrup
(recipe follows)

1 tablespoon elderflower cordial

Juice of ½ lime

Scant ½ cup (100ml) Fever-Tree
tonic water (or other craft tonic)

1 rhubarb stalk, trimmed

For this drink, I recommend a gin with herbal notes to give you a feeling of drinking in an Alpine meadow. And wearing a dirndl. Bruichladdich's Botanist works well, as does Meunier's (from France), which includes the usual gin aromatics but is made from beet alcohol.

Note: Make the rhubarb syrup ahead of time, so it's cold when you start mixing drinks. Elderflower cordial can be found on Amazon or at any specialty cocktail or barware store.

Fill a rocks glass or old-fashioned tumbler glass with ice cubes. Pour in the gin, rhubarb syrup, elderflower cordial, and lime juice.

Give everything a good stir and top with the tonic water. Stir again, then add the rhubarb and serve.

Rhubarb Syrup

MAKES ABOUT 1 CUP (240ML)

1⅓ pounds (600g) rhubarb stalks,
cut into 2-inch (5cm) pieces

1 cup (200g) sugar

1 cup (240ml) water

This delicious syrup is best served atop ice cream and pancakes, or most probably in gin cocktails.

In a heavy saucepan over medium-high heat, combine the rhubarb, sugar, and water and bring to a boil. Lower the heat and simmer, stirring occasionally, until the rhubarb is completely soft and the liquid has thickened slightly, about 20 minutes.

Set a fine-mesh sieve over a large bowl and pour in the rhubarb and its cooking juices. Let the rhubarb drain, pressing on the solids with the back of a spoon to extract all the liquid.

Carefully pour the syrup into a clean jar and cover. The syrup will keep in the refrigerator for up to 1 month.

THE ALMABTRIEB CATTLE PROCESSION

All over the European Alps, on the cusp of autumn when the nights start to cool, cattle that have spent the summer grazing on high Alpine meadows are escorted back to their barns, deep in the valleys. Since medieval times, this ritual is a full-blown procession in many high-altitude zones. The livestock is elaborately and colorfully decorated; some even wear headdresses made of fabric, fir branches, Alpine flowers, and feathers or ribbons. All cows wear their ceremonial bells. The dressing up is intended to ward off any bad spirits in the valley, so the cows have a peaceful return to their winter home.

No cows are harmed on the way down! In fact, if any cow happens to have been lost or died while summering at high altitude, none of the remaining cows wear any pageantry on the walk down. This celebration of transhumance isn't only for the cows, though; some herdsmen and -women wear traditional lederhosen and dirndl. Some even wear religious symbols; for example, a little picture of Saint Leonard, the patron saint of animals. The path down to the valley is lined with locals and tourists.

I haven't had a chance to witness the Almabtrieb ("the drive down the mountain"), but I hear that two drives in particular—in Alpbachtal and Fuschlsee in Austria—are beautiful. The seasonal migration is also celebrated in Switzerland, specifically in the Engelberg and Appenzell (where the event has graced many a back cover of *Artforum* magazine; see "Bischofberger and Alpine Art," page 246), as well as in Valtournenche, Italy.

Tyrolean Cake on a Spit

TIROLER PRÜGLETORTE

■■ **DIFFICULT**

SERVES 3 OR 4

YOU WILL NEED

Beechwood or other hardwood logs; you want the kind of wood that will ensure a long-burning flame

Rotisserie rod and horizontal spit setup

16- to 24-inch (40 to 60cm) long copper or metal pipe, about 2 inches (5cm) in diameter, that fits snugly onto the spit

Parchment paper

String

Large spoon or ladle

Painter's spatula

2¼ cups (500g) unsalted butter, at room temperature

2½ cups (500g) sugar

10 eggs

1 pound 2 ounces (500 g) all-purpose flour

½ teaspoon fine sea salt

Grated zest of 1 lemon

Whipped cream for serving

Berry purée for serving

When you're in the Alpbachtal, or better yet, close to Sigwart's Tiroler Weinstuben (see page 126), you *must* stop in Rattenberg, Austria's tiniest town, just adjacent to the Bradenberg River. It's very pretty in summer, and is full of quaint glassware shops and little bars. In the middle of its pedestrian promenade, you'll find the 250-year-old Café Hacker. Amid all the baked goods, there are two specialties: the Augustiner cake and the *Prügletorte*, a cake made from batter roasted over a spit.

Many years ago, I ordered a *Baumkuchen* (a German spit cake) online from a shop in Munich. When it arrived in Montreal, it was so stale that it was inedible (what should have been chewy, just verging on stale, was rock hard). I vowed to make my own. Before I could, my friend and collaborator Fred Morin set up a spit in the smoker at his restaurant Joe Beef to attempt it. But, just like that time we self-treated a bad case of shingles by rubbing ourselves with raw honey, we only ended up with a sticky mess. But I digress.

In Rattenberg, I walked into Café Hacker, where Reihard Hacker, the baker/owner (pictured opposite), was in the midst of wrapping a freshly made Prügeltorte. I just about tipped over with excitement. That cake is built over a wooden or metal cone (Austrians use a wooden rolling pin) that is turned over a live fire. You build a base layer of cake by pouring a ladle of batter along the cone as the spit turns continuously over the fire, continuing ladle by ladle to add more layers. Each addition of batter is allowed to brown slightly before a new layer is added. The more drips, the better; according to Tyrolean lore, those jagged edges and that gentle roasting are what make the cake.

Obviously, this isn't your everyday cake. In Tyrol, it's meant for feast days and weddings. Seeing as most of us don't have a wood-fired rotisserie setup in our home kitchen, this recipe is more an idea, an inspiration, a cultural footnote, if you will. Or perhaps, a challenge. Therefore, the method is loosely defined.

Note: The batter for the Prügeltorte is eischwerteig, *meaning that it calls for an equal weight of fat, butter, flour, and egg, just like a pound cake. Accordingly, you can increase or decrease the yield with some simple math.*

continued

Prepare a fire using beechwood. Set up a rotisserie frame onto which you can thread a copper or metal pipe. The fire is ready when it has started to turn to hot coals but is still flaming.

In a large bowl, using a spatula, beat the butter until lightened. Switch to a whisk to stir in the sugar, and continue to whisk as you add the eggs, one at a time. Sift the flour and salt into the batter mixture, add the lemon zest, and stir until well combined. Let the batter sit for 30 minutes.

Wrap the pipe with several sheets or layers of parchment paper, loosely tying it at each end with string to keep it snug. Depending on your rotisserie setup (that is, if it's not electrically powered), you'll need a friend to rotate the spit at a high and consistent speed (determined by trial and error)!

Bring the batter close to the fire. Using a large spoon, apply the first layer of batter to the pipe, while the spit is rotating, using the back of the spoon to spread it along the length of the pipe.

As the batter begins to set, you can use a painter's spatula to smooth the surface of the cake and to encourage the telltale drips. Once the first layer becomes light brown, apply the next layer. Repeat the procedure until you have used all the cake batter, making sure that the fire remains consistent.

Carefully lift the spit, remove the pipe, and stand the pipe upright in a dry, well-ventilated place to let the cake cool completely. Cut the string at the top end, then remove the cake by tugging on the top layer of parchment paper—this should ensure the cake and parchment slip off easily. Store in an airtight container at room temperature for up to 2 weeks.

When ready to serve, slice the cake along its length, through the center. It's naturally a bit dry, so I suggest accompanying it with whipped cream and berry purée, whatever is in season.

Karl and Rudolf Obauer run their eponymous restaurant and inn in Werfen. For a day outdoors, they recommend hiking through Eisriesenwelt, the world's largest ice cave, from May to October. In winter, you should ski the Ski Amadé area—they both favor the Werfenweng piste. A favorite Alpine dish is blueberry risotto with air-dried wood grouse and Alpine herbs. They love what Norbert Niederkofler is cooking at Rosa Alpina (see page 48) and try to visit there often, which is not often enough considering the pace of their own restaurant. In their minds, the best time to experience the Alps is in October.

SNAPSHOT

Hangover Soup with Cheese Dumplings

KATERSUPPE MIT KASPRESSKNÖDEL

 EASY

SERVES 4

SOUP BROTH

2 yellow onions, skin on, halved

5 juniper berries, coarsely crushed

5 whole cloves, coarsely crushed

2 pounds (900g) beef rump

2 pounds (900g) small marrow bones

1 leek, roots removed

2 carrots

1 small, fist-size celeriac or parsley root, coarsely diced

1 small bunch flat-leaf parsley

1 small bunch lovage

2 bay leaves

4 quarts (3.8L) water

2 empty eggshells

Fine sea salt and freshly ground black pepper

Splash of ruby port

1 tablespoon unsalted butter

1 yellow onion, finely diced

5 thin slices white bread, crusts removed

3 ounces (85g) chewy, soft pretzel, thinly sliced

⅔ cup (170g) mashed potato

7 ounces (200g) mixed cheeses (such as Tilsit and Emmental), diced

1 tablespoon minced fresh flat-leaf parsley

1 teaspoon minced fresh oregano

⅛ teaspoon freshly grated nutmeg

¼ teaspoon garlic powder

½ teaspoon caraway seeds

Fine sea salt and freshly ground black pepper

2 eggs, lightly beaten

¼ cup olive oil

Minced fresh chives for garnish

Philipp Rauscher, the current custodian at the Resterhöhe Berggasthaus & Lodge in the Kitzbühel Alps, is a warm, genuine host. If you arrive on foot, he will pick you up at the chairlift and drive you on a snowmobile the 200 meters (600 feet) or so to his mountain inn. When you're cold, he will stoke the century-old wood-burning cookstove and pour you some mulled wine. When you're hungry, he and his team will feed you. He offered me this elixir for a hangover (which happens when you spend the night there), and its marrow broth was revelatory enough for me to want to include it in the book. The cabin suites are comfortable, and nothing beats waking up at elevation to a full Alpine breakfast spread, complete with *Liptauer* (page 140) and freshly baked bread.

To make the soup broth: In a large stockpot over medium-high heat, place the onions halves facedown, add the juniper berries and cloves, and dry-fry, resisting the urge to stir, until quite seriously browned but not blackened, about 5 minutes. Then, add the beef, marrow bones, leek, carrots, celeriac, parsley, lovage, bay leaves, and water (add more water, if needed, to cover the ingredients). Turn the heat to high and bring to a boil, then turn the heat to very low and simmer for a minimum of 4 hours, but preferably overnight. Before you go to bed, add the eggshells to the pot; this will help clarify the liquid.

The next day, strain the liquid through a fine-mesh sieve into another large pot, pressing gently on the vegetables and meat to extract that last bit of flavor. Season with salt and pepper, then stir in the port. The alcohol will mostly dissipate, leaving a special aroma to linger over the hangover soup. Set aside to cool.

In a frying pan over medium-high heat, melt the butter. Add the onion and sauté until translucent and starting to brown, about 5 minutes. Set aside.

In a medium bowl, combine 1 cup (240ml) of the soup broth with the bread and pretzel pieces and soak for 15 minutes until very soft. Stir in the mashed potato, cheeses, parsley, oregano, nutmeg, garlic powder, caraway seeds, and onion until well combined. Season with salt and pepper. Stir in the beaten eggs.

Using your hands, divide the dough into eight rough balls, then press them flat.

In a large frying pan over medium-high heat, warm the olive oil until it shimmers. Add the flattened dumplings and fry until crispy and golden brown on each side, 2 to 3 minutes per side. Set aside on paper towels.

Place two dumplings in each bowl, ladle in a generous amount of broth, and garnish with chives. Serve immediately.

Spiced Cheese Spread

LIPTAUER

EASY

SERVES 4 TO 6

⅔ cup (145g) unsalted cultured butter, at room temperature

1 cup (200g) quark cheese

3 tablespoons crème fraîche

½ yellow onion, finely diced

1 teaspoon drained brined capers

3 canned anchovies, minced

10 gherkins, diced

3 tablespoons sour cream

1 tablespoon Dijon mustard

1 tablespoon caraway seeds

1 tablespoon sweet paprika

1 teaspoon fine sea salt

1 teaspoon freshly ground black pepper

1 tablespoon minced chives

1 tablespoon chopped fresh flat-leaf parsley

Take me to the *Heuriger*!

I love the kinds of more-ish dips served in Austrian wine bars, and Liptauer is certainly that and more: a mix of quark, paprika, and anchovies, with a dash of mustard and caraway. It's perfectly suited as a spread on freshly baked whole-wheat bread, as a dip with crackers, or as a filling in tiny bell peppers. And it's usually served at any good Austrian or German tavern (*Heuriger*) during the autumn harvest, accompanied by a glass of crisp Grüner Veltliner or seasonal Sturm (freshly fermented grape juice).

Note: Quark, one of the dairy bases for this dip, is technically a fresh soft cheese, though it tastes a lot like sour cream, and is used in many cooked and uncooked dishes in Germany, France (where it is called fromage blanc*), and in the Slavic countries. Look for quark in the refrigerated dairy section of your supermarket.*

In a small bowl, using a fork or a small whisk, whip the butter until smooth, then add the quark and crème fraîche, stirring until smooth again. Stir in the onion, capers, anchovies, and pickles.

Finally, adjusting amounts as desired, add in the sour cream, mustard, caraway seeds, paprika, salt, pepper, chives, and parsley. (You can also add a splash of the gherkin juice from the jar.) Transfer to a crock or glass jar for serving.

SKIING IN KITZBÜHEL

Sweet Bread Rolls with Jam

BUCHTELN MIT POWIDL

MEDIUM
MAKES 16 ROLLS

I've had these sweet bread rolls at a now-defunct tavern in Mayrhofen in the Zillertal Valley, as well as in the kitchen of Resterhöhe (see page 139) after a day of climbing and skiing Kitzbühel. Basically, they're puffy sweet rolls stuffed with plum jam and served with cream or vanilla custard on the side. If you're looking to fill your stube with a sweet brioche-orange scent in the morning, this is your go-to breakfast pastry. Most Austrians do not use sugar in the filling; they just reduce the plums to a spreadable paste. I prefer the recipe with a bit of sugar, and have adjusted for it.

YOU WILL NEED

Stand mixer fitted with the dough hook (optional)

Bench scraper or sharp knife

Digital scale (optional)

Two 8-inch (20cm) cast-iron or springform pans

¼ cup (60ml) whole milk

6 tablespoons (85g) unsalted butter, cut into ½-inch (12mm) cubes, plus ¼ cup (60g) unsalted butter, melted

½ cup (100g) granulated sugar, plus 1 teaspoon

1 teaspoon fine sea salt

4 eggs, lightly beaten

Splash of white rum

1 teaspoon grated orange zest

1 teaspoon grated lemon zest

1½ teaspoons active dry yeast

¼ cup (60ml) warm (105° to 110°F/40° to 45°C) water

1 pound 2 ounces (500g) all-purpose flour, plus more for dusting

About 6 tablespoons (90g) plum jam

Confectioners' sugar for dusting

In a small saucepan (or in a bowl using a microwave), combine the milk and cubed butter and heat until warm and the butter is melted, about 30 seconds. Stir in the ½ cup (100g) granulated sugar, salt, eggs, rum, orange zest, and lemon zest.

In a small bowl, combine the yeast with the warm water and remaining 1 teaspoon granulated sugar. Let sit for 5 minutes until bubbles appear.

Sift the flour into a large mixing bowl (if working manually) or the bowl of a stand mixer fitted with the dough hook.

Pour the warm milk mixture and yeast liquid into the flour and mix (at medium-low speed, or if working manually, with a wooden spoon) until a shaggy dough forms and starts to separate from the wall of the bowl. Continue to knead at low speed (or by hand working on the counter) for 5 to 8 minutes, until smooth. The dough should spring back when poked.

Cover the dough with a kitchen towel and let proof for 1½ hours or so in a warm place (such as inside a micro-wave with a cup of steaming water), until doubled in volume.

Butter two cake pans or coat with nonstick cooking spray.

Dust your work surface with a little flour before placing the dough on top. Using a bench scraper or sharp knife, cut the dough into sixteen equal pieces (a scale can be helpful here to portion the dough into equal balls, about 2 ounces [60g] each). Press each dough ball into a flat circle using the palm of your hand. Place 1 teaspoon of jam into the cen-ter of each round. Gather the dough circle up around the jam, twisting the edges together at the top to create a seal.

As you work, place each ball, seam-side down, into the prepared pans, leaving a small amount of space around each. Brush a little melted butter on top of each roll, and let them rise in a warm place until they look pillowy and fit snugly together, 40 to 45 minutes.

While the rolls are rising, preheat the oven to 350°F (175°C).

Bake the rolls until golden brown, about 25 minutes. Gently transfer the rolls to a wire rack to cool. Serve warm, dusted with confectioners' sugar. (Watch out, the jam inside will be hot!) The rolls will keep wrapped in plastic at room temperature for up to 2 days.

Wiener Schnitzel

▬▬▬ MEDIUM

MAKES 6 SCHNITZEL
(4 FOR DINNER, PLUS 2 FOR
SANDWICHES THE NEXT
DAY—NO ONE HAS EVER
COMPLAINED ABOUT A
SCHNITZEL SANDWICH)

YOU WILL NEED

**Deep-frying thermometer
or probe**

**Meat mallet (or ask your butcher
to pound the meat)**

**6 veal escalopes, 5 to 6 ounces
(140 to 170g) each**

**Fine sea salt and freshly ground
black pepper**

2 cups (240g) all-purpose flour

3 eggs, beaten

**2 cups (220g) fine dried
bread crumbs**

**1 quart (950ml) peanut oil or
canola oil**

**¼ cup (5g) minced fresh flat-leaf
parsley**

**3 tablespoons unsalted butter,
melted**

3 lemons, halved

**Cranberry jam, parsley potatoes,
or cucumber salad for serving**

Schnitzel is a quintessential Alpine dish, one that can be found on all the menus: whether it's a rifugio, hut, hostel, motorway stop, café, five-star hotel, low-end joint, high-end lodge—you name it, they serve it. I like to imagine Ötzi the Iceman (who was discovered in the Ötztal Alps on the border between Austria and Italy) had it on offer, with a side of foraged berries, in his cave dwelling.

And yet, Wiener Schnitzel does not come from the mountains. Despite the presumption that schnitzel is a German thing, the first cookbooks to record such a dish—a veal loin pounded thin—were Italian. Time Life's *Food of Italy* makes reference to a Milanese banquet in 1134 serving *lombolos cum panitio*, breaded veal chops. Not until the nineteenth century did it occur to an Austrian general to bring the Milanese recipe back to Vienna. It was, to be fair, the Viennese who thought to get rid of the bone; they knew they were onto something good when they then protected the Wiener Schnitzel with an appellation.

I would estimate my schnitzel count at more than two hundred over the course of traveling and eating to research this book. Ask me what my favorite one is, and the real answer is "wherever I ate the last one." At the same time, served on good china with a lemon wedge, a side of potatoes, and maybe cranberry jam or a cucumber salad, schnitzel is also a sophisticated, if not elegant, dish. And that's where a little technique comes into play.

In my opinion, the best schnitzel should have a bit of puff, meaning some nice air pockets between the meat and the breading. Austrians call this *souffléing*, and it happens when the schnitzel has room to float freely in the fat in which it's cooked.

When I tried the schnitzel recipes given to me by Austrian friends and cooks, they never tasted as good at home as they had in the mountains. So, with two friends to assist, I set out to develop my own recipe. Now when people ask me what's the best schnitzel, it's this recipe right here.

Team Schnitzel was torn over the use of oil versus clarified butter as the cooking fat. Clarified butter yielded a much richer flavor (some said too rich); oil ensured crispier breading. Because this recipe calls for a lot of cooking fat, we recommend you use oil only to fry the schnitzel. If you're feeling fancy, substitute 2 cups (430g) clarified butter (see page 146) for 2 cups (480ml) of the oil. Otherwise, a drizzle of melted butter on the meat when serving tastes just as luxurious. The temperature of the oil also turned out to be key: the schnitzel cooks more slowly at a lower temperature, but this resulted in a more-tender breading and meat, and—we think—better souffléing.

continued

THE SCHNITZEL PLAYBOOK

Your cheat sheet for all things meaty and breaded.

Chicken Parmigiana: Another Italian creation, chicken schnitzel baked with tomato sauce and mozzarella cheese.

Cordon Bleu: A schnitzel stuffed with Gruyère or Emmental cheese and cured ham, breaded, then fried. Believed to originate from Brig, Switzerland, my Toggi-Schnitzel (see page 250) is similar.

Cotoletta alla Milanese: The OG schnitzel, invented in Milan, Italy, using a bone-in veal chop.

Jagerschnitzel: Schnitzel topped with a creamy mushroom sauce.

Schnitzel à la Holstein: A German-style schnitzel topped with a sunny-side-up egg, garnished with anchovies and a lemon-caper sauce.

Schweineschnitzel: A German variation that showcases pork loin instead of veal.

Tonkatsu: A popular dish in Japan, this is pork crusted with panko rather than fine bread crumbs, and served with rice.

Torinese: A Milanese in a Piedmontese hazelnut coat. It hasn't yet taken over the world, but it should.

If your butcher hasn't pounded the meat for you, cover a chopping board with plastic wrap. Lay the veal down, then cover with another sheet of plastic. Use a meat mallet to pound the meat slices to a thickness of ¼ inch (6mm). Transfer the meat to a large tray. Season both sides of each slice with salt and pepper.

Set up a breading station by placing the flour on one plate, add the eggs to a shallow bowl, and put the bread crumbs on a second plate. Place a clean platter at the end to hold the breaded slices.

Preheat the oven to 300°F (150°C). Line a baking sheet with a layer of paper towels.

Pour the peanut oil into a large Dutch oven or cast-iron pan. The oil level should be about ¾ inch (2cm) deep (if you're using a very large pan, increase the amount of oil accordingly). Slowly warm the oil over low heat to 265°F (130°C) on a deep-frying thermometer.

Meanwhile, working with one slice at a time, dredge the veal in flour to coat completely, then shake off any excess. Next, dip the meat through the egg until well coated, then, with a fork, lift, allowing any excess egg wash to drip back into the bowl. Transfer to the bread crumbs, flipping to coat well on both sides, then shake off any extra crumbs. Place the breaded slice to the platter. Repeat with the remaining slices.

Working with tongs, slip one piece of veal into the hot oil and cook until pale golden brown, 3 to 3½ minutes. Keep an eye on the oil temperature, adjusting the heat regularly to keep the oil around 265°F (130°C). While the meat is frying, if you notice parts of the meat surfacing above the oil, gently lift your Dutch oven or pan by the handle, back and forth, to encourage the oil to wash gently over the meat. (If you are not a nervous fryer, you can instead baste the meat using a spoon, as needed.) Otherwise, leave the meat untouched and unflipped, to avoid puncturing the coating and releasing the valuable steam that creates the souffléed effect. Transfer the finished schnitzel to the prepared baking sheet and place in the oven to keep warm. Adjust your oil temperature before frying each new slice.

When you are finished frying all of the meat, drop the chopped parsley in the hot oil and fry for 10 seconds. Using a slotted spoon, remove from the oil and transfer to a paper towel.

Transfer the schnitzels to individual plates, then drizzle ½ tablespoon butter across each and garnish with a sprinkle of fried parsley. Serve with the lemon halves for squeezing, and your choice of a side of cranberry jam, parsley potatoes, or a cucumber salad.

HOW TO CLARIFY BUTTER

In a saucepan over medium heat, melt 1½ pounds (680g) unsalted butter. Bring the butter to a gentle boil; it will start to foam. The butter will keep bubbling and foaming as its water content evaporates; the milk particles in the foam will start to brown and settle at the bottom. Once the bubbling subsides completely, you know the water is completely gone. Strain the butter through a cheesecloth or a fine-mesh sieve to remove the milk solids. Refrigerate the clarified butter in an airtight glass jar for up to 1 month.

Tyrolean Hash

TIROLER GRÖSTL

SERVES 4

1⅓ pounds (600g) Yukon gold potatoes

1 tablespoon grapeseed oil

1 yellow onion, finely diced

9 ounces (250g) cooked beef, thinly sliced

1 teaspoon minced fresh flat-leaf parsley

½ teaspoon dried marjoram, or 1 teaspoon fresh marjoram

½ teaspoon caraway seeds

Fine sea salt and freshly ground black pepper

2 tablespoons unsalted butter

4 eggs

1 tablespoon minced chives

Klaus Plank at the Weisses Rössl stube in Innsbruck taught me how to use up leftover cooked or stewed beef with this hash recipe. This is one of the most typical dishes found in the Austrian Alps. It may seem strange that I've included this version from Innsbruck, a city (albeit the gateway to Tyrol) and not a mountain village, but hey, this is the most delicious version I tried. If you're going to go Tyrolean-style, you have to serve this in a frying pan.

In a saucepan, combine the potatoes with cold water to cover and bring to a boil over high heat. Turn the heat to medium-low and simmer until the potatoes are fork-tender, 25 to 30 minutes depending on their size. Drain and let cool until easy to handle, then peel and thinly slice.

Preheat the oven to 350°F (175°C).

In a cast-iron frying pan over medium-high heat, warm the grapeseed oil. Add the onion and beef and sauté until the onion has softened and started to brown, about 5 minutes. Stir in the potato slices, followed by the parsley, marjoram, and caraway seeds. Season generously with salt and pepper and transfer to the oven.

In a large nonstick frying pan over medium heat, melt the butter. Break the eggs, one at a time, into the pan, keeping space between them. Turn the heat to low and cook, uncovered, until the whites are fully cooked, 3 to 4 minutes.

Portion the hash onto four plates, top each with a fried egg, and sprinkle with the chives. Serve immediately.

KLAUS PLANK AT
WEISSES RÖSSI

Quark Cake with Peaches

TOPFEN-OBERS-TORTE MIT PFIRSICH

■■■■ EASY
SERVES 12 TO 14

YOU WILL NEED
9-inch (23cm) springform
cake pan or cake ring

CAKE
6 eggs

¾ cup plus 2 tablespoons (175g)
granulated sugar

Pinch of fine sea salt

1 teaspoon vanilla extract

1 teaspoon freshly squeezed
lemon juice, or ½ teaspoon
lemon extract

1¼ cups (150g) bread flour,
plus more for dusting

2 tablespoons unsalted butter,
melted

CREAM-PEACH FILLING
7 sheets leaf gelatin

1¾ cups (175g) quark cheese,
at room temperature

¼ cup (60ml) milk

⅔ cup (135g) granulated sugar

1 teaspoon vanilla extract

1 teaspoon freshly squeezed
lemon juice, or ½ teaspoon
lemon extract

2¾ cups (650ml) heavy cream

6 canned peach halves, patted dry

Confectioners' sugar for dusting

In all the years I spent researching this book, the only time I was *really* snowed in was in the Stubai Alps, southwest of Innsbruck and north of the Ötztal Alps. I was staying at a *Jagdschloss* (hunting lodge) in the small, compact, yet very dramatic village of Kühtai. To get there, you drive so far up into the mountains that you pass glaciers along the way. Kühtai is known as the highest ski resort in Austria; the base camp lies at about 1,950 meters (6,400 feet). I suppose that the altitude, combined with the darkest of skies, combined with the fact that the hotel is owned by a count should have been obvious clues to the bumpy night ahead. After a failed ski trip—due to black skies and zero visibility—to find huts in the surrounding mountains, I gave up and returned to the lodge for beef broth with strips of pancake (*Rinderconsomme mit Frittatensuppe*), and this sponge cake. And schnapps. Lots of schnapps.

Note: Canned peaches and frozen quark (fresh cheese) have long shelf lives— which is ideal for remote, isolated hotel kitchens, the kind that require cogwheel trains to reach, the kind that may need to go many days, sometimes weeks, without fresh produce or a new delivery. I guess you could use fresh peaches for this recipe, but that would take away from that snowed-in feeling.

To make the cake: Preheat the oven to 325°F (160°C). Butter and flour a springform cake pan or cake ring.

Using a stand mixer fitted with the whisk attachment, on medium speed, combine the eggs, granulated sugar, salt, vanilla, and lemon juice, beating until pale and fluffy, 3 to 4 minutes. Add the flour, mixing it in on low speed until smooth. Add the melted butter and mix briefly to incorporate. Pour the batter into the prepared cake pan.

Bake until the top is golden brown and cake springs back when pressed in the center, about 25 minutes. Transfer the pan to a wire rack and let cool for 5 to 10 minutes before releasing the springform (or ring). Dust the cake lightly with flour before inverting it onto the wire rack. Let cool completely.

To make the cream-peach filling: Prepare a water bath by bringing a pot of water to a simmer. In a bowl of

cold water, soak the gelatin sheets until the sheets become limp, 5 to 10 minutes.

In the meantime, in a heatproof bowl, combine the quark, milk, and granulated sugar. Place the bowl over the pot of simmering water and whisk until the mixture is well combined and lukewarm. Remove the bowl from the pot and set aside.

Gently pick up and squeeze the sheets of gelatin to get rid of excess water and transfer them to a medium bowl.

Ladle a third of the warm quark mixture into the bowl with the gelatin and whisk together until the gelatin has melted into the quark and no lumps remain. Return the quark-gelatin mixture to the rest of the quark, and mix until fully combined. Stir in the vanilla and lemon juice.

In a medium bowl or using a stand mixer fitted with the whisk

continued

attachment, whip the cream to stiff peaks. Transfer a third of the whipped cream to the quark-gelatin mixture and whisk gently until lightened. Then, using a spatula, gently fold the remaining whipped cream into the batter.

Using a serrated cake knife, slice the cooled cake in half horizontally. Lay the cleaned cake ring or the springform part of the cake pan onto a flat plate. Place the bottom of the cake into the ring.

Spread half of the quark mixture across the cake. Arrange the peach halves, pit-side up, evenly over the cream. Cover with the remaining quark mixture, then top with the remaining half of the cake. Refrigerate until set, at least 6 hours but preferably overnight.

Remove the springform or cake ring, sprinkle the cake with confectioners' sugar, and slice. Serve immediately.

STREETS OF INNSBRUCK

Poppy-Seed and Currant Roll

MOHNSTRUDEL

■■■■ MEDIUM

SERVES 8 TO 10

YOU WILL NEED

High-speed blender or
food processor

4 by 12-inch (10 by 30 cm) terrine
dish or baking sheet

YEASTED DOUGH

½ cup (120ml) whole milk,
warmed to 105° to 110°F
(40° to 45°C)

2⅓ cups (280g) all-purpose flour

1 tablespoon active dry yeast

1 tablespoon plus 1 teaspoon
sugar

3 tablespoons unsalted butter,
melted

¼ cup (60ml) warm (105° to
110°F/40° to 45°C) water

1 teaspoon fine sea salt

POPPY-SEED FILLING

⅓ cup (50g) raisins

¼ cup (60ml) dark rum

1¼ cups (170g) poppy seeds

1¼ cups (300ml) whole milk

⅓ cup (65g) sugar

1 vanilla bean, split and seeded

¼ teaspoon ground cinnamon

Pinch of fine sea salt

¼ cup (30g) semolina flour

2 tablespoons plus 1 teaspoon
marzipan, crumbled

Grated zest of ½ orange

Grated zest of ½ lemon

CURRANT FILLING

¼ cup (70g) strained store-bought
blackcurrant jam

Scant 1 cup (130g) currants

1 egg yolk, beaten

Vanilla Sauce (recipe follows)
for serving

The Ice Q at the summit of Gaislachkogl, above Sölden, is a stunning glass cube with two restaurants, a bar, a wine cave, and a lookout built on rock at 3,000 meters (9,840 feet). It was a key location in the James Bond film *Spectre*, and could very easily feel like a tourist trap. But it doesn't, because civil engineering in remote locales (and Willy Bogner Jr., a retired ski racer who choreographed many a Bond ski stunt) is as authentic to the Alps as Heidi herself.

I loved the Ice Q's poppy-seed roll with raisins and blackcurrant jam. Making the yeasted dough is very doable (and less daunting than its Viennese paper-thin cousin; see page 175), as is the poppy-seed filling. (In German, this is still called a *strudel*. For our purposes and to avoid confusion, we're calling it a roll.)

To make the yeasted dough: In the bowl of a stand mixer, stir together the warm milk, ⅓ cup (40g) of the flour, the yeast, and sugar. Let this mixture rest until small bubbles start breaking through the surface, 3 or 4 minutes.

Using the stand mixer fitted with the dough hook, add the remaining 2 cups (240g) flour, the melted butter, warm water, and salt to the bowl. Knead the mixture at medium-low speed until a dough forms, about 1 minute, then increase the speed to medium-high and continue to knead until the dough looks smooth, about 5 minutes more. Remove the bowl from the mixer and cover the dough, still in the bowl, with a kitchen towel. Transfer to a warm place and let the dough rise until doubled in size, 45 to 60 minutes.

To make the poppy-seed filling: While the dough is proofing, in a small bowl, combine the raisins and rum and let sit until plump, about 30 minutes.

In a high-speed blender or food processor, grind the poppy seeds until sandy, about 10 seconds.

In a medium saucepan, combine two-thirds of the milk, the sugar, vanilla seeds, cinnamon, and salt and stir to mix. Place over medium-high heat and bring to a boil. Stir in the poppy seeds, turn the heat to medium-low, and cook, whisking constantly, until the milk is absorbed and the mixture thickens, about 3 minutes. Remove from the heat.

In a separate saucepan over medium-high heat, bring the remaining one-third milk to a boil. Turn the heat to medium, stir in the semolina, and cook, stirring constantly, until the liquid is absorbed and the batter pulls away from the sides of the pot, 1 to 2 minutes.

In a large bowl, combine the poppy-seed and semolina mixtures, using a spatula to mix. Stir in the marzipan until well distributed, then stir in the orange zest, lemon zest, and rum-soaked raisins. Transfer to the refrigerator.

To make the currant filling: In a small bowl, stir together the blackcurrant jam and currants.

If using a terrine dish, butter it generously. You can also bake as a free-form roll on a baking sheet lined with parchment paper.

continued

With a lightly dusted rolling pin, roll out the dough to form a rectangle, about ¾ inch (2cm) thick, trimming off any uneven edges with a sharp knife to make a neat border. Using a spoon, coat the rectangle of dough entirely with the poppy-seed filling. Gently spread the currant filling over the poppy-seed mixture.

Starting on the long side, carefully roll up the dough completely and transfer, seam-side down, into the prepared terrine dish or onto the baking sheet. Set aside to rise at room temperature until it starts to puff up, about 20 minutes.

Gently brush the beaten egg yolk over the top of the risen dough. Place the roll in a cold oven and then turn the oven temperature to 300°F (150°C). (Yes, you read this correctly.) Bake for 30 minutes until puffed and golden brown. Remove from the oven and let cool completely before unmolding and slicing.

Serve the roll with vanilla sauce alongside.

Vanilla Sauce

MAKES 3½ CUPS (830ML)

9 egg yolks

7 tablespoons (85g) sugar

1½ cups (360ml) milk

1½ cups (360ml) heavy cream

1½ vanilla beans, split and seeded

This is a perfect accompaniment to any strudel.

In a large bowl, whisk together the egg yolks and sugar until smooth and pale, about 2 minutes.

In a medium saucepan, combine the milk, cream, and vanilla bean pods and seeds. Place over medium heat and bring to almost the boiling point, then quickly remove from the heat. Discard the vanilla pods.

Slowly pour one-third of the milk-cream mixture into the egg mixture while whisking continuously. Pour the combined egg-milk mixture back into the saucepan with the rest of the vanilla-infused milk and cream and whisk to combine. Over medium heat, stir constantly until the sauce starts to thicken and the temperature reaches 180°F (82°C).

Remove from the heat and transfer to a clean bowl or container; place plastic wrap directly on the surface to prevent a skin from forming as it cools. Refrigerate for at least 1 hour or up to 3 days.

BOND IN THE ALPS

It turns out that Ian Fleming, James Bond's creator, attended the small Tennerhof private school in Kitzbühel, an institution run by a former MI6 member, to improve his German. There he fell in love with an Austrian woman (and the Alps), and began writing and skiing. I can only assume that he became fascinated by the Alps more generally after that—note the Swiss banking codes, winding roads, love of watches, and remote hiding spots for his books' villains (not to mention the Olympic biathlon henchmen). Following are some quintessential Alpine moments, as seen in Bond films.

Goldfinger (1964). Along the Furka Pass—the high mountain pass that borders the Swiss regions of Valais and Uri—there is a series of hairpin bends and turns. This is where Tilly Masterson, on a revenge-fueled car chase, fires her rifle at Goldfinger, narrowly missing Bond.

On Her Majesty's Secret Service (1969). In Mürren (Bernese Highlands, Switzerland), the Piz Gloria revolving restaurant serves as the lair for criminal mastermind Ernst Stavro Blofeld (who was inspiration for *Austin Powers*'s Dr. Evil).

The Spy Who Loved Me (1977). The opening ski chase culminates with Bond skiing off a cliff in the fictional "Berngarten" (Austria) and opening his Union Jack parachute.

For Your Eyes Only (1981). Bond stays at the Miramonti Majestic hotel in Cortina d'Ampezzo (Dolomites/Southern Alps, Italy).

GoldenEye (1995). The opening scene famously shows Bond swandiving off the 220-meter (720-foot) concrete face of Verzasca Dam near Locarno, Switzerland.

The World Is Not Enough (1999). Bond and love interest/oil heiress Elektra King heli-ski for pleasure in Chamonix (France), only to be attacked by villainous paragliding snowmobilers. Spoiler alert: Bond lives.

Quantum of Solace (2008). Bond eavesdrops on a terrorist network's conference call during a performance of *Tosca* at the Bregenz open-air opera house (Lake Constance, Austria).

Spectre (2015). While tracking down the mastermind behind the titular global criminal organization, Bond ends up at the Ice Q (pictured opposite)—standing in as a remote private psychiatric clinic—at the summit of Gaislachkogl (Sölden, Ötztal Alps).

Kaiserschmarrn

■■■■ EASY
SERVES 1 ADVANCED EATER
OR 2 BEGINNERS

1 cup (120g) all-purpose flour, sifted

1 cup (240ml) whole milk

3 eggs

¼ cup (55g) unsalted butter, melted

Fine sea salt

¼ cup (60ml) grapeseed oil

½ cup (60g) confectioners' sugar

2 tablespoons rum (optional)

Apple jam or compote and/or cranberry jam for serving

TRAVEL HACK

Gampe Thaya is open for dinner after the cable cars have closed for the day. Because the lodge is halfway up the mountain, most taxi services will drop you at the midway point and expect you to walk the remaining 30 minutes to the hut (a beautiful hike when it's still light out). Taxi Lenz in Sölden, however, will drive you door-to-door.

Of all the Austrian dessert classics, this imperial one reigns supreme over Alpine menus.

Though Kaiserschmarrn originated in Vienna, it's not exactly something you'd bring to a kaffeeklatsch or that you'd crave on a warm summer day. It is big, it's easy to make, and it's a whole lotta rustic. Served right from the frying pan it was cooked in, it's a jumble of buttery shredded pancake generously dusted with confectioners' sugar. In other words, it's best made and enjoyed in a 300-year-old hut in Tyrol.

So that's how I came to try it at the Gampe Thaya hut (see Travel Hack), located at 2,000 meters (6,560 feet) in the southern Ötztal Valley. In the summer, Gampe Thaya is also a dairy farm set in a meadow chock-full of cows and Alpine pastures, flora, and fauna. In the winter, it's a ski-in/ski-out lodge right on the Gampe Alm piste. Regardless of the season, owner Jakob Prantl (featured on the following spread) will welcome you, pour you a beer, and just maybe make you Kaiserschmarrn with his own two (very large) hands.

Note: The possibilities for Schmarrn *(translated as "shredded or chopped pancake") variations are endless! To make Apfelschmarrn (apple) or Kirschschmarrn (cherry), simply add a few thin slices of apple or a handful of pitted and halved cherries to the batter before you pour it into the pan. You can also add 2 tablespoons raisins to the batter, or stir in the finely grated zest of one lemon if you prefer.*

In a large bowl, combine the flour, milk, eggs, melted butter, and a pinch of salt and whisk well to combine into a loose batter. Let rest at room temperature for 20 to 30 minutes.

In a large, well-seasoned frying pan over medium heat, warm the grapeseed oil until it shimmers. Pour in the batter and let it sit in the pan, untouched, so it can start to slightly brown on the bottom. Using a flat spatula, or a deft flick of the wrist, flip the pancake and continue to cook until brown on the other side, about 2 minutes.

Using two forks (or a saber, like Jakob), and working directly in the pan, coarsely cut the pancake into pieces, 1 to 2 inches (2.5 to 5cm) in size. Sprinkle liberally with the confectioners' sugar.

Harness your Alpine bravado by splashing the rum onto the pancake, then setting the pan aflame. Let the fire subside and serve up the Kaiserschmarrn warm in its pan, accompanied by apple and/or cranberry jam.

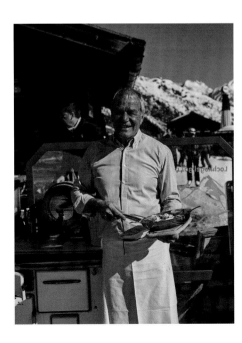

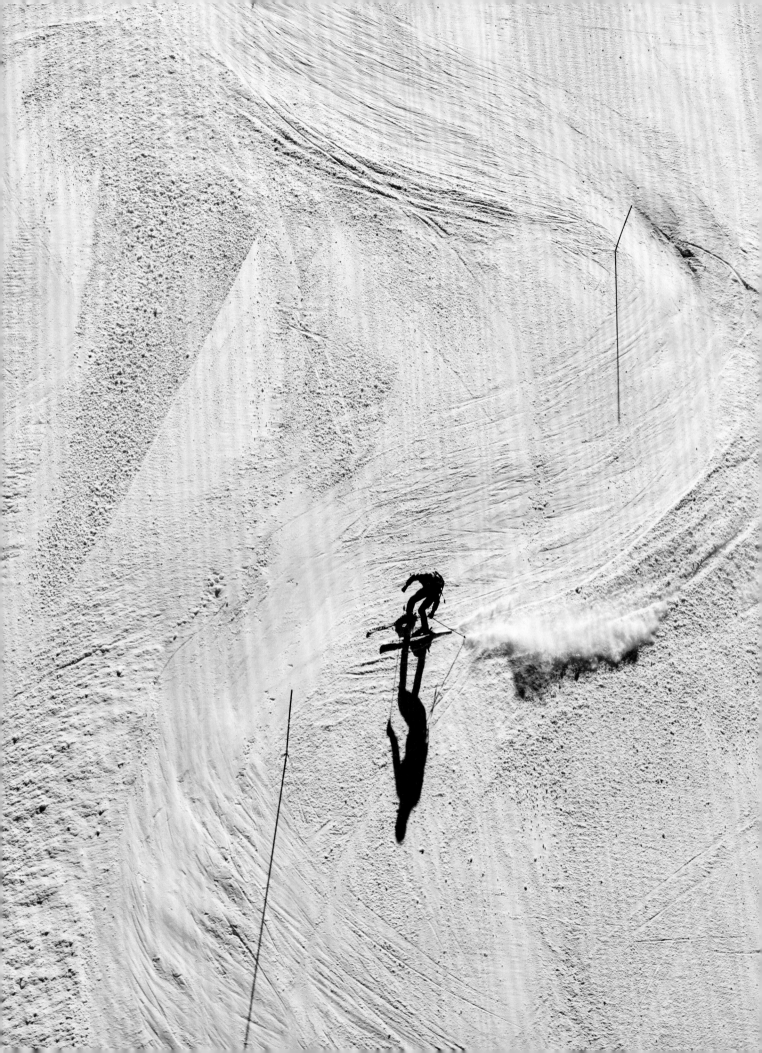

Apricot Dumplings

MARILLENKNÖDEL

■■■■■ MEDIUM

SERVES 6 TO 8

(MAKES 12 DUMPLINGS)

12 fresh apricots

12 sugar cubes

¼ cup (55g) unsalted butter, at room temperature, plus 1 cup (220g) unsalted butter, cubed

¾ cup (90g) confectioners' sugar, plus more for dusting

2 eggs

4 ounces (115g) fresh crustless white bread slices, ripped into pieces

2½ cups (500g) quark cheese

⅔ cup (85g) all-purpose flour, plus more for dusting

1¼ cups (150g) panko bread crumbs

Vanilla sugar (see page 118) for sprinkling

Almost as famous as Kaiserschmarrn (page 161) as far as Austrian desserts go, this recipe's more traditional name is *Wachauer Marillenknödel*, as apricots are emblematic of the Wachau region just west of Vienna along the Danube River. Stone fruits thrive (as do wine grapes) in that valley, and because the rest of the ingredients in this recipe are shelf-stable, cold-room/pantry staples, you often see this on dessert menus throughout the Austrian Alps. I love the apricot dumplings at Almhof Schneider; after spending a morning on the mountain, this dessert along with a good coffee or glass of bubbles, preferably enjoyed in the Almhof's living room looking down onto the village of Lech, makes for a perfect afternoon.

Note: Some recipes use potato for the starch; I use flour and plain white sliced bread. Remove the crusts before weighing.

Begin by pushing the handle of a wooden spoon through the center of each apricot to ease out the kernel while keeping the fruit whole. Insert a sugar cube into the center of each apricot. Set aside in a shallow bowl.

In a stand mixer fitted with the paddle attachment, working at medium speed, cream the ¼ cup (55g) butter and confectioners' sugar until homogenous and light, about 1 minute. With the machine still running, add the eggs, one at a time. Turn the speed to medium-low, add the ripped bread, then the quark, and finally the flour and paddle until well incorporated, 3 to 4 minutes.

Cover the mixer bowl with plastic wrap and refrigerate for at least 3 hours or up to overnight.

Dust a large plate or baking sheet and a clean work surface with flour. Scrape the cold dough out of the bowl and onto the work surface. Flour your hands generously and shape the dough into a roll, approximately 12 inches (30cm) long. Slice the roll into twelve even pieces.

Dust your hands again and, using the palm of one hand, flatten each slice to form a circle wide enough to wrap around an apricot, about 3 inches (7.5cm) across—this will depend on the size of the apricots. Place the dough circle in your hand, center an apricot in the dough, and use your other hand to wrap the dough around the fruit. Gently roll the covered apricot between your hands to complete the seal and even out the dough, then transfer to the prepared plate. Repeat with the remaining dough and apricots.

Bring a large pot of water to a boil.

Transfer the apricot dumplings one by one into the boiling water and gently nudge them around in the water so they don't stick to the bottom of the pot. Simmer until a knife poked through a dumpling comes out hot, 10 to 12 minutes.

In the meantime, in a large frying pan over medium heat, melt the remaining 1 cup (220 g) butter. When the butter is bubbling, stir in the bread crumbs and toast them until golden, but not too dark, 5 to 7 minutes. Turn off the heat.

Using a slotted spoon, remove the apricot dumplings from the water and transfer them to the frying pan. Roll each one in the toasted crumbs to cover completely, using a shake of the pan and a spoon to help coat, then transfer to a serving dish. Sprinkle with confectioners' sugar and vanilla sugar and serve immediately.

Gerold and Katia Schneider are my favorite Alpine couple. Together they run an architectural practice, the hotel Almhof Schneider, and the Allmeinde Commongrounds cultural space (pictured here) in Lech. They're responsible for the gorgeous and utility-driven design of the two locations and for Skihütte Schneggarei, a wooden restaurant and bar next to the hotel run by Gerold's brother, Andi. Gerold is a fourth-generation maître de maison and heir to a family history that goes back to 1450 in the very same place. In winter, Gerold and Katia routinely take the first lift each morning and ski together. They prefer the pistes at Stierfall and Gams, and like to go off-piste on the Omeshorn. When staying at their hotel, at around 9:30 a.m., I waited for them to return from skiing to get their ski report over eggs and smoked fish. In summer, they like to go running together. After a busy day as gracious hosts, they love to eat smoked trout with mushrooms. Fun Fact: Katia played Heidi in the eponymous German TV series that premiered in 1978.

—

SNAPSHOT

Cheese Spaetzle

KÄSESPÄTZLE

▮▮▮▮ MEDIUM
SERVES 6 TO 8

YOU WILL NEED
Spaetzle maker or potato ricer, or colander with large perforations

Flexible dough scraper

ONION GARNISH
1 yellow onion, sliced into thin rounds

⅓ cup (40g) all-purpose flour

1½ teaspoons sweet paprika

½ cup (110g) unsalted butter

SPAETZLE
Fine sea salt

2 cups (240g) all-purpose flour

2 cups (240g) semolina flour

5 eggs

½ cup plus 2 tablespoons (150ml) whole milk

⅓ cup (80ml) sparkling water

Pinch of freshly ground black pepper

Pinch of freshly grated nutmeg

¼ cup (60ml) beef or chicken stock or low-sodium beef or chicken broth

3½ cups (400g) grated Emmental or Gruyère cheese

2 tablespoons minced fresh chives or flat-leaf parsley

The earliest record of cheese spaetzle ("shpetz-luh")—essentially boiled noodles fried with fresh mountain-hut cheese—dates back to medieval times in the region of Swabia (in what is now southwestern Germany, but the region used to stretch as far as western Austria). A little noodle meditation: You see spaetzle on almost all mountain menus in the German Bavarian Alps and across Austria. In some parts of Austria, spaetzle with cheese is referred to as *Kasnocken* (see variation). I've come across spaetzle in Switzerland, but there it's mostly rösti—spaetzle's Swiss carb counterpart. The English terminology can become confusing: I refer to spaetzle as "noodles," but in German-speaking parts, spaetzle are "little dumplings." I think of dumplings as something bigger, similar to *knödel* (in Austria and Germany) or *canederli* (in Alto Adige). Some mountain menus even translate *spätzle* as "gnocchi," which these noodles definitely are not, their dough being made of egg and flour, not freshly riced potatoes. Does this, in the end, really matter? As long as the spaetzle is delicious, no! But if an Alpine cookbook can't be a reference on this matter, what can?

Back to the recipe—I'm not sure when fried onions became the standard garnish, but they're what you see in every traditional restaurant in the Vorarlberg area (the westernmost part of Austria). And this is where I had my first Käsespätzle, in the most traditional of mountain restaurants at Alter Goldener Berg in Oberlech. I've been lucky enough to try the entire menu at Goldener Berg, and I've included their recipes for Spinach and Cheese Mezzaluna (page 60), Weisswurst (see page 108), and this cheese spaetzle as my favorite dishes to share.

Note: While some people use a potato ricer to make spaetzle, I like to use a flexible dough scraper and a perforated hotel pan balanced directly over a pot of boiling water; an industrial-size colander would work too (the holes in a standard colander are too small). Spaetzle makers are, however, easily purchased online.

To make the onion garnish: In a large bowl, toss the onion with the flour and paprika.

In a large frying pan over medium-low heat, melt the butter. Shake off any excess flour from the onion rounds and then add them to the pan. Let them slowly become golden brown, resisting the urge to stir, except very occasionally, 30 to 45 minutes. Don't let the onions get too dark, however, as they will become bitter. Drain on paper towels and set aside.

To make the spaetzle: Bring a large pot of water to a boil, then add a generous pinch of salt and turn down the heat, so the water just simmers throughout the cooking process.

In a large bowl, combine both flours, the eggs, milk, sparkling water, pepper, nutmeg, and a pinch of salt. Using a whisk at first, followed by a spatula, thoroughly mix to form a dough; it should feel elastic and not be runny, just soft enough to pass

continued

through the holes in the spaetzle maker or colander.

Work the dough quickly through the spaetzle maker or the colander. Once in the water, the spaetzle will cook in less than 2 minutes after the water returns to a simmer. Give the strands a good stir, and when the spaetzle float to the surface, drain the noodles, discarding the cooking water, then give the noodles a good rinse in cold water to stop them from overcooking. Drain again.

In the same pot (or in a cast-iron or enamel stove-to-table serving dish of your choice), warm the stock over medium heat, then return the spaetzle to the pot (or serving dish). Shake the pot (or dish) a few times to evenly distribute the stock and reheat the spaetzle, then add the grated cheese and mix well, until the cheese is nicely melted.

Serve family-style or portion the spaetzle into shallow bowls, then top with the onion garnish and minced chives.

VARIATION

The Pinzgau region has its own version of Käsespätzle, known as Pinzgauer Kasnocken. The main difference lies in the cheeses; in Pinzgau, they use a mix of Bierkäse, Tilsit, and Gouda. The best Kasnocken I tasted in the Alps was at the Valeriehaus, at the bottom of Sportgastein (see Travel Hack, page 122). To make Kasnocken, proceed as described in the main recipe, but replace the 3½ cups (400g) Emmental or Gruyère with 1 cup (120g) grated Bierkäse, 1½ cups (160g) grated Tilsit, and 1 cup (120g) grated Gouda.

BESIDES BEING THE BEST INTRODUCTION TO TRADITIONAL ALPINE CUISINE, ALTER GOLDENER BERG ALSO HAS A GREAT VIEW OF THE PETERSBODEN HOTEL AND A LIFT FROM OBERLECH UP TO KRIEGERALPE.

Apple Strudel

APFELSTRÜDEL

■■■■ MEDIUM

SERVES 8

YOU WILL NEED

Large cotton or linen
kitchen towel

Pizza wheel

1¼ cups (200g) all-purpose flour,
plus more for dusting

½ cup (120ml) water

2 tablespoons grapeseed oil

¼ teaspoon fine salt

½ teaspoon apple cider vinegar

2½ cups (300g) peeled, very finely
diced tart apples

¼ cup (50g) granulated sugar,
plus 2 teaspoons

1 teaspoon ground cinnamon

⅔ cup (50g) panko bread crumbs

1 tablespoon unsalted butter,
plus ½ cup (110g), melted

Confectioners' sugar for dusting

Vanilla Sauce (page 156),
ice cream, or freshly whipped
cream for serving

The Klösterle hut is run in a centuries-old preserved *Walserhaus,* or log cabin. From Lech, following the path pointing to the end-of-the-line and very cute micro-village of Zug, you'll find the hut at the very end of the only road. Owned by Hannelore Schneider, the matriarch of the Almhof Schneider (see page 106), you can reach this fairy tale of a hut by sleigh, or you can ski there with a very easy off-piste detour. The day I was there, it was snowing heavily, and the more adventurous skiers had just arrived for a late lunch, complete with cakes and schnapps to calm the nerves.

The pièce de résistance is an oak table in the foyer, just in front of the fireplace with an offering of desserts, including a rich *susi torte* (flourless chocolate cake) and the most traditional—an apple strudel. I went with the strudel and never looked back. This is my version of the recipe.

Note: The secret to the best apple strudel flavor? The apples should be tart and firm, like a Boskoop, Braeburn, or Granny Smith, and definitely not mealy. Substitute any tart russet apple. And the dough needs to rest overnight for maximum stretch.

In a stand mixer fitted with the dough hook, combine the flour, water, grapeseed oil, salt, and vinegar and mix at low-medium speed until a shaggy dough forms, 5 to 6 minutes, then knead at medium-high speed until soft, smooth, and pliable, 5 to 7 minutes. Wrap in plastic and refrigerate overnight (the dough will stretch better if you work with it when it's truly cold and very well rested).

In a bowl, combine the diced apples with the ¼ cup (50g) granulated sugar and cinnamon.

Line a plate with paper towels.

In a nonstick frying pan over medium heat, melt the 1 tablespoon butter until frothy. Stir in the bread crumbs and remaining 2 teaspoons granulated sugar and cook, stirring occasionally, until golden brown, 2 to 3 minutes. Transfer to the prepared plate and let cool.

Preheat the oven to 350°F (175°C).

Lay a large kitchen towel on a work surface and dust it with flour. Lay out a sheet of parchment paper longer than 20 inches (50cm) for transferring the strudel onto a baking sheet.

Roll out the dough onto the towel and shape it into a square. Working quickly, so the dough doesn't dry out, lift and start stretching the dough at its edges, rather than at the center, using your closed fists; you'll find the dough almost stretches by itself thanks to the weight of the thicker edges and gravity. Work your way around the square, leaving the sections of dough you're not actively stretching to rest on the floured kitchen towel. Continue until you have at least a 20-inch (50cm) square, and the dough is thin enough for you to see your hand or some text printed on a card through it. Brush the dough with three-fourths of the melted butter, reserving the rest for the top of the rolled strudel.

Using a pizza wheel or a sharp knife, trim the thicker edges off the dough (discarding them) to make a 20-inch (50cm) square of very thin dough.

continued

Spread the bread crumb mixture all over the square of stretched dough, leaving a 1-inch (2.5cm) margin all around. Then add the apples along the bottom quarter of the dough, on top of the bread crumbs. Fold in the side edges of the dough over the filling, to keep it tucked in.

Using the kitchen towel for support, tightly roll up the dough around the filling, then keep rolling it onto the parchment paper, before transferring the parchment and the strudel onto a baking sheet. Brush the top and sides with the remaining melted butter.

Bake until golden, 30 to 40 minutes. Let cool slightly, then dust with confectioners' sugar.

Serve with vanilla sauce, ice cream, or freshly whipped cream. If you don't immediately eat all of the strudel, keep at room temperature, up to overnight, covered with a clean kitchen towel so the pastry doesn't dry out.

MOUNTAIN JUICE: ALPINE WINES

The Prié Blanc grape that grows in Italy's Valle d'Aosta behaves like an untamed wild vine, wrapping itself around anything close by for security. As if afraid of heights, it crouches low to the ground, clinging to a tree, a cliff, to gravity. I would do the same, because at 1,200 meters (3,940 feet) in Aosta's *alta valle* ("high valley"), the terraces are steep, and the ground is rocky and unforgiving.

Not only does the Valle d'Aosta have some of the highest-elevation vineyards in Europe, it also has many centenarian vines. Why? Because *Phylloxera*—the louse that decimated almost all of Europe's vineyards in the nineteenth century—was never able to attack. Up there, it's simply too high, too cold. Another fun fact? The vines don't need any grafting (connecting a vine to a rootstock); here in Aosta, you just stick the plant right into the ground.

There I was on a cold March day, near the town of Morgex La Ruine about 30 minutes south of Courmayeur, with winegrower Ermes Pavese in these Aosta vineyards, *his vineyards*, in awe. Not at the scenery, but at the desolation and back-breaking work needed to cultivate this escarpment. It truly looks like the land time forgot: below the steep terraces is the SS26 highway that curves from Gran Paradiso in Italy to the summit of Mont-Blanc in France; at the top, abandoned castles sit here and there on high ridges.

Making wine here, in the DOC (*Denominazione di Origine Controllata*) zone of Blanc de Morgex et de la Salle, is risky business. In the two years prior to my visit, the yield was close to zilch because of frost. Even in a great year, Pavese produces around 12,000 bottles, an amount

WHERE TO DRINK (GOOD) WINE IN THE ALPS

In the Alps and want to drink (good) wine? Here are a few places to start.

AUSTRIA

Almhof Schneider LECH

Döllerer GOLLING

Enoteca Settemilia SALZBURG

FRANCE

Café des Alpes CHÂTILLON-EN-DIOIS

Chachacha CHAMONIX

Kamouraska ANNECY

Le Clos des Sens ANNECY

Le Vin des Alpes GRENOBLE

Restaurant Palégrié
CORRENÇON-EN-VERCORS

Saint Bruno GRENOBLE

Zinc Bar GRENOBLE

ITALY

Ballardini MADONNA DI CAMPIGLIO

Bellevue Hotel Restaurant COGNE

Ciasa Salares SAN CASSIANO

Enoteca Valentini CANAZEI

ErbaVoglio AOSTA

Osteria della Mal'Ombra TRENTO

Restaurant Sissi MERANO

Siegi's CALDARO

SWITZERLAND

Enoteca Hischier BRIG

Hangar 41 SION

Hotel Jungfrau Wengernalp WENGERNALP

The Red Bottle SALGESCH

small enough to be called "niche." Winemaking in Aosta, at least at this altitude, seems more like an exercise in survival, for both the winemakers *and* the grapes, than a successful business.

So, why do it? The answer lies in the glass. The wine is nervy. It tastes of grapes tough enough to hold on to the rocky cliffs, trying to make it through a summer close to the sun, only to be harvested by hand, sometimes in a snowstorm, in September. The wine tastes like it bubbled up from a glacier: cold, effervescent, and refreshing, with a hint of acid. (And yes, for those who are wondering, there *is* ice wine in the Alps, though it is rare. Ermes Pavese makes my favorite, called Vino de Uve Stramatura Ninive.)

Like other feats of Alpine engineering, it's hard to believe that growing grapes here could ever work. But it does. And like the local Valdôtain patois, the wine is completely unique to this place. But, unlike those cryptic languages, it's very easy to drink; and I must say, I do like the taste.

Pavese's Prié Blanc may be a singular wine, but this kind of encounter on a steep slope is one I had many times when meeting winemakers across the Alps. Though his vineyard is not as high up (it's closer to 500 meters [1,640 feet]), Jean-Yves Péron output a similar amount of wine (15,000 bottles) and is a natural wine fan's go-to winemaker.

JEAN-YVES PÉRON CLIMBING HIS VINEYARDS

Jean-Yves lives in the medieval town of Conflans, and when I went to visit him one summer, he had been up since 5 a.m. and hadn't eaten once during the 35°C (95°F) day. There was simply too much work to do on his hundred-year-old property just outside of Albertville. His estate is divided into several microparcels containing the grapes of Mondeuse, Jacquère, Altesse, and Roussanne; and, after a couple of hours touring the vineyard (which felt more like mountain climbing), we sat to eat under a fig tree for protection from the sun, and I began to understand why some Alpine winemaking is referred to as "heroic viniculture."

Actually, hiking into the world of Alpine wine was one of my favorite parts of researching this book. The grapes of the Alps are like its people: survivors with a thick skin and the ability to weather the storms. For me, Alpine wine is about geography and poetry. It's about tinkering with what you have, but giving it enough space to let Mother Nature have a say.

The wine regions of the Alps, from east to west, are in Italy, including Trentino and South Tyrol, Lombardy's Valtellina, and the Aosta Valley; Switzerland's Valais; and in France, the Savoie, Isère, and Bugey regions. Though I touch on places such as Sauze d'Oulx, Sestriere, and Torino (all located in Piedmont), the wines of Piedmont do not originate in Alpine areas. And while I love the weird and wonderful world of *Heurigers* (taverns) and Austria's wine culture, Austrian vineyards are all on the eastern side of the country in Burgenland, Styria, and Upper and Lower Austria, and do not come close to the Alpine Arch (see page 8). That said, there are a *few* winemakers in Carinthia and at least one in the Vorarlberg I know and really like.

To cover four countries over such a wide range of terrain would involve addressing differences in soils, exposure to the sun, and a host of cultural challenges. (I've suggested books on specific wine regions in

ERMES PAVES AND SON

Further Alpine Reading on page 334.) Indeed, covering just the Savoie region of France could fill a book of this size. In Italy, Alois Lageder is a gentleman winemaker with vineyards in Margreid, the southernmost German-speaking village in Europe. But just a 20-minute drive south, and you're at the Foradori's rustic domain in Mezzolombardo, a very Italian-feeling village. Similarly, it's hard to compare how Jean-Yves Péron grows his black Mondeuse near Albertville with how Sandrine Caloz works with Petite Arvine in the Valais, let alone to connect them to what Elisabetta Foradori is doing with her wild vines of Teroldego in Trentino. Each is seemingly different, but they are all using native varietals to express terroir. And they are all challenged by altitude, which has taught them how to work with the mountain.

Proximity to high mountains, relative isolation, and quickly shifting weather systems affect all of the agriculture in the Alps. If you have ever been caught on a mountain during a storm or when the weather changes suddenly, you know how prepared you have to be. And so, I learned during my travels that Alpine producers need an additional tool in their arsenal—or perhaps just a sharper one—agility. Because at elevation, everything is more extreme. The sun is closer. The wind is stronger. The temperatures are colder. You have to be completely in tune with the energy of the mountains and react quickly. And, like Prié in the Aosta Valley, the native Alpine varieties themselves have adapted and evolved over centuries to meet these meteorological conditions head-on.

You can detect the direct influence that altitude has on wine style in the freshness and acidity of the wines—in all Alpine wines, across all countries. In the Alps, there are extremely cool nights but solid daytime heat, keeping the acidity of the fruit balanced. Higher vineyard locations are typically cooler (air temperature drops about 0.6°C [1°F] with every 100 meters [330 feet] of altitude), which makes for a longer, slower growing season and means the grapes hang from the vine longer without becoming overripe. *Overripe* usually means a sugar bomb or a wine without the structure of acid to support it. But with Alpine wines, the cool air is a savior and provides a shifting balance.

Something else Alpine vineyards have in common: Each and every square meter of land is used. Vertical growth is the norm. Because winter tourism is so popular and requires the space necessary for sporting activities, finding and acquiring new land is also extremely difficult. Winemakers have learned to really read the land they have in detail; soil, exposure, grape variety—all of these factors are crucial to a successful production.

When it comes to Alpine wine and food pairings, I take a page from the French and Italians and stay regional. For example, Teroldego (a grape from Trentino) loves rabbit with polenta, cheese, dumplings, and very simple mountain food. Altesse and Jacquère (both from the Savoie) pair beautifully with seafood and seem to highlight salinity. Both Gringet and Chasselas, two grapes that are nonaromatic and quite neutral but fresh, support shellfish with creamy sauces. And Prié is the perfect bottle to start an evening paired a few snacks or with nothing at all. If you want

Sandrine Caloz is a *vigneronne* (winegrower) working at her family's Cave Caloz in the Valais. Her favorite Alpine restaurant is Cabane des Violettes in nearby Crans-Montana. There, she loves to ski on the Plaine Morte pistes. She also loves to hike, and completed the famed Tour du Mont-Blanc trek with her sister in 2010. She has two daughters, one of whom has a (delicious) wine named after her: Sélene, a blend of Cabernet Franc, Gamaret, and Diolinoir.

SNAPSHOT

to make fondue, use a wine from the Valais close to the pastures of the Vaud. And if you want to poach a fish, try a wine from a vineyard close to where the fish was caught.

Today, Alpine farmers and winemakers are becoming more progressive and, in some cases, they realize the best thing to do to old vineyards with native varietals is basically nothing. The first step is to allow space for vines to grow in the mountains—and this is already happening. But our mindset is also changing. We're no longer in the era of celebrating the taste of corporate wine. Quirky wine is honored. We've loosened up a bit, and this is good news for mountain juice.

Climate change also encourages a lighter touch in terms of viniculture, meaning, no pesticides and less intervention. For that reason, many of the winemakers I've suggested here are making low-intervention wines. I am by no means dogmatic, but in a book that champions the terroir of the Alps, I want you to get as close to the mountain as possible with your wine choice, and additives and chemicals are direct obstacles to that goal. Interest in natural wines and native varietals opens new opportunities for Alpine winemakers—let's hope they continue to preserve and champion the Alpine character of their regional varieties. As Elisabetta Foradori put it to me, "It takes a lot of precision and observation to let the Alps speak their truth in your glass."

Mountain Juice: Alpine Wines

MAIN ALPINE VARIETALS TO KNOW

These are the main players in each region. Please note this list includes native and nonnative varietals. Austrian varietals are not listed as so few grapes grow in the Austrian Alps.

AOSTA (ITALY)

White

Moscato Bianco
Malvoisie
Müller-Thurgau
Prié
Torrette

Red

Cornalin
Fumin
Mayolet
Nebbiolo (Picotener)
Petit Rouge
Prié Rouge
Vien de Nus
Vuillermin

TRENTINO-ALTO ADIGE (ITALY)

White

Chardonnay
Gewürztraminer
Kerner
Manzoni Bianco
Moscato Giallo
Nosiola
Pinot Bianco
Pinot Grigo
Sauvignon Blanc
Sylvaner

Red

Lagrein
Marzemino
Merlot
Moscato Rosa
Pinot Nero
Rebo
Schiava family
Teroldego

VALTELLINA, LOMBARDY (ITALY)

White

White Nebbiolo

Red

Nebbiolo (Chiavennasca)

VALAIS (SWITZERLAND)

White

Amigne
Chardonnay
Chasselas (Fendant)
Marsanne
Petite Arvine
Pinot Gris
Sauvignon Blanc
Sylvaner

Red

Cornalin
Diolinoir
Gamaret
Gamay
Garanoir
Humagne Rouge
Merlot
Pinot Noir
Rèze

SAVOIE (FRANCE)

White

Altesse
Bergeron (Roussanne)
Chardonnay
Chasselas
Gringet
Jacquère

Red

Douce Noire
Etraire de la Dhuy
Gamay
Mondeuse
Persan
Pinot Noir
Poulsard

PRODUCERS TO LOOK FOR

Due to the remoteness of locations, having access to the beautiful wines produced in the Alps can be tricky. Here is a list of great producers with a lot of integrity; almost all of their wines (many of them organic) are available in North America. Many of the names of Italian wineries are simply the name of the winemakers; but to avoid confusion, the name of the winery is also listed.

ITALY

Alois Lageder
ALOIS LAGEDER

Angelo Sega
BARBACAN WINE

Arturo Pelizzatti Perego
AR.PE.PE.

Conti Sertoli Salis
CONTI SERTOLI SALIS

David Fasolini and Pierpaola di Francoi
DIRUPI

Elisabetta Foradori
FORADORI

Ermes Pavese
ERMES PAVESE

Eugenio Rosi
EUGENIO ROSI

Gino Pedrotti
GINO PEDROTTI

Grosjean Frères
GROSJEAN FRÈRES

Marco Zabi
CASTEL NOARNA

Martin Gojer Pranzegg
MARTIN GOJER PRANZEGG

Sandro Fay
SANDRO FAY

AUSTRIA

Georg Lexer
WEINGUT KARNBURG

Hubert Vittori, Andrea and Alfred Riedl
WEINGUT TAGGENBRUNN

Josef Möth
WEINGUT MÖTH

Markus Gruze
WEINGUT GEORGIUM

SWITZERLAND

Jacques Grange
DOMAINE DE BEUDON

Marc Balzan and Andrea Grossman
DOMAINE DE CHEROUCHE

Marie-Thérèse Chappaz
DOMAINE CHAPPAZ

Paul-Henri Soler
PAUL-HENRI SOLER

Romaine and Hans-Peter Schmidt
MYTHOPIA

Sandrine Caloz
CAVE CALOZ

FRANCE

Adrien Berlioz
CRAY CELLAR

Dominique Belluard
DOMAINE BELLUARD

Gilles Berlioz
DOMAINE PARTAGÉ

Jacque Maillet
JACQUE MAILLET

Jean-Yves Péron
DOMAINE JEAN-YVES PÉRON

Marie and Florian Curtet
DOMAINE CURTET

Michel Grisard
DOMAINE PRIEURÉ ST-CHRISTOPHE

Nicolas Gonin
DOMAINE NICOLAS GONIN

Thomas Finot
DOMAINE FINOT

Weissweine
SCHWEIZ
Genève

Chardonnay, Dom. du Grand Clos   12   70.—
Jean Michel Novelle, Satigny
Grand Cru - Riesling - Sauvignon   14/15 75.—
Jean Pierre Pellegrin, Peissy

Vaud

La Côte   Sauvignon Blanc, Aoc   16   46.—
           H. Cruchon, Echiens-s-Morges

Lavaux   St. Saphorin-les Blassinges, Aoc 15/16 48.—
           P. L. Neyroz, Chexbres
           Dézaley Médinette-Gr. Cru, Aoc   15/16 5b.—
           L. Bovard

Chablais   Yvorne Clos de la George 1er Gr. Cru/50cl 15/16 52.—/25.—
           Dom. Clos de la George

SWITZERLAND

The Swiss Alps: An Overview

The mountain pass of Kleine Scheidegg, which translates as "minor watershed," sits on a plateau in the Bern Oberland, aka the Bern highlands. It is also a railway station where a cogwheel train from Lauterbrunnen reaches its peak (see Travel Hack, page 196). Located between the towns of Wengen and Grindelwald, both major hubs for skiing and hiking, the area on the mountain is car-free and has a panoramic vista of three Bernese giants: the Eiger, the Mönch, and the Jungfrau, which rises to 4,158 meters (13,642 feet). It's as beautiful as it is disorienting. To arrive there, you must take the cogwheel train that lurches up the mountain and into the clouds.

When my boyfriend and I arrived in Wengen en route to Kleine Scheidegg station, fog and clouds mixed interchangeably, which was an extraordinary sight from a wooden bench on the train but less relaxing for the skiers on the adjacent pistes (as I would come to realize). The cogwheels turned and as the gradient increased, a ski-racing course came into view and my mouth dropped at the scene. My boyfriend explained it was the site of the Lauberhorn, a downhill ski race he used to watch when he was young. It's the longest World Cup downhill in the world at 4.5 kilometers (2.8 miles) and what I saw from the train was the famous 2-meter (7-foot) drop. As we moved forward, I swiveled in my seat so I could watch time-trialing teens whiz down chutes, less than a traffic lane wide, at 85 kilometers (55 miles) per hour. The next day, while traversing down the hill (yes, to get to lunch), I took a wrong turn—or rather, I *didn't* take the turn—and I wound up on the Lauberhorn course. I know (now) that ski maps can't help you if there is no visibility, and so I bore down, the clouds parted, and all was fine—save for some mild shaking between forkfuls of (really good) sausage and rösti (Switzerland's national dish; see page 253).

Of Switzerland's twenty-five *cantons* (regions), eight lay in the path of the Alps: Bern, the Valais, Vaud, St. Gallen, Uri, Appenzell, Ticino, and Graubünden. Compared to Italy, Austria, and France, Switzerland is the smallest country; however, approximately 65 percent of Switzerland is in fact "Alpine." And of the eighty-two 4,000-meter (13,000-foot) peaks in the Alps, forty-eight are Swiss and almost all of the remaining thirty-four are within 20 kilometers (12 miles) of the Swiss border . . . which is a statistical way of saying that we have a lot of rösti ground to cover here.

The major subranges of the Swiss Alps are the Pennine (Zermatt!), the Bernina (St. Moritz!), and yes, the Bernese Alps.

One notices the umlauts and feels a more back-straightening atmosphere in the Bernese mountains, at least as compared to Italy and most of the Savoie region of France. In Bern, you hear German almost exclusively compared to French (which you hear in the cantons of Vaud and Valais) or Italian (which is spoken in Ticino). The nickname for this cultural boundary is *Röstigraben*—or "rösti ditch." Rösti is so prevalent in every aspect of Swiss German cooking, it's said that the real boundary between the German-speaking and French-speaking Swiss is determined by how prevalent rösti is on local menus. This somewhat imaginary yet somewhat real ditch runs from the Jura mountains in the northwest to Zermatt in the south.

TRAVEL HACK

The only way to reach Kleine Scheidegg is via the Wengernalp railway. If you're staying at any of the hotels on the mountain, you can call ahead with your arrival information and a porter will meet you at the railway. There are two possible routes: from Lauterbrunnen via Wengen or from Grinderwald-Grund. I traveled via Lauterbrunnen, where you can leave your car in a parking lot at the railway station. Take note of the Wengernalp Railway timetable when planning your journey; the trains run every half hour.

While I was visiting, I heard travelers compare the Jungfrau to Disney World—twice!—and it made me wonder if they had ever truly been on the Mad Tea Party teacups ride. While it is perhaps true that arrival at the Kleine Scheidegg train station—a slightly desolate stop where porters help you with your luggage *and* a Clint Eastwood movie was shot—feels a bit like Frontierland, this is where any sort of Disneyesque comparison ends. This area of Bern is many things, but it's *not* easily accessible, and that's what makes it wonderful. If you're looking for a Swiss Alpine adventure that's out of your comfort zone, this is a perfect place to start.

We spent the night at the Hotel de Bellevue des Alpes, a splendidly pre-served, one-of-a-kind nineteenth-century grand hotel in the mountains. It is difficult to reach, otherworldly, glamorous, and authentically rooted in the era of the great mountaineers; the air in this region feels thick with history. Here you can have fondue on the terrace (as we did) while appreciating the north face of the Eiger, a mountain so fierce and abundant with unsuccessful climbs that it's known as the "graveyard of the Alps." When a snowstorm blew in the next day, we played board games and ate local venison charcuterie for lunch followed by *Schwarzwälder Kirschtorte* (Black Forest cake) in the afternoon. The snow drifts began piling up, and before nightfall the first-floor windows were completely covered. The place is eerily romantic; you can feel the ghosts of Alpinists past while walking the hotel's toile-lined walls. Which makes sense, as this is the epicenter of what was known as the Golden Age of Alpinism. From 1854 to 1865, most of the four-thousanders were first conquered by international (and Swiss) mountaineers. It was here, at the Wetterhorn in nearby Grindelwald, where the first *recorded* ascent took place.

Many tourists take the cog train to Kleine Scheidegg and then board the Jungfraubahn Railway to the Aletsch Glacier, a human-made tourist destination (there is a snow park and a Lindt chocolate shop) called "The Top of Europe." This is indeed the highest railway in Europe, and at the terminus is a simple restaurant that serves sausages and french fries, as well as little confections called *Eigerspitzlis*, a sort of Toblerone clone. (However, I prefer the *Jungfrauspitzlis*, little chocolates with vanilla tips and a cherry filling that are made at the Bäckerei Konditorei Vincenz down in Wengen.) We didn't visit the glacier, however; instead, we skied the Jungfrau region from Mürren to Wengen to the town of Grindelwald, seeking interesting people cooking tasty fare in what can be impenetrable locations.

At the Ringgenberg bakery in Grindelwald, I tasted a unique Alpine sourdough bread (Swiss mountain salt plus rye from Bern plus Alpine spring water) that I'm dreaming of for next summer's hiking trip. And after a rough traverse on skis, at the beautiful Victorian-style Hotel Jungfrau Wengernalp I had an incredible meal: a comforting schnitzel with perfect rösti, and apple strudel. Down the mountain, but still in the Bernese Oberland, are the villages of Unterseen, Wilderswil, and Habkern, all of which are Alpine towns with simple Swiss restaurants serving traditional foods such as three-year-aged *Hobelkäse* (mountain cheese), local sausages, lake trout, and wild mountain mushrooms. A favorite recipe I brought back is *Nussgipfel* (page 231), a hazelnut

AUTOVERLAD!

On my way from Klosters to the tiny town of Lavin (to check out Hotel Piz Linard), my GPS showed a gray diagonal line that, suspiciously, cut straight through the Swiss Silvretta Alps. About 10 minutes into the drive, I saw a sign for *Autoverlad* (car train). Like a car ferry across water, this kind of train transports cars through mountains where the passes are too arduous or snowed in to drive over. You simply drive up and *onto* the train carriage, turn off the engine, and let the train barrel under some of the highest peaks in the world. Straight *through* the eerily empty, pitch-black mountain. Things get interesting when another car train is coming from the other direction on the adjacent tracks. It's like that scene in *Willy Wonka & the Chocolate Factory,* when they are riding on the boat through the tunnel of terror: it's very fast and strangely psychedelic. Taking the Autoverlad may add extra time to your trip, but it's usually not much, as this is Switzerland, and these things run on time. Within this book, there is mention of two self-loading Autoverlad, both in Switzerland: the Vereina-Klosters and the Realp-Oberwald through the Furka Pass Tunnel.

PARK YOUR TOBOGGAN OUTSIDE CHEZ VRONY, ZERMATT.

croissant-like pastry that photographer Christina Holmes and I found in the pretty little town of Habkern, which has one small ski lift for four idyllic pistes.

Farther down, wedged between two lakes (Brienzersee and Thunersee), the city of Interlaken is not exactly Alpine, but it is an opening to the Bernese Oberland from the Valais region in the south. When I stopped at a roadside hotel/restaurant called Salzano, I found cooks outside in subzero temperatures smoking trout, which they then prepared with fresh beet tagliatelle (see page 235). For dessert, I had little pine-smoked marshmallows served on pine twigs. It brought to mind the rule of the Alpine Club: When in doubt, stop for lunch.

When I think of the Swiss Alps, yes, I think of rösti, but also of raclette, watches, trains, and engineering—and the famous ski resort of Zermatt has all of that and more. Similar to Kleine Scheidegg, Zermatt is a car-free zone, and as one of the most-touristy Alpine towns in the world, the resort has made transportation easy with its Glacier Express (see page 204) and *elektromobiles* that shuttle locals and tourists around. You simply leave your car in Täsch, a village 5 kilometers (3 miles) away. Zermatt is situated at 1,620 meters (5,300 feet) and its mountains are at least another 1,200 meters (3,900 feet) higher, an altitude that gives Zermatt one of the longest ski seasons in Europe (that I know of). To visit Zermatt, regardless of season, is to have a skiable/hikeable buffet of options (both on and off piste), including access to the town of Cervinia, Italy, which is a whole *other* Italian buffet right across the Swiss-Italian border. And no, you do not need to bring your passport. From Zermatt, the views of that great pyramid of the Alps, the Matterhorn, still thrill me with every glimpse.

Zermatt is in the canton of Valais, an area that's synonymous with Swiss wine. I've been down the industrial motorway from Täsch to Sierre more times than I remember, but I always feel uplifted visiting with winemakers in the summertime, when the vineyards are lush with fruit and the adjacent Crans-Montana ski resort is vacant except for workers preparing the lifts for the next season. Branching out from the Valais's main vein are hidden Alpine towns just waiting to be explored, as well as hundreds of little rifugios and shelters for those who choose to explore the Alps on foot.

In the town of Grimentz, I stayed at the petite Hotel Alpina and walked the small cobblestone paths of the Val d'Anniviers. In this valley, the Walser-style homes uniformly burst with red geraniums in summer, while the Alps are packed with dairy cows. Within a 15-minute drive from Zermatt, you can visit the Moiry Dam, which holds Lac Moiry, a jade-blue lake that looks to be (but isn't) the watershed of the French Alps, with the Dents du Midi mountains right there in the distance. Almost atop the dam is a little restaurant called Clems and Fabs that serves local wines, meats, and cheeses and has a fun little Prosecco and Swiss wine list (for a restaurant on top of a dam).

From Grimentz, I traveled to Verbier and then back through the Vaud and the French-speaking town of Rougemont. The pretty hamlets of the Vaud region give way to the very pretty chalets of Gstaad. I wasn't expecting to

LAC MOIRY

like Gstaad as much as I did. What I had heard of the town's reputation didn't include culinary heights, and for the purpose of writing a cookbook of substantive and authentic recipes, I didn't anticipate having such good eats. Although I toured and hiked the local area (including the Eggli and Wispile ski areas), it's clear that all the action, eating and otherwise, happens in the town and valley. I made salsify soup (see page 215) and *Zürcher Geschnetzeltes* (page 212) with chefs from two of Gstaad's best hotels, and I ate fresh chamois (a type of mountain goat/antelope) from local hunters. The village's best-known restaurant, Chesery (see page 220), translates as "the dairy." And it's no wonder; with nearly a hundred dairy farms in the area, it is said that there are more cows than people in Gstaad (the rumor I heard is 7,000 cows to 5,000 human souls).

Just outside of Gstaad, there are two locations that I absolutely love. The first is Lauenen, where I ate hearty Herdsman Macaroni (page 228) at the low-key Hotel Alpenland, and the second is the area of Les Diablerets (from the French, meaning "the Devils") in the canton of Vaud. This area and its famous glacier were thought to be cursed. It is common mythology that terrible things happen in the mountains—that beasts, goblins, and dark secrets are hiding beneath or among the rocks. (In German, *Eiger* translates to "the ogre.") But accidents do happen here, both human and geological. In the 1700s, part of a rockface from Les Diablerets fell onto the town below, burying the inhabitants. This and other lore give an appealing but melancholy sense that stays with you while visiting. It's a wild outpost from which to hike and ski and it is a really interesting alternative to the resorts of Gstaad and Verbier, which are less than an hour's drive away. Food-wise, your mind will not be blown, but I was enamored with a little lo-fi shack called Les Cosmos that sold hamburgers, dried beef, and beer and reminded me of a Quebecois *casse-croûte* (snack bar).

The Appenzell is a region with a rich cultural history. (See "Bischofberger and Alpine Art," page 246). In addition to the famous Appenzeller cheese, there is depth in these regional menus as well. It was there in a quaint *gasthaus* (small inn) on a lake that I had my first *Forelle Blau* (page 256) while hiking the Rotstein Pass.

Nestled beside the Appenzell is the Toggenburg region, where I spent time touring butcher shops with sausagemaker Eli Cairo of Olympia Provisions and had perhaps my best bratwurst (not Alpine) at a very cozy hotel and restaurant called Stump's Alpenrose in Wildhaus (very Alpine).

Beside Uri and below the Appenzell is the large canton of Graubünden. It is home to *Pizokel* (see page 259), a dish I adore in the resort town of Klosters. It's also where a lovely pink hotel called Piz Linard is situated (and where I encourage you to stay), and where you'll find the less-than-lovely town of Davos. My Swiss tour ends in the Graubünden's Engadin Valley, and specifically in the town of St. Moritz, where the authentic is not so obvious, but there is much to experience if you know where to look.

ROOM KEYS AT
HOTEL PIZ LINARD

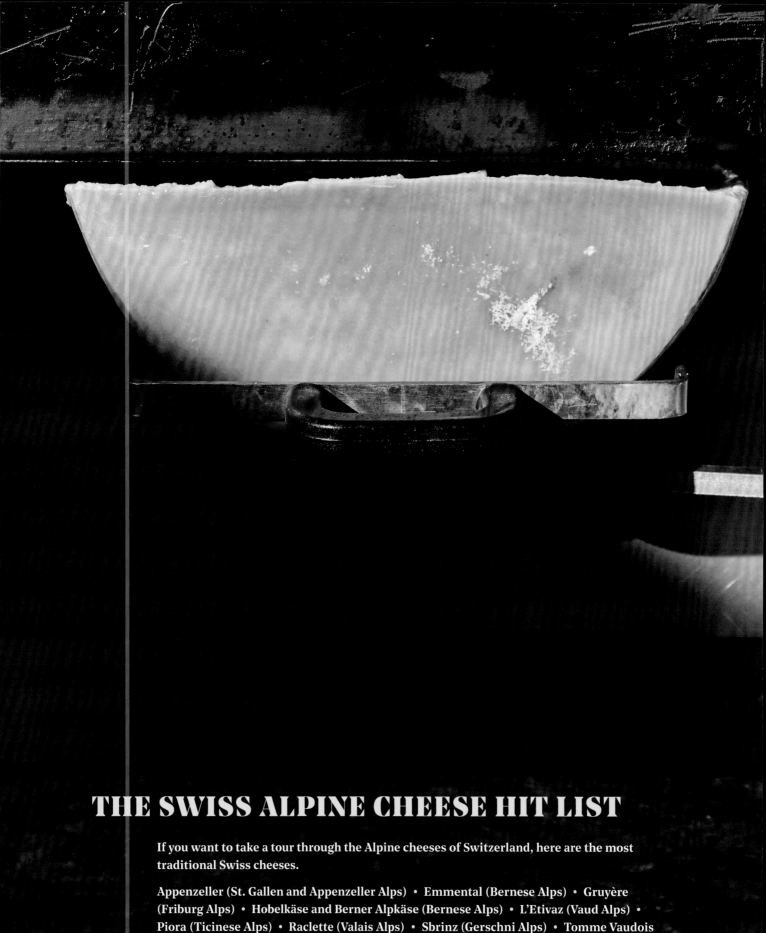

THE SWISS ALPINE CHEESE HIT LIST

If you want to take a tour through the Alpine cheeses of Switzerland, here are the most traditional Swiss cheeses.

Appenzeller (St. Gallen and Appenzeller Alps) • Emmental (Bernese Alps) • Gruyère (Friburg Alps) • Hobelkäse and Berner Alpkäse (Bernese Alps) • L'Etivaz (Vaud Alps) • Piora (Ticinese Alps) • Raclette (Valais Alps) • Sbrinz (Gerschni Alps) • Tomme Vaudois (Vaud Alps) • Uri Alpine Cheese (Gnov Alp) • Vacherin (Fribourg Alps)

One of the first chefs I ever met in the Alps, Hans Nussbaumer, worked at the Kulm Hotel for fifty years and was trained in the grand hotel style of Escoffier and French technical cooking. This was the old way of St. Moritz and many of the other resort towns that had tourism as a main industry. Hans always had a pencil sticking up from the lip of his toque, and although it is one old-school detail of kitchens past that I miss, I think St. Moritz and the Engadin have been successful in keeping old traditions while welcoming new.

Some of my new St. Moritz favorites include the stag carpaccio at Veltliner Keller, a December-only tradition, and *pizzoccheri*, a buckwheat noodle dish from the Italian Valtellina. The Bullshot cocktail from the Cresta Club is a St. Moritz classic, the recipe for which (see page 245) I managed to cajole from a member in a moment of weakness. And the Engadin walnut cake from Bakery Hanselmann in the center of the village is the Swiss equivalent to an Italian panettone. (Just across the border in Italy, I also love the St. Moritz outpost of Da Vittorio and have included their paccheri [see page 248]). The photos are over-the-top *Italiano* and the pasta is so easy and so good. And Italy is right there! About 2 hours away, just past Pontresina and over the Bernina Pass.

It is there where the canton of Graubünden, and our primer to Switzerland ends, but before snow-diving into the dishes, let's end where we began: on the train.

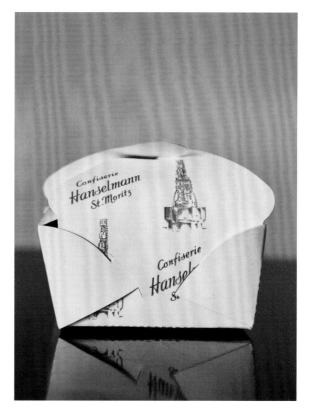

THE ALPINE EXPRESS

Switzerland gains major points on the Alpine leaderboard for its wonderfully efficient and often-breathtaking rail options. And because you cannot drive laterally *across* the Swiss Alps, the only way to travel directly *through* the Alps is by train. An important signifier of Alpine tourism, the construction of mountain train lines coincided with the building of huts, restaurants, and hotels in the mid-nineteenth century (and the Swiss Alpine Club, too, in 1863). The first line, the Rigi, had its inaugural ascent from Vitznau to Rigi Staffelhöhe, in May 1871. Mt. Pilatus Rail (the steepest cogwheel train in the world, from Alpnach to Mt. Pilatus) followed in 1889. From there, it was the Gornergrat in 1898 and the Jungfraubahn in 1912. And it continues! (See "Autoverlad!" page 197).

Although this list is by no means exhaustive, here are some of my favorite Alpine railway routes.

The Glacier Express: From St. Moritz to Zermatt in 8½ hours, apparently the Glacier Express has been dubbed the "world's slowest train," but does that really matter when there is a Champagne trolley and a dining car with great views?

The Gornergratbahn: From Zermatt to the top of the Gornergrat. In the summer you can see ibex on the Alps. If you're staying the night at Riffelalp above Zermatt, this is the train you will take.

The Gotthard Panorama Express: This route, mostly by train but also partly by boat, takes you from Lugano to Lucerne (or vice versa) and travels through Ticino and Bern, including passage through the Gotthard Tunnel. Note: This train runs in the summer season only.

The Bernina Express: A railway that connects Chur, Davos, St. Moritz, Tirano, and Lugano, it crosses the Bernina Pass, a mountain passage much more relaxing to navigate from a train seat than from behind a steering wheel, I assure you.

The Mont-Blanc Express/The St. Bernard Express: This small excursion train has two routes—Martigny to Châtelard to Chamonix (France) and Martigny to Orsières to Grand St. Bernard. The second route ends just before the St. Bernard Tunnel and is only available in summer.

The Montenvers Railway: A short 5.1-kilometer (3.2-mile) cogwheel taking you from Chamonix to the Montveners site that overlooks the Mer de Glace glacier.

The Brienz Rothorn: The oldest steam cogwheel railway in Switzerland chugs from the tiny town of Brienz up to the Rothorn, where you'll find the Alpine Lodge Restaurant and a hundred beds to stay the night (spring and summer only).

The Apres-Ski Train: This train travels from Andermatt (Uri) over the Oberalp Pass to Disentis (Graubünden) and is essentially a rolling party with a fully stocked bar. There are six disembarkation points, and if you have an Andermatt ski pass, it's free (not the booze, just the ticket). They serve *Nussgipfel* (see page 231) on this train, alongside charcuterie and cheese boards.

The Wengernalp Railway: Links the towns of Lauterbrunnen, Wengen, and Grindelwald with Kleine Scheidegg. The world's longest cogwheel railway, it's responsible for getting people and foodstuffs up to the villages on the mountain.

Fondue

FONDUE NEUCHÂTEL

 EASY

SERVES 4

YOU WILL NEED

Fondue set with burner (I favor a Le Creuset enameled cast-iron set) and fuel (see manufacturer's instructions)

1 garlic clove

1½ cups (360 ml) dry white wine, such as Chablis or dry Riesling

1 teaspoon freshly squeezed lemon juice

1 tablespoon cornstarch

3 tablespoons kirsch

2 cups (230 g) grated Emmental cheese

2 cups (230 g) grated Gruyère cheese

Freshly ground white pepper

Freshly grated nutmeg

Sweet paprika

Day-old French bread or country loaf, cut into 1-inch cubes, or apple slices for serving

Cornichon pickles for serving

Pickled onions for serving

I'm not sure when a Swiss person first dipped into flavorsome, melted cheese, but wedding registries haven't been the same since. Relatively speaking, fondue is still fairly new in North America. As the story goes, fondue was first marketed to Americans during the 1964 World's Fair in New York via the Swiss Pavilion's Alpine restaurant. From there, North Americans embraced the *caquelon* (fondue pot), especially in the 1970s when sharing food (and your partner) became more popular.

But let's get to the cheese. Fondue can be as highbrow (see variation) or as casual (see Wine Cave Fonduta, page 52) as you want. This is our baseline fondue; if someone says *fondue*, assume *this* is what they're talking about. Neuchâtel is the capital of the canton of Neuchâtel. The cheese in a Neuchâtel is a mix of Gruyère and Emmental.

In Switzerland, boutique cheeses are often used as a stamp of quality. For example, at Chesery restaurant in Gstaad, the cheese fondue is made from L'Etivaz and Vacherin Fribourgeois. L'Etivaz is made by a small cheese co-op in a town of 150 people; it's essentially a Gruyère made as it was 100 years ago: a creamier, less sharp version of its newer self. Vacherin Fribourgeois is produced by a very small number of cheese artisans and, consequently, is very difficult to find. There is fun to be had tasting fondues around Switzerland, because you're likely to come across cheeses from local dairies that are rare and fresh from the *alpage* (high mountain pasture), reflecting local flavors.

In France, you're more likely to come across either Fondue Savoyarde (half Beaufort or Comté, half Emmental) or Fondue Jurassienne (100 percent Comté). In the French chapter, I included a "take-away" fondue housed in a brioche (see page 308). Apologies to my *terre d'adoption* (adopted land), but I'm not including Montreal-favorite Fondue Chinoise here (nor a Bourguignonne); neither dish is Alpine, and I've never loved the idea of dipping meat into an open vat of hot oil on my dining-room tablecloth.

Notes: Fondue sets are more versatile than you think—they are the perfect vessel, in fact, for any kind of low-and-slow melting or tempered sauce making. I like to whip up a béarnaise sauce in mine, while pan-frying sirloin steaks for two. Bring the pot to the table and dip your steak directly in the warm sauce.

Just because you are gluten-sensitive doesn't mean you should miss out. Replace the bread with slices of apple (I sometimes prefer this to bread).

I like to begin cooking the fondue on the stove top until a bit of the liquid has evaporated and then move to the set above the fuel burner.

continued

Rub the inside of the fondue pot with the garlic. With the caquelon over stove-top medium heat, warm the wine with the lemon juice.

In a small bowl, use a fork to whisk the cornstarch and kirsch until smooth.

Gradually add both cheeses to the pot, stirring continuously in a figure-eight motion. When the mixture begins to bubble, stir in the kirsch-cornstarch paste. Continue to cook for another 3 to 5 minutes, and season with a little white pepper, nutmeg, and paprika.

Should your melted cheese begin to separate, increase the heat and whisk or stir the mixture quickly to bring it together again.

Carefully light the flame on your fondue set, following the manufacturer's instructions. Turn off the stove-top heat and carefully transfer the pot to your fondue set.

Serve the fondue with bread cubes or sliced apples, cornichon pickles, and pickled onions.

VARIATION

To make a Champagne Fondue in the style of the Gstaad Palace, replace the wine with the same amount of Champagne and omit the lemon juice. Feel free to grate a truffle onto the fondue just before serving. It might seem baller to pour most of a bottle of Krug into your fondue caquelon; let me suggest these two sparkling wines instead: Belluard's Perles du Mont Blanc (Savoie) and Christoph Hoch's Kalkspitz (Austria). I like them for three reasons. The wines are both biodynamic and made in the style of Champenois vintners. They add a nice aromatic element to the cheese, but still have enough minerality and structure to prop the cheese up (unlike Krug, which has too much sugar to do so). They are in our Alpine circle (Hoch is Upper Austria, but relatively close). I don't think it's a coincidence that fondue's best accomplices are made from grapes grown at the altitude where neighboring cows like to graze.

HOT TIPS FOR FONDUE

There is perhaps no dish that comes with more rules than fondue. And that is very, very Swiss.

The Swiss say that combining hot cheese with a cold beverage causes the cheese to coagulate in your stomach, leaving you with severe pain and indigestion; for this reason, room-temperature kirsch or white wine or tea is advised. To this I say, let common sense prevail. If you eat 3 pounds (1.4kg) of cheese, I don't think it's the cold wine that's causing your stomachache. Accordingly, spend a little more for good-quality cheese and maybe eat a little less of it?

- Never double-dip.

- Do reach your fork all the way to the bottom of the pot. The cheese in the central area directly above the burner will have crisped and toasted into delicious morsels of caramelized goodness—it's known as *la religieuse* (the nun), perhaps because of its otherworldly flavor. You'll want to fight others for it.

- To accompany the cheese, try a cellared Hock (German white table wine) or perhaps that gifted bottle of Etter Kirsch you never knew how to use. Or whatever wine you used for the fondue. Stemware should be as tacky or esoteric as your fondue pot.

- For dessert, I like the sound of pears poached in Gewürztraminer, and a maybe a shard or two of dark chocolate.

Hot Chocolate with Alpine Herbs

SERVES 2

YOU WILL NEED

Large loose-leaf tea sachet or tea ball infuser

1¼ cups (300ml) milk

⅓ cup (80ml) heavy cream, plus ½ cup (120ml) (optional)

⅓ cup (50g) grated or chopped dark chocolate (70% cocoa)

1 teaspoon dried lemon verbena

1 teaspoon dried chamomile flower

1 teaspoon chopped fresh mint

1 tablespoon sugar (optional)

The mountains are for early risers. Fresh snow to be skied, cows to be milked, butter to churn, the summer sun rising from behind the hilltops . . . all of this happens before 8 a.m. And so, strong coffee is a must (as is schnapps, but later). I realize not everyone loves coffee, so I've included this no-fail hot chocolate recipe with an Alpine twist. The addition of easy-to-find Alpine herbs elevates the chocolate to adult-level enjoyment, though that shouldn't stop children from also having a cup at breakfast or any other time of day.

Note: Now's the time to pull out your serving set. A nice copper pot with side spout wouldn't hurt for pouring the infused chocolate milk.

In a small heavy saucepan over medium heat, warm the milk and ⅓ cup (80ml) cream until steaming, then stir in the chocolate. Stir constantly while simmering until the chocolate has fully melted, 2 to 3 minutes. Do not let the milk boil.

Fill a sachet or tea ball with the verbena, chamomile, and fresh mint and drop it into the hot chocolate. Let this sit for 4 minutes to infuse fully.

In the meantime, if you are planning on serving whipped cream, whip the remaining ½ cup (120ml) cream and sugar to make Chantilly cream.

Have a little taste of the hot chocolate to determine if you wish to infuse any longer. If it tastes Alpine enough, transfer into a copper hot chocolate pot, and serve with or without whipped cream.

Veal Strips in Cream Sauce, Zürich-Style

ZÜRCHER GESCHNETZELTES

EASY

SERVES 4 TO 6

1 tablespoon grapeseed oil

1½ pounds (680g) veal tenderloin, cut into 1- to 1½-inch (2.5 to 4cm) strips

Fine sea salt and freshly ground black pepper

¼ cup (60g) unsalted butter, cubed

1 pound (450g) white mushrooms, thinly sliced

⅓ cup (50g) minced shallots

Juice of ½ lemon

¾ cup plus 2 tablespoons (200ml) white wine

½ cup (120ml) veal demi-glace

1¼ cups (300ml) heavy cream

2 tablespoons minced fresh flat-leaf parsley

1 tablespoon minced fresh chives

The best veal I've had was at Kronenhalle, Zürich's famous fine-dining restaurant. I also think Zum Weissen Kreuz, also in Zürich, does an incredible (and much less expensive) version. (Apologies to Zürich, though, the image pictured here is from the Bellevue Hotel in Gstaad, 160 kilometers [100 or so miles] away.) This is perhaps my favorite Alpine dish. High-quality veal is cut into thin strips, gently sautéed in butter with mushrooms and white wine, and served simply over rösti (see page 253; no surprise, we're in Switzerland). You could also accompany this with spaetzle or rice or mashed potatoes. It feels hearty and hut-worthy, but still sophisticated (maybe because of the demi-glace?) and somewhat lighter than a lot of mountain cuisine. It's appropriate no matter the season or occasion; consider it the Alpine version of a *blanquette de veau* (French veal stew).

Note: Veal demi-glace can be purchased at any good butcher, or you can substitute Venison Glaze (page 224).

Preheat the oven to 285°F (140°C), or its lowest setting.

Warm a large sauté pan over high heat, then add the grapeseed oil. When the oil is shimmering, add the veal strips and sauté briefly, until they just start to brown; season with salt and pepper. Transfer the meat strips to a plate and keep warm in the oven.

Turn the stove-top heat to medium and then add the butter to the pan. When the butter starts to foam, add the mushrooms and sauté until the liquid from the mushrooms has evaporated, 5 to 7 minutes, but the mushrooms haven't colored.

Stir the shallots into the mushrooms and sauté until translucent, about 3 minutes. Season with salt, pepper, and the lemon juice. Pour in the wine, turn the heat to medium-high, and cook until the liquid has almost completely evaporated.

Turn the heat to medium, stir in the demi-glace and 1 cup (240ml) of the cream, and cook until the sauce reduces enough to coat the back of a spoon. Return the warm veal strips to the pan, and return to a simmer.

With a small whisk, whip the remaining ¼ cup (60ml) cream to soft peaks. Gently stir the whipped cream, parsley, and chives into the stew.

Serve immediately.

Salsify Soup

SCHWARZWURZELSUPPE

■■■ EASY
SERVES 4

YOU WILL NEED
High-speed blender or
food processor

2 medium beets, peeled
and cubed

1½ cups (360ml) beet juice

Fine sea salt and freshly ground
white pepper

1¼ pounds (570g) salsify roots

1½ lemons

¼ cup (55g) unsalted butter

2 small yellow onions, finely diced

½ teaspoon sugar

1 bay leaf

2 sprigs thyme

¾ cup plus 2 tablespoons (200ml)
dry white wine

1 cup (240ml) low-sodium
vegetable broth

½ cup (120ml) freshly squeezed
orange juice

1 cup (240ml) heavy cream

Scant 1 cup (200g) sour cream

Choosing a root vegetable soup as the dish to represent the luxury hotel Gstaad Palace was an exercise in restraint, as well as therapy, as it revealed not only my middle-class roots (bad pun) but also my contrarian nature.

The hotel recently celebrated its 100-year anniversary, and the good people there allowed me to review old menus, on which I flagged dishes such as *Potage Léopold* (a vegetable consommé that was one of Austrian King Leopold's favorites) and *Sorbet Mandarin*. My original idea was to re-create a dish based on the palace's infamous parties from yesteryear. The problem is that all of these dishes are straight out of Escoffier's hotelier manual (like all the older luxury hotel menus) and not particular to Gstaad or the Alps in any way. And because of the five-star-ishness of it all, the ingredients were quite luxe and inaccessible to home cooks. And so, the hotel's chef, Franz Faeh, and I went deeper . . . into the ground that is! And we pulled out a thick, dark, muddy root of salsify.

Salsify is perhaps the most European of root vegetables. Though it's about as pretty as an unwashed beet, it's white on the inside, and when cooked, becomes completely creamy. (It's also known as the oyster plant, because some people think it tastes like a delicate oyster when cooked.) Salsify is especially popular in France, Italy, and, yes, Switzerland. Its flavor is absolutely superior in a soup.

Note: Salsify can be hard to find in North America; try a specialty greengrocer in the winter months or inquire at your local farmers' market. When peeling salsify, you'll notice that its white interior has a tendency to discolor very quickly, so peel with a sharp knife and soak in a bowl of ice water with the juice of a lemon to preserve the root's natural hue.

In a small saucepan, combine the beets and beet juice and simmer, covered, until tender, about 45 minutes. Transfer to a blender and purée until smooth. Season with salt and white pepper, then set aside.

Peel the salsify and cut into 1-inch rounds. Place immediately in a bowl of ice water with the juice of 1 lemon.

In a Dutch oven over medium heat, combine the butter, onions, and salsify and sauté, stirring regularly, until the onions become translucent, about 5 minutes. Sprinkle with the sugar and ½ teaspoon salt and stir. Add the bay leaf and thyme, then pour the wine into the pot and stir well.

Increase the heat to high, bring to a boil, and reduce the wine by a third, 3 to 4 minutes. Then pour in the vegetable broth, orange juice, and heavy cream. Return to a boil, then lower the heat, cover, and simmer for 30 minutes or so, until the salsify is absolutely tender. Discard the bay leaf and thyme.

In a high-speed blender or food processor, purée the soup until completely smooth. Adjust the seasoning with salt, white pepper, and lemon juice, as needed.

Spoon a generous amount of puréed beet into four bowls and dot with the sour cream. Bring a pitcher of the hot soup to the table and pour into each bowl. Stir and enjoy.

Switzerland

Dîner

Tortue claire des Indes en tasse
Bâtonnets au Sbrinz

Suprême de sole Impératrice
Cœur de filet de bœuf Rossini
Pommes croquettes
Haricots fins au beurre
Salade

Parfait glacé à la vieille Chartreuse
Mignardises

13 février 1960

Dîner de Gala

avec

BENNY GOODMAN
and his Big Band

GSTAAD PALACE MENUS FROM OVER THE YEARS

Le Menu

Tassette de nids d'hirondelles

*

Coquille St. Jacques
au champagne flanquée
d'un petit vol-au-vent
Joinville

*

Aile de Reine de France
Duc de Rohan
Pommes noisettes
Quartiers printanière

---

llandaise

t foie
ny
s sucrés

Sherry
e No81

WINTER PALACE
staad

Menu

MENU du 25 Décembre

807
Lunch:

Cock-tail de fruits au Sherry
Gousse d'or au fumet de céleri
Vacherins
Cœur de filet de Bœuf Nasalbeth
Pommes pont-neuf
Artichauts de Nice à la Clamart
Cœurs de laitues Vinaigrette
Surprise étoile du berger

Dîner

Crème à la Reine
Fricandeau de veau glacé à la Vichy
Pommes croquettes
Endives Ardennaise
Salade
Ananas Royal
Biscuits

Pers.

Potage
Ragout de Bœuf
aux carottes
p. fines herbes
salade

Consomé aux étoiles
Roti de veau aux lég.
Cornettes au beurre
salade
Biscuit glacé

Gerne bestätige ich, dass Maggi's Produkte bei zweckmässiger Verwendung die besten Hilfsmittel der führenden Küche sind; unübertroffen in Feinheit, Geschmack nnd Zuverlässigkeit.
November 1944
G. Schächtelin, Chef de cuisine,
Hotel Verenahof, Baden.

14

MENU du 26. Décembre
238
Lunch:

Filet de perc...
fr. Pom...
Pointe de culotte de...
chev-vei
pommes parse...
fenouils fines he...
Salade
Les assortiments

255 Dîner

Potage Léopo...
Foie de Veau à la elerm...
pommes fines her...
Chou-fleurs à la chit...
Salade
Bordure Nesselrod...

Pers.

Potage
Bisch aux carottes
p. purée
salade

Potage
Thon au...
p. en ro...
salade

Maggi's Produkte: Real Turtle und Oxtail clair flüssig, sowie Mag...
und Sulze verwende ich seit Jahren. Diese vorzüglichen Produkte...
in allen wechselreichen Fällen eines Küchenbetriebes stets die beste...
erwiesen.
Oktober 1945
H. Güthlin, Chef d...
Restaurant Schützenh...

DINER DE GALA

Le caviar Malossol sur glace
Toast Melba et beurre
***
La tortue Lady Curzon
Paillettes dorées
***
Le filet de charolais Wellington
Le fond d'artichaut Riviera
Les pommes noisettes
La salade de chicorée rouge
***
Le soufflé glacé Paquita
Les friandises
***

Mardi, le 17 janvier 1956
Supplément clients de l'hôtel Frs. 12.
Passants Frs. 25.

Fr. 50.—
Fr. 50.—   Fr. 25.—
Fr. 50.—
7   Fr. 50.—
945 Fr. 50.—
1945 Fr. 100.—
Fr. 50.—

Suprêmes de soles Winter Palace

Cœur de filet de bœuf Impériale
Croquettes parmentier
Haricots verts au beurre
Salade

Bombe glacée Télévision
Friandises

Mercredi, 29 décembre 1954

GRAND HOTELS AND BASEMENT WORKSHOPS

It's not uncommon for grand Alpine hotels to have workshops where the hotel furniture is custom-made and repaired. And, as we're talking about the Alps here, these hotels are often located in areas too difficult to reach with large transport trucks and only accessible via mountain passes that could be closed for days (and sometimes weeks!) due to weather. So, these workshops are necessary even today.

And so, when the Gstaad Palace staff took me on a tour through the nooks and crannies of the hotel, I was intrigued by the basement workshop, where two full-time workers were repairing chairs that naughty children broke and, likewise, broken bed boards of even naughtier adults. These inner workings are the marrow of the Alpine hotel's bones of the past: best to dig in and savor every little bit.

Chamois Pie

GÄMSE KUCHEN

■■■ DIFFICULT

SERVES 4

4 savoy cabbage leaves (5 to 6 inches [12 to 15cm] in diameter)

Four 3- to 4-ounce (80 to 100g) chamois medallions or venison loin medallions

Fine sea salt and freshly ground black pepper

2 tablespoons grapeseed oil

¼ cup (55g) unsalted butter, plus 2 tablespoons melted butter

1 cup (70 g) trimmed, very finely diced fresh chanterelles

1 tablespoon minced shallot

1 tablespoon minced fresh rosemary, flat-leaf parsley, or thyme

1 egg, beaten; plus 1 egg yolk

½ slice white bread, crusts removed, shredded into small pieces

1 pound (450g) butternut squash, peeled and cut into 2 by ¼-inch (5cm by 6mm) sticks

1 teaspoon sugar

Sour-Cream Pastry Dough (page 223), rolled out and refrigerated

2 tablespoons heavy cream

¼ cup (60ml) white wine vinegar

3 tablespoons olive oil

2 tablespoons fresh rosemary leaves

1 cup (240ml) Venison Glaze (page 224)

12 whole candied chestnuts (*marrons glacés*)

1 black truffle (optional)

In Lord Byron's poem *Manfred,* the protagonist (Manfred) longs for a dead lover while living in the Bernese Alps. He attempts to throw himself off the Jungfrau in suicidal desperation . . . when along comes a chamois hunter. In a twist of fate, the hunter convinces Manfred to join him for a meal.

A type of mountain goat/antelope native to the Alps, the chamois is an almost mythical animal existing atop the world's highest crags and crevices. Living at high altitude in Alpine meadows in the summer, chamois then migrate down Furka Pass to the lower-altitude forests in the winter.

Not easy to find, thriving in solitude, and completely fearless, they are the embodiment of the astrological Capricorn (hence the restaurant name Il Capricorno, see page 71).

Chamois also makes for very popular game meat. During hunting season, it appears on menus throughout the region, sparingly though; as it's always wild, never farmed. I will never forget the braised chamois at the Berggasthaus Rotsteinpass at 2,125 meters (6,970 feet) near the Säntis mountain in Appenzeller.

A more sophisticated version of the braised dish is the chamois pie from Chesery restaurant. Located next door to a Louis Vuitton store (this is Gstaad, after all), in the site of an old cheese dairy, Chesery has been helmed since 1990 by chef Robert Speth. He prepared this dish with his typical French technique (it's somewhat similar to a *pithivier*) combined with a hint of Alpine elegance. Essentially a venison pie with a sour-cream crust, this recipe is one of the more difficult in the book, but the result is a spectacularly special dinner at home.

Notes: Chamois is likely impossible to source outside of continental Europe and its mountain zones, but you can make a delicious version of this pie with venison instead. Trust me, this is a delicious alternative.

The bones and aromatics for the venison glaze have to marinate for 2 days, and you'll want to make the sour-cream dough ahead of time.

*Candied chestnuts (*marrons glacés*) can be purchased online or in any classic French or Italian pâtisserie or grocer that carries specialty European products.*

Bring a pot of salted water to a boil, and fill a large bowl with water and ice cubes.

Place the cabbage leaves in the boiling water and blanch for 30 seconds. Remove the leaves and plunge into the ice water to stop the cooking. Drain, pat dry, and set aside in the refrigerator.

Season the chamois medallions with salt and pepper.

In a frying pan over medium-high heat, warm the grapeseed oil until it shimmers. Add the meat and sear until nicely browned, about 2 minutes on each side. Transfer the meat to a rack and let cool.

continued

CHEF ROBERT SPETH

In the same pan over medium heat, melt the ¼ cup (55g) butter. When the butter is foaming, add the chanterelles, shallot, and rosemary and sauté until the mushroom liquid is fully evaporated and the mixture looks fairly dry, about 7 minutes. Transfer to a shallow bowl and let cool a little. Stir in the beaten egg and white bread, mixing well and seasoning to taste.

Preheat the oven to 425°F (220°C). Line a baking sheet with parchment paper. Line a plate with paper towels.

Toss the squash sticks with the melted butter and sugar, then lay them on the baking sheet and set aside.

Spread the blanched cabbage leaves on a kitchen towel or clean counter. Lay 1 tablespoon of the mushroom mixture in the middle of each leaf. Place the seared meat on top of the mushroom mixture, flattening it a little. Lay another 1 tablespoon of the mushroom mixture onto each piece of meat. Carefully roll up the cabbage leaf to enclose the meat and make a round parcel.

From the pastry dough, cut out four circles, each approximately 6 inches (15cm) in diameter. Lay one cabbage ball onto each circle of dough. Fold the dough up and around the cabbage, pinching tightly to make a seam. Transfer the dough parcels, seam-side down, to the prepared baking sheet.

Make an egg wash by whisking together the cream and remaining egg yolk. Coat the parcels twice with egg wash. Transfer the squash and the meat pies to the oven.

Bake until the crust on the meat pies turns golden brown, 8 to 10 minutes. Remove from the oven and let rest for 5 minutes. Keep baking the squash until tender, another 2 to 4 minutes. Splash the vinegar onto the baking sheet and deglaze the hot pan, scraping up any browned bits as well as stirring the squash to coat.

In a small saucepan over medium heat, warm the olive oil. Add the rosemary and fry until crisp, about 3 minutes. Transfer to the prepared plate.

In another small saucepan over medium heat, warm the venison glaze. Transfer to a gravy boat or your preferred serving vessel.

Lay one meat pie onto each plate. Scatter the squash sticks, 4 candied chestnuts, a sprinkle of fried rosemary leaves, and a shaving of truffle, if desired, on each plate. Serve with the venison glaze.

Sour-Cream Pastry Dough

MAKES 14 OUNCES (390G)

1¾ cups (220g) all-purpose flour

1 teaspoon fine sea salt

¼ cup (55g) cold unsalted butter, cubed

½ cup (115g) sour cream

1 tablespoon apple cider vinegar

This dough is tender and flaky and very easy and quick to make, but also quite sturdy—a great dough to use as a wrap for handheld pies.

In a mixing bowl, combine the flour and salt. Using your fingertips, rub the butter into the flour until it has been reduced to pea-size pieces. Add the sour cream and vinegar and mix gently until the dough starts to come together. (You can also make the dough in a food processor by pulsing the flour, salt, and butter together five or six times, then adding the sour cream and vinegar and pulsing another three or four times.)

Turn the dough out onto your work surface and gently knead two or three times. Pat the dough into a disk shape, wrap tightly in plastic, and refrigerate for 2 hours. (The dough will keep a day or two refrigerated if you wish to make it ahead of time.)

On a lightly floured surface, roll out the dough into a circle about 12 inches (30cm) in diameter. Keep refrigerated until ready to assemble, according to the recipe.

MY FUTURE CHALET IN GSTAAD?

Venison Glaze

HIRSCHGLASUR

MAKES 1 CUP (240ML)

VENISON STOCK

6 to 7 pounds (2.7 to 3kg) venison bones

1 quart (950ml) dry red wine

1 cup (240ml) ruby port

1 cup (240ml) Madeira

1 tablespoon red wine vinegar

8 ounces (225g) celeriac, diced

3 yellow onions, diced

1 carrot, diced

2 garlic cloves

1 sprig thyme, 1 sprig rosemary, 4 bay leaves, and 4 whole cloves, tied together into a small bouquet garni

2 tablespoons grapeseed oil

2 tablespoons tomato paste

1 cup (100g) fresh or frozen cranberries

1 cup (240 ml) dry red wine

½ cup (120ml) ruby port

½ cup (120ml) Madeira

2 yellow onions, thinly sliced

3 bay leaves

5 whole cloves

2 tablespoons dried cranberries

2 tablespoons balsamic vinegar

½ teaspoon grated orange zest

½ teaspoon freshly squeezed lemon juice

Fine sea salt and freshly ground black pepper

1 to 2 tablespoons cold unsalted butter (optional)

This venison glaze is made with a trio of aromatic wines and homemade concentrated venison stock. To make the stock, the vegetables and bones must marinate for 48 hours, so be sure to give yourself a couple of days' lead time. You'll need to find a butcher who can order venison and venison bones, unless you have friends who hunt.

This concentrated sauce is excellent with venison or wild fowl, and yes, it's worth your trouble. It's also a decadent sauce for dumplings or *canederli* (see page 45).

To make the venison stock: In a large pot, combine the venison bones with the wine, port, Madeira, red wine vinegar, celeriac, onions, carrot, and garlic and add the bouquet garni. Cover, place in the refrigerator, and let marinate for 48 hours.

Preheat the oven to 450°F (230°C).

Strain the marinade into a container, allowing excess liquid to drip off the bones and vegetables. Reserve the bouquet garni.

In a large roasting pan over medium-high heat, warm the grapeseed oil. Add the bones and vegetables to the pan and spread them out, then transfer to the oven and roast until golden brown, 20 to 30 minutes. Stir in the tomato paste and continue to roast until the tomato paste acquires a golden hue, about 7 minutes.

Transfer the contents of the roasting pan to a stockpot or a large Dutch oven. Place the roasting pan over medium-high heat, pour in the strained marinade, and deglaze the pan, stirring with a wooden spoon to scrape up any browned bits. Pour this marinade into the stockpot.

Place the cranberries and reserved bouquet garni in the pot and add enough water to cover the bones. Over medium heat, bring to a boil, then immediately turn the heat to the lowest setting and simmer for about 3 hours, skimming regularly to remove any impurities or foam.

Strain the stock through a fine-mesh sieve and remove the fat (the easiest way is to refrigerate the stock overnight, then pick off the congealed fat cap the next day).

Transfer the stock to a clean pot, return to a boil, and reduce the liquid by half, until you have about 1 quart (950 ml) of stock. Remove from the heat and let cool. (At this point, you can transfer the stock to an airtight container or two, seal, and freeze for up to 3 months.)

In a large stainless-steel saucepan over medium-high heat, combine the wine, port, Madeira, onions, bay leaves, and cloves. Bring to a boil and reduce the liquid until almost completely evaporated. Add the venison stock and dried cranberries, bring to a boil, and continue to boil until reduced by half. Strain through a fine-mesh sieve, return to the saucepan, and further reduce by half again, down to about 1 cup (240ml) of liquid. Season with the balsamic vinegar, orange zest, lemon juice, and salt and pepper as needed. If necessary, thicken the consistency of the sauce and add a nice glossy sheen by whisking in the butter.

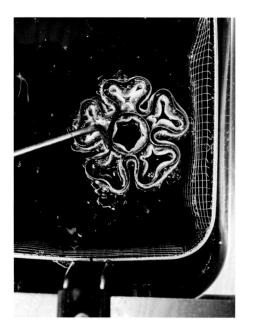

Rosettes with Berries

ROSETTES AUX BAIES

■■■■ MEDIUM
SERVES 6 TO 8

YOU WILL NEED
Rosette iron with handle
Deep fryer (optional)
Deep-frying thermometer or digital instant-read thermometer with probe

ROSETTES
¾ cup (100g) all-purpose flour
¼ cup plus 2 tablespoons (50g) cornstarch
½ teaspoon fine sea salt
2 tablespoons granulated sugar
1 vanilla bean, split and seeded
3 eggs
½ cup (120 ml) milk
1 quart (950 ml) canola oil or peanut oil

BERRY TOPPING
¼ cup (50 g) granulated sugar
Juice of 1 lemon
Water as needed
2 tablespoons unsalted butter
1½ cups (240g) fresh blueberries

Confectioners' sugar for dusting
1 cup (240ml) crème fraîche (optional)

You might have noticed that this recipe name is translated from French rather than German; I'm representing Gstaad's border with France here. These rosettes are essentially deep-fried cookies made in the intricate shape of the rosette iron of your choice. The iron is heated to a very high temperature in oil, dipped into the batter, then again immersed in the hot oil to create a crisp shell around the metal. The iron is removed from the oil and the rosette is separated from the iron. Usually, the edges of the rosette are dipped into frosting or sugar. In the Alps, restaurants often have their own ironworks, which is how convenient it would have been to come by a rosette iron. Thanks to the World Wide Web, finding an iron rosette mold is much easier than you think.

To make the rosettes: In a medium bowl, combine the flour, cornstarch, salt, granulated sugar, vanilla seeds, eggs, and milk and whisk to mix well and work through any lumps. Set aside for 2 hours.

Start up your deep fryer or pour the oil into a Dutch oven over medium heat—it should be about 2 inches deep. Set up a thermometer probe and heat the oil to 360°F (180°C). Line a baking sheet with paper towels.

Carefully heat a rosette iron in the hot oil for 2 minutes. Bring the bowl of batter close to the stove top (you will be able to dip more efficiently if you've transferred the batter to a tall and narrow vessel like a vase or a deli container—wide enough still to fit the rosette). Give the batter a stir.

Lift the hot rosette iron up, allowing excess oil to drain back into the pot, then lower it to the surface of the batter (being careful not to submerge it or the batter will wrap around the iron and be impossible to remove), lift it up, and lower it back into the hot oil. Hold the iron in place and fry the batter until golden brown, 1 to 2 minutes.

Remove the iron from the oil and, using a fork, gently nudge off the fried dough, working your way carefully around the shape, and onto the prepared baking sheet. This might prove tricky on first try—the iron is likely not seasoned enough yet. The more rosettes you make, however, the easier they will slide off. (The rosettes can be fragile so patience is required.) Repeat the dipping and cooking procedure until all the batter is used.

To make the berry topping: In a heavy saucepan over medium-high heat, combine the granulated sugar, lemon juice, and a splash of water and cook for 5 to 6 minutes. Remove from the heat and stir in the butter. Toss in the blueberries while the mixture is still warm.

Place one rosette onto each plate, spoon the warm blueberry topping over them, and dust with confectioners' sugar. Serve with a heaping spoonful of the crème fraîche, if desired.

Herdsman Macaroni

ÄLPLERMAKKARONEN

████ EASY

SERVES 4

1 pound (450g) Yukon gold
potatoes, peeled and cubed

9 ounces (250g) dried macaroni
or penne

2 tablespoons unsalted butter

2 yellow onions, diced

5 ounces (140g) thick-sliced
bacon, cut into lardons

¼ cup (60ml) white wine

2 cups (480ml) low-sodium
vegetable broth

1 cup (240ml) heavy cream

Fine sea salt and freshly ground
black pepper

1 tablespoon minced fresh
flat-leaf parsley

½ cup (50g) grated Berner
Hobelkäse cheese

Applesauce for serving

Hotel Alpenland in Lauenen is small and simple—one of those hotels
I love. At breakfast, two ski-lift operators were at the next table having
their morning coffee. It feels homey and miles from the ritz and glitz
of Gstaad, though it's just a 20-minute drive away.

I've had many iterations of this macaroni dish, which Appenzell claim
as its own, but my favorite version is from Hotel Alpenland, due to its
simplicity. This is pure mountain food for shepherds and herdsmen: cream,
cheese, potatoes, bacon, and shelf-stable dried pasta, complemented
by applesauce. It's basically mac and cheese on steroids—without the
side effects.

*Note: If you can't find Berner Hobelkäse, a hard raw-milk Swiss cheese without
holes, you can substitute any aged cow's-milk cheese, such as réserve Gruyère
or Emmental Switzerland Premier Cru.*

Bring a large pot of salted water to a
boil. Add the potatoes, stir, and boil
for 3 minutes before adding the pasta,
then cook together until the potatoes
are just tender and the pasta is firmly
al dente, 3 to 4 minutes. Drain and
set aside.

In a large sauté pan over medium
heat, melt the butter. Stir in the
onions and bacon and cook until
the onions become translucent
and the bacon has rendered its fat,
5 to 7 minutes. Pour in the white
wine, stirring to loosen any caramelized onion or bacon bits. Turn the
heat to high and simmer the wine
until slightly reduced, about 1 minute. Add in the vegetable broth and
cream, followed by the potatoes
and pasta.

Bring to a boil, then turn the heat
to low and simmer until almost all
of the liquid has been absorbed,
about 10 minutes. Season with salt
and pepper and stir in the minced
parsley.

Divide the pasta-potato mixture into
individual ramekins or transfer to an
ovenproof serving dish, then sprinkle
with the grated cheese and broil
until nicely browned, about 3 minutes, keeping a watchful eye on the
proceedings.

Serve with applesauce on the side.

LOCAL SKI OPERATORS
HAVING BREAKFAST AT
ALPENLAND HOTEL

Hazelnut Croissants

NUSSGIPFEL

■■■ MEDIUM
MAKES 12 SMALL ROLLS

HAZELNUT CREAM

½ cup (50g) hazelnut meal
(hazelnut flour)

2 tablespoons all-purpose flour

½ teaspoon ground cinnamon

¼ cup packed (50g) light
brown sugar

¼ cup (55g) unsalted butter,
at room temperature

1 egg, beaten

1 teaspoon vanilla extract

1 pound (450g) butter puff pastry
dough, defrosted and refrigerated

1 egg yolk whisked with
1 tablespoon heavy cream,
for egg wash

A hard-and-fast rule of the Alpine Eating Club: When you're driving and you spot an intriguing sign on your way to somewhere else, hit the brakes and follow the sign. Photographer Christina Holmes and I were driving up from Interlaken through the tiny mountain village of Habkern when we saw a sign for Gässli-Beck (Bakery Gässli). The fog was so dense, our chances of finding the T-bar lift for a morning of hut-exploring were shot—so we had some time for a detour. As we walked up to the window of the bakery, I spotted a pastry I hadn't seen before, with a little sign that identified it as *Nussgipfel*. We bought two and ate them standing up, mumbling happy food sounds. I asked about the recipe, and owner Christina Ringgenberg said it has been in the family for ages and is a secret. Like buying a vowel on *Wheel of Fortune*, I stood in the bakery guessing at ingredients: "Ground hazelnuts?" Yes. "Cinnamon?" Yes. "Almond powder?" No.

I later found out that *Nussgipfel* is available throughout Switzerland. I'm sure there are recipes all over the internet, but I didn't want just *any* recipe, I wanted to approximate the *secret* recipe from Gässli-Beck. When I got home, I enlisted help from my friend Kendra McKnight, ace recipe developer and tester. I described the flavors and texture (nut roll meets rugelach) of what is essentially a croissant wrapped around a hazelnut cream. This recipe is pretty darn close.

Notes: Hazelnut meal, or hazelnut flour, is available in many natural foods stores or online. But you can also make your own. Toast 4 ounces (115g) hazelnuts in a 275°F (135°C) oven for 15 to 20 minutes, until fragrant, then rub them with a clean kitchen towel to peel away the darkened skins. Pulse the naked hazelnuts and ¼ cup (60g) all-purpose flour in a food processor until finely ground, then proceed with the recipe. Don't be tempted to replace hazelnut flour with almond flour. The result will taste much less interesting.

There's no shame in using store-bought puff pastry (found in the freezer aisle)— just make sure the dough is made with 100 percent butter, rather than a mix of butter and palm oil. Thaw the frozen puff pastry in the fridge overnight.

Alternatively, you don't even need to deal with commercially made puff pastry— just revamp yesterday's bakery-bought plain croissants by halving them horizontally, spreading the hazelnut cream inside, and then baking them for 7 to 10 minutes at 350°F (175°C) and you have these hazelnut delights.

Cutting the pastry triangles works best if you measure your cuts in centimeters rather than the less-precise inch equivalent—use a ruler that includes metric measurements.

continued

To make the hazelnut cream: In a small bowl, whisk together the hazelnut meal, all-purpose flour, and cinnamon to combine.

Using a stand mixer fitted with the paddle attachment, at medium speed, cream the brown sugar and butter until pale and fluffy, about 2 minutes. While still mixing, slowly pour in the egg, followed by the vanilla, pausing the mixer as needed to scrape down the sides and bottom with a spatula. Turn the speed to low and incorporate the hazelnut-flour mixture until just combined. Set aside.

Line a baking sheet with parchment paper.

Working on a lightly floured surface, roll out the puff pastry dough into a rectangle that is 8 by 20 inches (20 by 50cm) wide—the dough should be about ⅛ inch (3mm) thick. Trim any errant, irregular edges. Rotate the rectangle so the long side is facing you.

Starting from the top-left corner of the rectangle, measure a little over 1¼ inches (3.5cm to be exact) to the right and make a notch in the top edge of the dough with a knife. From the bottom-left corner of the rectangle, measure 2¾ inches (7cm) to the right, and make a notch there. Cut diagonally from the bottom-left edge of the dough up to the 1¼-inch (3.5cm) notch, discarding the scrap of dough to the left. Next cut from the 2¾-inch (7cm) notch up to the 1¼-inch (3.5cm) notch. You have your first triangle of dough. Transfer to the prepared baking sheet.

For the next triangle, starting in the (new) top-left corner, measure 2¾ inches (7cm) to the right. Cut diagonally from the 2¾-inch (7cm) mark down to the (new) bottom-left corner. You have your next triangle. Set aside on the baking sheet. Measure 2¾ inches (7cm) from the bottom-left corner and cut through to the top-left corner—this is your third triangle. Repeat accordingly until you have twelve triangles of dough. Each triangle should be 2¾ inches (7cm) wide at the base and about 8 inches (20cm) tall. You can discard or reuse any dough scraps as you see fit.

Dollop 1 tablespoon of the hazelnut cream onto the bottom third of each triangle, leaving a clean margin around the edges. Roll up each triangle of dough fairly snugly, starting at the base and ending at the point. Make sure to tuck the point underneath as you transfer the croissants back to the baking sheets. Press down on the top of each croissant very gently with the palm of your hand to help the seal. It's okay if hazelnut cream is peeking out of the rolls. Refrigerate for 30 minutes.

Preheat the oven to 425°F (220°C).

Gently paint the croissants with the egg wash. Bake the croissants until they are deep golden brown and the hazelnut cream has started to crisp around its edges, 15 to 17 minutes. Transfer to an airtight container and store, at room temperature, for up to 4 days.

Serve at room temperature.

Smoked Trout with Cabbage and Beet Tagliatelle

GERÄUCHERTE WINTERFORELLE MIT KOHL UND RÜBEN-TAGLIATELLE

■■■■■ MEDIUM

SERVES 4

YOU WILL NEED
Pasta machine or stand mixer fitted with the pasta attachment

Charcoal-fired grill

Wooden plank, that will fit on the grill, soaked in water

CABBAGE
1 medium green or white cabbage

1 quart (950ml) water

1 quart (950ml) apple cider vinegar

2½ cups (500g) sugar

1½ cups (160g) sliced ginger

5 whole star anise

2 small red chiles

12 lime leaves

BEET TAGLIATELLE
3 eggs, plus 2 egg yolks

Water as needed

2⅓ cups (290g) all-purpose flour or semolina flour, plus more for dusting

1 teaspoon fine sea salt

1 tablespoon beet powder

TROUT
½ cup (100g) sugar

½ cup (100g) kosher salt

Grated zest of 1 orange

Grated zest of 1 lemon

1 tart or sour apple, grated

1 whole trout (about 1 pound [450g]), cleaned, gutted, and portioned into 4 skin-on fillets

¾ cup (165g) unsalted butter

¼ cup (60ml) apple juice

1 apple, finely diced

Salzano, in Interlaken, is the best kind of Alpine roadside hotel and restaurant. The afternoon I walked in, there was a storm descending on the nearby Bernese Mountains (where I was heading), but the dining room was a cozy stube where the local police were having coffee and cakes, and telling jokes in a corner booth. But the kitchen there is *serious,* and uses only local products on the menu: ravioli filled with pork and quark cheese, Jerusalem artichoke soup with speck—even little marshmallows infused with pine served on an edible twig! This place is a pared-down Noma in a *Twin Peaks* diner set against the menacing north face of the Eiger (i.e., the "cemetery of the Alps"). What a trip!

I settled on a whole trout that was cedar-smoked in the snow just outside the window and served with electric-pink beet tagliatelle and a little cabbage, kraut-style. If you don't want to smoke your own fish, you can, of course, just grill it.

Note: It takes 24 hours to cook, cool, and press the cabbage, and 4 hours to cure the fish before cooking. Any leftover cabbage can be kept in an airtight container, in the refrigerator, for up to 1 week.

To prepare the cabbage: In a large stockpot over high heat, combine the cabbage, water, vinegar, sugar, ginger, star anise, chiles, and lime leaves. Bring to a boil and reduce to about 1 quart (950ml) of liquid, 20 to 25 minutes.

Remove the cabbage from the cooking liquid and, when cool enough to handle, slice it into very thin threads and transfer to a large bowl. Pour the cooking liquid over the cabbage and cover with plastic wrap. Place a heavy pot or another bowl filled with cans on top of the cabbage mixture to press it. Let it sit for 24 hours at cool room temperature.

To make the tagliatelle: In a glass measuring cup, combine the eggs and egg yolks and add enough water to measure ¾ cup plus 2 tablespoons (200ml) total.

In a large mixing bowl, combine the flour, salt, and beet powder and whisk to combine. Make a well in the center of the flour and pour in the egg mixture. Using a fork, swirl the mixture, slowly incorporating the flour into the center of the well. When the flour is completely incorporated, gather and knead the dough together for about 5 minutes to form one large ball. Wrap the ball in plastic and rest and refrigerate for 45 to 60 minutes.

To prepare the trout: In a large bowl, combine the sugar, salt, orange zest, lemon zest, and grated apple and stir well. In a shallow dish, lay out the trout fillets, flesh-side up, cover with the salt-citrus mixture, and refrigerate for 4 hours.

Heavily dust a baking sheet with flour. Divide the rested dough into fourths. Keep the dough covered while working with one piece at a time.

Roll the dough through the widest roller setting of your pasta machine (or attachment, if you're using a stand mixer), dusting with all-purpose flour along the way to ensure the dough

continued

doesn't stick, but not too much as you don't want the dough to become dry. Fold the sheet of dough in half onto itself, and roll it through this initial setting ten to fifteen times, folding it again after each pass.

Change the machine setting to the next, narrower setting and roll the sheet through once. You'll notice your sheet will become longer and longer as you work it through each successive setting. Keep rolling until Setting 7 (on most pasta machines); you want the sheet to be thin enough to just see your hand through it. Lay the pasta sheet out on the prepared baking sheet. Repeat the rolling procedure with the remaining three pieces of dough.

Tightly roll each sheet of pasta, from short end to short end. Cut crosswise into ⅜-inch (1cm) wide strips. Unroll the strips and toss with flour; spread on the baking sheet. Let dry for 30 minutes.

Start a fire in a charcoal grill about 1 hour before the fish has finished curing.

After the 4 hours have elapsed, thoroughly rinse the curing mix off the trout under cold running water. Pat the fish dry.

In a small frying pan over medium heat, melt ½ cup (110g) of the butter. As the butter melts, it will begin to foam and the color will change from yellow to tan to brown, 4 to 5 minutes. Once you smell a nutty aroma, take the pan off the heat and transfer the browned butter into a heatproof bowl to cool, leaving behind the milk solids settled on the bottom of the pan.

Lay the trout fillets, skin-side down, on a wooden plank and place on the grill, rather than directly on the coals, away from direct heat. Baste regularly with the brown butter until the fish is cooked, 15 to 20 minutes.

Bring a large pot of salted water to a boil. Add the tagliatelle and cook until al dente, 2 to 3 minutes once the water has resumed boiling.

Meanwhile, in a large sauté pan over medium-high heat, melt the remaining ¼ cup (55g) butter, pour in the apple juice, and stir, cooking slightly. Strain the pasta, then transfer to the sauté pan to combine with the sauce. Stir in the diced apple.

Divide the trout among four plates, then add the beet pasta and a generous spoonful of lukewarm cabbage. Serve immediately.

Pan-Fried Calf Liver

GESCHNITTENE KÄLBERLEBER

■■■■ MEDIUM
SERVES 4

MIXED HERB SAUCE

⅓ cup (15g) fresh herb leaves
(a mix of marjoram, sage, thyme,
and rosemary)

1 cup (50g) flat-leaf parsley leaves

½ cup (120 ml) extra-virgin
olive oil

Fine sea salt and freshly ground
black pepper

2 tablespoons unsalted butter

2 tablespoons extra-virgin
olive oil

½ yellow onion, finely diced

2 garlic cloves, minced

1½ pounds (680 g) fresh calf liver,
cut into thin slices

Fine sea salt and freshly ground
black pepper

Rösti (page 253) for serving

When people ask me where to eat in Zermatt, whether they're skiing or hiking, I always recommend Zum See. It's a beautiful trip to the namesake hamlet at 1,700 meters (5,575 feet). To get there, simply take the cable car up to Furi from Zermatt and enjoy a short hike or ski down, stopping in for an espresso at one of the small huts along the way. This restaurant is almost always packed, with people drinking small beers on the terrace as they wait for a table. You'll see wooden tables laden with slabs of mille-feuille or Sachertortes or apple pies, protected by the roof overhang.

In the tiny kitchen you'll find Max, the lovable owner, alongside his wife, Greti, working their magic. When Max was fourteen, he apprenticed with a butcher, and his adoration for the tertiary cuts shows: they've been the menu go-to since 1984. Seeing kids with rosy cheeks and snowy boots feverishly polishing off his calf liver and kidneys warmed my heart. This recipe is Max's. Oh, and for the coffee fanatics who note it's almost impossible to find a good cup in Switzerland, Max sources his beans, which he grinds daily, from Italy.

Note: The mixed herb sauce in this recipe is an excellent seasoning for all kinds of meat. You'd be wise to make a large batch. Store it in a glass jar in the refrigerator for up to 2 weeks, as long as the minced herbs are covered with olive oil.

To make the herb sauce: In a blender or food processor, combine the herbs and parsley and pulse until coarsely chopped. Add the olive oil and continue to pulse, until the consistency of the mixture looks like pesto. Season with salt and pepper, then set aside.

Warm a large cast-iron pan over medium-high heat. Add the butter, olive oil, and onion and sauté until the onion is nicely browned, 5 to 7 minutes. Stir in the garlic and mixed herb sauce and turn the heat to high.

Lay the liver slices in the pan, leaving some space between them. Once the slices are nicely browned, 1 to 2 minutes, flip them and cook for another minute or two, until the other sides are browned as well. Season with salt and pepper.

Serve immediately, with the rösti alongside.

Raclette

■■■■ EASY
SERVES 4

YOU WILL NEED
Raclette maker

8 new potatoes

1½ pounds (680 g) raclette cheese, cut into ⅛-inch (3mm) thick slices

1 small jar cornichons pickles

1 small jar pickled onions

8 ounces (225g) Bündnerfleisch or viande des Grisons, cut in paper-thin slices

Freshly ground black pepper

The Valais is the native land for raclette (a traditional dish in which a piece of cheese is heated and the melted parts scraped off, named after the French verb *racler*, "to scrape," onto the plate), and the absolute best place for raclette in the Valais is Château de Villa. Per its name, it is an actual château in the village of Sierre. I arrived on a very cold and snowy February night after an afternoon of wine tasting with Sandrine Caloz (see snapshot, page 186), whose family winery is just up a winding narrow road from the castle.

Upon entering, I was greeted by a 6-foot-7-inch (2m) giant with a 12-inch (30cm) wide wheel of cheese in his hands, all 13 pounds (6kg) of it. The giant, who was a *racleur* (scraper), was manning a raclette station: two wooden tables holding forty or more wheels of cheese. Behind him was a blackboard with the night's Appellation d'Origine Protégée (AOP) offerings, along with their provenance: Bagnes 1 (Verbier), Mondralèche (Lens), Wallis 65 (Turtmann), Simplon (Simplon-Dorf), Illiez 6 (Alpage Berroix). All the cheeses were from Valais. For raclette, the wheels are cut in half, placed onto a handled shelf, and pushed under a larger metal broiler. The racleur came over, looked me up and down, and said he'd start at the top of the list.

At the table, the raclette is served with small cornichons, pickled onions, country bread, and boiled potatoes. The cheese went from mild to more intense, and as my friend and I worked through them, we referred to the map, wondering why the milk from a Simplon cow would have such a kick compared to the brown beauty from the next valley over.

To harness your inner racleur or racleuse at home, buy 1½ pounds (680g) of raclette cheese from the best cheeseshop in your area. Be sure to ask the cheesemonger if he or she has more than one; most worthy shops will have Raclette de Valais AOP as well as more niche options.

As a postscript, I returned to Château de Villa in the summer with my photographer, Christina Holmes, eager to capture the moodiness of the room and that imposing racleur. Instead, we found an outdoor garden packed with locals eating raclette, served to them by a jaunty waitress, who was wearing a white blouse and red kerchief. No darkness. No wall of cheese. Just a pretty little garden with people drinking rosé.

Notes: To host a raclette night at home, you will need a raclette maker/grill (someone you know likely has one you can borrow). If you do buy a raclette set (and you should), also look for a decent wire cheese cutter. It will make raclette night that much easier.

If you can't find Swiss Bündnerfleisch, substitute another cured meat of your liking.

For wine and dessert options, see "Hot Tips for Fondue," page 209.

Fun Fact: Raclette is lactose-free. During the maturation period of the cheese, lactose is fully decomposed.

continued

Scrub the potatoes (do not peel), put them in a pot, and cover with salted water. Bring to a boil and boil until tender (test with a sharp knife), about 20 minutes. Keep warm until ready to serve.

Using a sharp knife, carefully remove the rind from the cheese. Arrange the pickles, onions, and meat on a platter and set aside.

Preheat the raclette grill.

Each guest should then help themselves to a slice of cheese and melt it in their individual grilling tray. It takes approximately 2 minutes to melt to a creamy consistency, or 3 minutes for a crispier top. Hold the pan on its side to scrape the cheese onto your plate, using your wooden spatula, and season with pepper. The potatoes and any other warm accompaniments can be kept warm on the grill top.

ST. MORITZ IN MARCH

A Proper Bullshot

■■■ (WAY TOO) EASY
SERVES 4
(MAKES 1 PINT [475 ML])

Ice cubes

¾ cup (175ml) Van Hoo vodka

One 10½-ounce (298g) can condensed beef consommé (preferably Campbell's)

2 teaspoons freshly squeezed lemon juice

3 dashes of hot pepper sauce (preferably Tabasco)

Generous dash of Worcestershire sauce (preferably Lea & Perrins)

1 teaspoon creamy horseradish

1 teaspoon freshly ground black pepper

½ teaspoon celery salt

St. Moritz has long been a dashing winter destination for the fast-living über-rich. The St. Moritz Tobogganing Club (SMTC) is a members-only private club founded in 1887—with the sole purpose of gathering its international members for the conduct of skeleton racing (that's head-first) on the Cresta Run, a natural-ice run built every winter between St. Moritz and the hamlet of Cresta, 1.2 kilometers (¾ mile) away. The ice course is now owned and operated exclusively by the SMTC for its members and comes with club rites and rituals nonmembers can never know. What we *do* know, however, is this: Club members have a habit of gathering for lunch at the Kulm Hotel (the "outdoor amusements committee" of the Kulm originally came up with the idea for the Cresta Run back in the early 1880s); the SMTC has elected the Bullshot as its club drink.

And now that we've snuck this recipe out of the club, let's have a Bullshot in the comfort of our own homes, please—without the whole speeding head-first down a skeleton run at 130 kph (80 mph) bit. The mark of a great Bullshot is a good layer of pepper grinds in the bottom of the glass.

As per tradition, fill a pitcher with plenty of ice. Pour in the vodka, consommé, lemon juice, hot pepper sauce, Worcestershire, horseradish, black pepper, and celery salt and stir vigorously. Strain the drink into four small tumblers. Serve immediately.

BISCHOFBERGER AND ALPINE ART

Galerie Bruno Bischofberger is a Zürich-based art gallery that has been advertising on the back cover of *Artforum* magazine since 1986. (In 1989, the back of the magazine was reserved exclusively for them.) The full-page ads feature photographs typically depicting a Swiss tradition, ceremony, or some aspect of daily Alpine life: a fisherman on Lake Lucerne, seasonal haying in the Alpstein, cheesemaking in copper vats in an Appenzell hut, farmers herding pigs down a mountain path, or guerilla-style shots of Silversterklaus, a New Year's Eve celebration high in the Appenzell Hinterland.

Who are these people? What is this world?

The images always made me so curious—at first, I thought they were ads for a specific Alpine photography exhibition. But then I came to see them as an alluring identification card for the gallery, a sort of peculiar Alpine gateway. Bruno Bischofberger operated a satellite gallery in St. Moritz, which is surely why most of the art world ever ascended to the Engadine Valley. These images chronicle harder-to-read forms of folk knowledge—alluring, highly regionalized story worlds—that remind us that there is a lot hiding in the mountains, especially if you know where to look.

PORTRAITS   4 DECEMBER – 11 MARCH

GALERIE
BRUNO BISCHOFBERGER
UTOQUAI 29
8008 ZURICH, SWITZERLAND
TEL. 262 40 20
FAX 262 28 97
www.brunobischofberger.com

IN EXCLUSIVITY: BARCELÓ, BIDLO, CUCCHI
REPRESENTING: CLEMENTE, CONDO, DOKOUPIL,
HALLEY, MCDERMOTT & MCGOUGH, SALLE, SCHNABEL, SOTTSASS
WORKS BY: BASQUIAT, TINGUELY, WARHOL

PORTRAITS   4 DECEMBER – 31 MARCH

GALERIE
BRUNO BISCHOFBERGER
UTOQUAI 29
8008 ZURICH, SWITZERLAND
www.brunobischofberger.com

IN EXCLUSIVITY: BARCELÓ, BIDLO, CUCCHI
REPRESENTING: CLEMENTE, CONDO, DOKOUPIL,
HALLEY, MCDERMOTT & MCGOUGH, SALLE, SCHNABEL, SOTTSASS
WORKS BY: BASQUIAT, TINGUELY, WARHOL

GALERIE BRUNO BISCHOFBERGER
UTOQUAI 29, 8008 ZURICH, SWITZERLAND
TEL 41 1 262 40 20 FAX 41 1 262 28 97
WWW.BRUNOBISCHOFBERGER.COM

IN EXCLUSIVITY: BARCELÓ, BIDLO, CUCCHI, DOKOUPIL
REPRESENTING: CLEMENTE, CONDO, HALLEY, SALLE, SCHNABEL, SOTTSASS
WORKS BY: BASQUIAT, TINGUELY, WARHOL

Galerie
Bruno Bischofberger
Utoquai 29

represented:
MIGUEL BARCELÓ
JEAN-MICHEL BASQUIAT
MIKE BIDLO
FRANCESCO CLEMENTE
GEORGE CONDO
ENZO CUCCHI
DAVID SALLE
JULIAN SCHNABEL
JEAN TINGUELY
ANDY WARHOL

UNTIL 1 MARCH
UNTIL 13 MAY

GALERIE BRUNO BISCHOFBERGER
UTOQUAI 29, 8008 ZURICH
SWITZERLAND
TEL 41 44 250 77 77
FAX 41 44 250 77 88
WWW.BRUNOBISCHOFBERGER.COM

IN EXCLUSIVITY: BARCELÓ,
CUCCHI, DOKOUPIL
REPRESENTING: BIDLO,
CLEMENTE, CONDO, HALLEY,
SALLE, SCHNABEL, SOTTSASS
WORKS BY: BASQUIAT,
TINGUELY, WARHOL

GALERIE BRUNO BISCHOFBERGER
UTOQUAI 29, 8008 ZURICH SWITZERLAND
TEL 41 44 250 77 77 FAX 41 44 250 77 88
WWW.BRUNOBISCHOFBERGER.COM

BARCELÓ, BASQUIAT, BIDLO, CLEMENTE,
CUCCHI, DOKOUPIL, HALLEY, SALLE,
SCHNABEL, SHINKAREV,
SOTTSASS, TINGUELY, WARHOL

DON'T DO IT ETC.
UNTIL 25 JUNE

SUMMER SHOW
VIA MAISTRA 37, 7500 ST. MORITZ SWITZERLAND, TEL 41 81 833 50 00
16 JULY UNTIL 17 SEPTEMBER

THE 80S REVISITED, PART 2 | KUNSTHALLE BIELEFELD
WORKS FROM THE BISCHOFBERGER COLLECTION
UNTIL 19 JUNE

GALERIE BRUNO BISCHOFBERGER
FOUNDED 1963
UTOQUAI 29 · 8008 ZURICH
WWW.BRUNOBISCHOFBERGER.COM

VIA MAISTRA 37 · 7500 ST. MORITZ
MID JULY – MID SEPTEMBER

BARCELÓ, BASQUIAT, BIDLO,
CLEMENTE, CUCCHI, DOKOUPIL,
HALLEY, SALLE, SCHNABEL,
SHINKAREV, SOTTSASS,
TINGUELY, WARHOL

THE BRUCE HIGH QUALITY FOUNDATION
THE RAFT OF THE MEDUSA / LE RADEAU DE LA MÉDUSE
SEPTEMBER 22 – OCTOBER 27

GALERIE BRUNO BISCHOFBERGER
UTOQUAI 29, 8008 ZURICH SWITZERLAND
TEL 41 44 250 77 77 FAX 41 44 250 77 88
WWW.BRUNOBISCHOFBERGER.COM

GALERIE BRUNO BISCHOFBERGER
FOUNDED 1963

GALERIE BRUNO BISCHOFBERGER
FOUNDED 1963
TEL +41 44 250 77 77

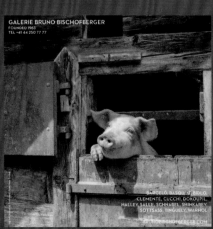

GALERIE BRUNO BISCHOFBERGER
FOUNDED 1963
TEL +41 44 250 77 77

BARCELÓ, BASQUIAT, BIDLO,
CLEMENTE, CUCCHI, DOKOUPIL,
HALLEY, SALLE, SCHNABEL, SHINKAREV,
SOTTSASS, TINGUELY, WARHOL

WWW.BRUNOBISCHOFBERGER.COM

GALERIE BRUNO BISCHOFBERGER

WIESENSTRASSE 1
8834 MÄNNEDORF/ZURICH
TEL +41 44 250 77 77
GALERIE@BISCHOFBERGER.COM

Vittorio's Paccheri

■■■■ EASY
SERVES 4

⅓ cup (80ml) extra-virgin olive oil, plus more for drizzling

1 garlic clove

8 ounces (225g) San Marzano tomatoes, coarsely chopped

3 ounces (85g) Oxheart or heirloom tomato, coarsely chopped

Fine sea salt and freshly ground black pepper

2 ounces (55g) Datterini or cherry tomatoes, finely chopped

9 ounces (250g) paccheri

2 tablespoons unsalted butter

¾ cup (75g) grated Parmigiano-Reggiano cheese

10 fresh basil leaves

¼ teaspoon red pepper flakes (optional)

From Bergamot to the Bernina Pass, the Vittorio family has taken their famous *paccheri* (a large, tubular dried pasta) from the north of Lombardy to the Carlton St. Moritz, where they have an outpost—Da Vittorio. Like a (very good) Italian restaurant in Las Vegas, the food and service are theatrical with a dose of glitz (see photo), which is fine because . . . look at this pasta.

Note: You can find paccheri at almost any Italian grocery store.

In a Dutch oven or heavy saucepan over medium heat, warm the olive oil. Add the garlic and cook until golden, 3 to 4 minutes. Add the San Marzano and Oxheart tomatoes, ½ teaspoon salt, and a good grinding of pepper. Lower the heat and simmer until thickened and chunky, 25 to 30 minutes. Transfer to a blender and purée until smooth. Return the tomato sauce to the pan over low heat, stir in the Datterini tomatoes, and let simmer.

Meanwhile, bring a large pot of salted water to a boil and cook the paccheri until al dente (refer to the timing on the box). Drain the pasta and transfer to the pot with the tomato sauce. Stir in the butter and cheese, then add the basil, a drizzle of olive oil, and the red pepper flakes, if desired.

Serve immediately.

Toggi-Schnitzel with Apple-Chive Slaw

TOGGI-SCHNITZEL MIT APFEL SCHNITTLAUCH SALAT

■■■ MEDIUM
SERVES 4

APPLE-CHIVE SLAW

1 apple (Gala or Pink Lady will do), julienned

1 tablespoon minced fresh chives

2 teaspoons grain mustard

Four 4-ounce (115g) boneless pork loin chops, about ¾ inch (2cm) thick

5 ounces (140g) cured ham or speck, thinly sliced and divided into 4 portions

5 ounces (140g) Appenzeller cheese, very thinly sliced and divided into 4 portions

3 eggs

1 tablespoon fine sea salt

1 tablespoon sweet paprika

1 cup (120g) all-purpose flour

2 cups (120g) panko bread crumbs

Canola oil or peanut oil for frying

2 lemons, halved

It's said that the cordon bleu (a cutlet with a cheese filling) originated in Brig, which is the first Swiss town you hit after crossing the Simplon Pass from Piedmont, Italy. The terrain here is rocky and unpredictable; the plateaus are vast, and very windy. And the region's local dish abides: a veal or pork loin is pounded as for schnitzel, with a stuffing of speck or ham filled with a thin portion of local *Alpkäse* (hut cheese) or Gruyère. It's ample and it's delicious.

I ate this dish while hiking around the Toggenburg (far north from Brig) along with a regulating *Fitness Teller Salat* (page 254). The real deal is almost impossible to re-create outside of Switzerland because it requires the traditional and local (fresh) Alpkäse. However, this adaptation—a Toggenburger's take on a cordon bleu chop—is just as mouthwatering. A digestive friend to help ease the path is recommended—enter the apple slaw.

"Toggi-Schnitzel" is my way of paying homage to the region that inspired this recipe; I just shortened the region's name accordingly. (You can do this with any place: in Montreal, for example, a thin layer of Schwartz's smoked meat in place of the speck would make a Mont-Schnitzel—and wouldn't be a bad idea.)

Notes: Use a meat tenderizer or rolling pin to pound out the meat. If you're a fan of schnitzel, invest in the mallet. Besides looking cool, it actually works.

If you can't find Appenzeller, use Gruyère.

To make the slaw: In a small bowl, mix together the apple, chives, and mustard with a fork until well combined. Set aside.

Pat the pork chops dry. Using a very sharp knife, butterfly each chop, slicing horizontally all the way to the fat cap, *without cutting all the way through*. Open each chop like you would a book.

Using the smooth side of a meat mallet (or a rolling pin), hit the meat pieces directly, starting in the middle of each and working your way out from the center. You want to pound the meat, not tear it. This should take two or three good hits. Then flip the pieces of meat and give them two good hits on the reverse side, trying to get it nice and even and about ¼ inch (6mm) thick.

Lay the pounded meat on a cutting board so the side with the fat cap is facing down. Lay half of one portion of cured ham on one half of the pork slice. Next, lay one full portion of cheese on top of the ham and then cover it with the remaining portion of ham. Fold the pork slice over the ham and cheese, making sure the filling is contained within the pork. It should look like a tiny delicious packet within a larger tasty package. Repeat with the remaining loins, ham, and cheese.

In a shallow bowl, whisk the eggs with the salt and paprika until fully combined. Put the flour and bread crumbs into two separate shallow bowls or onto large plates. Set out a large platter.

Using your hands, carefully dredge each stuffed loin chop in the flour on both sides, shaking off any excess flour. Dip the meat into the egg, making sure both sides are fully covered and then draining off any excess—you can use a fork to help you turn and lift the meat from the egg wash. Nestle the pork into the bread crumbs, making sure it gets fully coated on all sides. Transfer the stuffed chops to the platter.

Warm a pan (large enough to hold all of the schnitzels) over medium-low heat. (It's okay to use two smaller pans or to work in batches.) Add enough canola oil to reach ½ inch (12mm) up the sides of the pan.

When the oil starts to shimmer (you do not want the oil to smoke, just to sizzle nicely), add the stuffed meat and let it brown, about 3 minutes. Using tongs or a fish spatula, carefully flip each loin, working away from your body to avoid splatters. Fry until the second side is golden as well, another 3 minutes. You'll know you've hit the sweet spot if a little cheese starts to melt out just then.

Transfer each chop to a plate (or to a low oven, if you're working in batches). Serve with two spoonfuls of apple slaw and a halved lemon each.

Peter Zumthor is a world-renowned Swiss architect. He was born in Basel and originally trained as a cabinetmaker before studying architecture. He's known as a regionalist who prefers to use local materials (stone, wood) in a very raw or pure way, often riffing on traditional building techniques and vernacular. An architect I know says there's something about his work that makes you want to go up and touch it. You can do just that at one of his most famous and beautiful projects, Therme Vals, a spa and hotel built in the mountain hamlet of Leis in Vals. Zumthor likes to work out of a wooden barn in Haldenstein, a small village in Graubünden.

SNAPSHOT

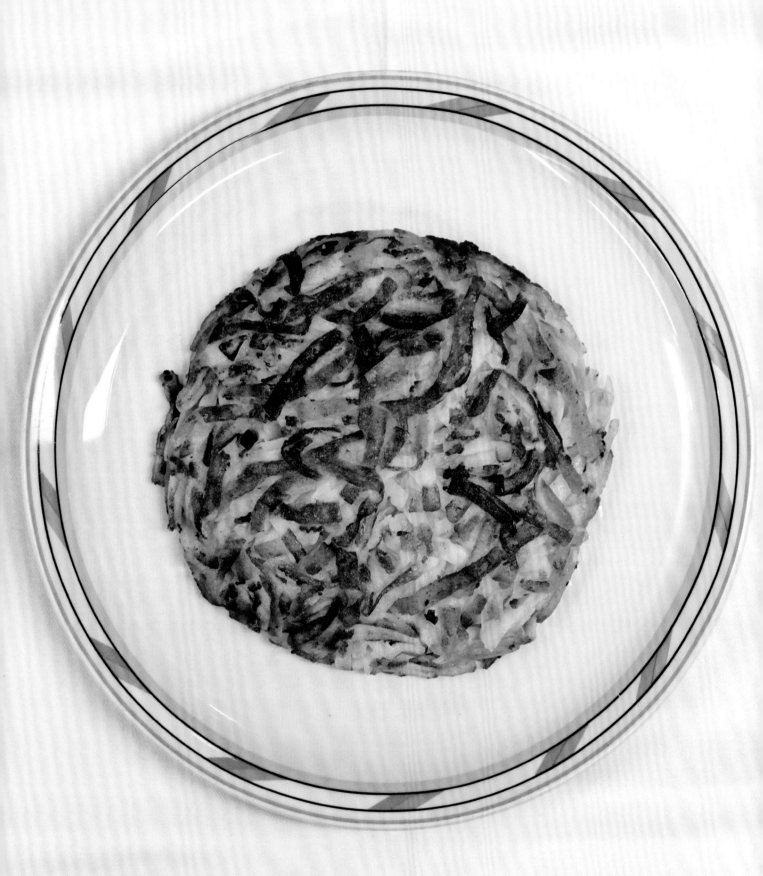

Rösti

■■■■□□ MEDIUM

SERVES 4 TO 6

1½ pounds (675g) Yukon gold potatoes

Kosher salt

½ cup (110g) unsalted butter, cubed

Freshly ground black pepper

Grated Appenzeller or Gruyère cheese for sprinkling (optional)

One of the most dramatically situated restaurants I visited is the Berggasthaus Aescher-Wildkirchli, perched on the edge of the Ebenalp, an Appenzeller cliff—no road, no address, no accessible purveyors, no access to public water—near a system of caves and a small chapel. How does such a place exist, and function as a busy restaurant?

Provisions arrive on a pallet via cable car three times a week and lowered into the adjacent cave, which acts as the restaurant stockroom. There, the temperature hovers around 5°C (40°F)—ideal for potatoes. In that cave is a swimming pool–size tub accumulating 120,000 liters (31,680 gallons) of spring water that drips from the rocks above. This reserve has to last from May through November, the entirety of Aescher's season.

And so, rösti is the house specialty by necessity (pasta and rice would use too much cooking water). The potatoes are steamed in a gigantic pressure cooker off to the side of the hut, but you don't have to cook them this way at home.

Note: If you don't have a well-seasoned cast-iron pan, using a nonstick pan makes the process much easier. (That said, you would never be allowed to use such a pan in a Swiss kitchen!)

Place the potatoes in a large pot over medium-high heat and *just* cover with water. Add 2 tablespoons salt and simmer until the potatoes are tender on the outside but resistant in the middle when poked with a sharp knife, about 30 minutes. You want them slightly undercooked. Drain the potatoes and let them sit at room temperature overnight.

Using the dull side of a paring knife, peel the potatoes. Do not be tempted to use a peeler; the potatoes are too fragile. Using a box grater, grate the potatoes into a large bowl, keeping the strands as long as possible.

In a large cast-iron or nonstick frying pan over medium heat, melt ¼ cup (55g) of the butter; do not let it brown. Transfer the potatoes to the pan and stir to coat with butter. Stir gently and occasionally for 3 to 4 minutes, seasoning with about 1 teaspoon salt and 1 to 2 teaspoons pepper.

Melt the remaining ¼ cup (55g) butter in the microwave.

Still working over medium heat, press the potatoes into a round shape with a wooden spoon. Press the edge of the rösti together so that it forms a small wall, away from the edge of the pan (as if it just came out of a ring mold): gather all of the rösti from the sides of the pan, returning the errant potatoes to the middle, like you're gathering sand into a pile for a sand castle). Pour half of the melted butter around the outside edge of the potatoes, lifting the edge gently with a spatula so that the butter can run underneath the rösti. Let the rösti turn golden brown on the first side, 7 to 10 minutes.

Lay a plate facedown over the pan and flip out the rösti, then add the remaining melted butter to the pan and slip the rösti into the pan to fry the second side, another 7 to 10 minutes. Reshape the rösti, so it's packed tight into a cake. If you're going to serve with cheese, sprinkle with the grated cheese 5 minutes before you finish cooking.

Serve immediately.

Fitness Salad

FITNESS TELLER SALAT

█████ **EASY**
SERVES 4

If you ate as much schnitzel, sausage, cured meat, and cheese as the Swiss, you would eat this salad on a daily basis too. It's pro-digestion, anti-gout, and actually tasty. You can find this medley of salads, similar to an *assiette de crudités* in France, on almost every menu in the Ostschweiz (or Eastern Swiss Alps). It typically consists of three to five different and simply treated vegetables on a plate. Here, I've included my favorite combination: marinated daikon, carrot rémoulade, beet and arugula slaw, potatoes and chives, and cucumber salad. Über-simple, always necessary.

Marinated Daikon

1 shallot, finely diced

1 teaspoon white wine vinegar

2 teaspoons extra-virgin olive oil

1 bunch fresh chives, coarsely chopped

Pinch of kosher salt

1 small daikon, peeled and sliced into thin rounds (1/16 inch [1.5mm] or less)

3 radishes, tops intact, cleaned and thinly sliced horizontally

Fine sea salt

In a small bowl, use a fork to whisk together the shallot, vinegar, olive oil, chives, and kosher salt until well combined. Add the daikon and radishes and toss to coat. Sprinkle with a generous pinch of sea salt to finish before serving.

Carrot Rémoulade

2 large carrots, coarsely grated

1 tablespoon apple cider vinegar

2 tablespoons mayonnaise

1 bunch green onions, white and green parts, thinly sliced

Fine sea salt

In a medium bowl, use a spoon to mix together the carrots, vinegar, mayonnaise, and green onions. Sprinkle with a generous pinch of salt to finish before serving.

Beet and Arugula Slaw

3 large beets, cooked, peeled, and cut into 1-inch (2.5cm) cubes

Grated zest of ½ orange

1 tablespoon extra-virgin olive oil

2 teaspoons balsamic vinegar

1 teaspoon sherry vinegar

1 handful tarragon leaves, minced

1 handful arugula, coarsely chopped

Fine sea salt

In a medium bowl, use a spoon to mix together the beets, orange zest, olive oil, balsamic vinegar, sherry vinegar, tarragon, and arugula. Sprinkle with a generous pinch of salt to finish before serving.

Potatoes and Chives

4 Yukon gold potatoes, peeled

2 teaspoons extra-virgin olive oil

1 bunch fresh chives, thinly chopped

Fine sea salt

Place the potatoes in a large pot and cover with generously salted water. Bring to a boil over high heat, then turn the heat to low and simmer until completely tender, 25 to 30 minutes. Drain the potatoes, refrigerate for 20 minutes to chill, and then slice into thick rounds.

In a large bowl, use a spoon to mix together the potatoes, olive oil, and chives. Sprinkle with a generous pinch of sea to finish before serving.

Cucumber Salad

2 English cucumbers, peeled, seeded, and sliced into ¼-inch (6mm) half-moons

2 tablespoons white wine vinegar

2 tablespoons grapeseed oil

2 sprigs dill, finely chopped

Fine sea salt

In a medium bowl, use a spoon to mix together the cucumber, vinegar, grapeseed oil, and dill. Sprinkle with a generous pinch of salt to finish before serving.

Blue Trout

FORELLE BLAU

■■■■ MEDIUM
SERVES 1 OR 2

1 quart (950ml) water

1 cup (240ml) dry Riesling

½ cup (120ml) white wine vinegar

1 yellow onion, sliced

1 celery stalk, sliced

2 teaspoons fine sea salt

1 live trout

1 lemon, quartered

⅓ cup (80ml) melted butter

Boiled salted potatoes for serving

Berggasthaus Forelle (which translates as "Trout Mountain Inn"; see Travel Hack) is a magical inn and restaurant at the foot of the Seealpsee, a lake in the Alpstein region. Located in a narrow valley surrounded by trees and high peaks, it's the kind of place where you would expect to see wizards and elves. Instead, you'll find groups of Swiss Germans swimming naked and drinking Alstätten wines. The summer I visited, friends and I sat down to some pretty, little bottles of Heini Haubensak (a local AOC wine from St. Gallen, Switzerland) and ordered a few *blau* trout and a couple of plates of spaetzle with *Alpkäse* (local hut cheese) and crispy onions (see page 126). I suggest you do the same.

Note: For this recipe, you need a freshwater lake filled with trout, a net, and a bat. Catch a trout in a freshwater lake. Place it in a holding device of your own creation. (At Forelle, there's a concrete bunker filled with lake water, right outside of the kitchen.) Keep the fish alive!

In a large pot over medium heat, combine the water, Riesling, vinegar, onion, celery, and salt. When the liquid begins to simmer, scurry to your holding device with a net. It may help to wear gloves or have a dish towel handy. Make sure your bat is nearby! The next step relies on you being decisive, quick, and humane.

Grab the trout by its tail and club it once on the back of its head. Say a little prayer as you transfer it to a cutting board and, taking good care, slice into and across the belly lengthwise. Remove the guts and rinse the cavity thoroughly, but *do not* wash the outside of the fish; the slime and its interaction with the vinegar is what turns the fish blue.

When the cooking liquid is barely simmering, drop the trout into the pot. Cook for 9 to 12 minutes; the fish should flake off the bone easily. If you've followed these steps correctly, the trout will turn bright blue within a minute of hitting the liquid.

Transfer the fish whole to a plate. Serve with fresh lemon wedges, melted butter, and boiled salted potatoes.

TRAVEL HACK

To reach the Berggasthaus Forelle, take the *Luftseilbahn* (aerial cable car) to the Sutter family's Berggasthaus Ebenalp restaurant and stop for lunch. The views from the Ebenalp are endless. To the north is Lake Constance (the Bodensee, in German), with Germany just beyond. To the east are the snow-capped Austrian Alps; if you squint, you can see the mountains of Lech.

From the Ebenalp summit, it's a 2-hour or so walk to Seealpsee. The descent is not difficult, but children should be secured. Or, you can walk on the road, which will take about 1½ hours and offers only a 200-meter (650-foot) drop in elevation (Forelle is around 1,200 meters [4,000 feet]). Either way, the Berggasthaus Aescher Wildkirchli (see page 253) is very close by (you can see Seealpsee from its terrace).

So, a morning hike, lunch at Ebenalp (or Aescher), then another hike and a swim at Seealpsee, followed by dinner at Forelle. The perfect one-day Alpine excursion.

Grape and Walnut Pizokel

PIZOKEL WYNEGG

■■■ EASY

SERVES 4

YOU WILL NEED
Spaetzle maker (see Note, page 171; optional)

Fine sea salt

3½ cups (420g) all-purpose flour

¾ cup plus 2 tablespoons (200ml) milk

1 cup (200g) quark cheese

4 eggs

Freshly ground black pepper

Generous grating of nutmeg

2 tablespoons grapeseed oil

½ yellow onion, finely diced

1⅓ cups (200g) seedless red and green grapes, halved

¾ cup (90g) walnuts, coarsely chopped

⅓ cup (80ml) white balsamic vinegar

¼ cup (85g) honey

½ cup (120ml) low-sodium vegetable broth

¼ cup (55g) unsalted butter

1½ cups (160g) ⅜-inch (1cm) Taleggio cubes

2 tablespoons minced fresh flat-leaf parsley, plus 1 tablespoon flat-leaf parsley leaves

The area around Klosters in the far-eastern Swiss canton of Graubünden has been a renowned winter-sports resort ever since the British royals and Hollywood celebrities started favoring it in the 1950s (Davos is about 10 kilometers [6 miles] away). However, the area isn't all glitz and glamour, especially in the more remote corners of the Prättigau region. Since the Walser settled in the valley between 1180 and 1313, life has been marked by the hard work of subsistence agriculture. People used what they could grow, breed, and harvest themselves.

Common in the region, *Pizokel* is a humble, nutritious entree made from flour, milk, and eggs—a type of fresh pasta not unlike spaetzle. There is no absolute pizokel recipe, because there are as many variants as there are grandmothers in the valley. The dough for pizokel could include potatoes, quark, or . . . even pork liver. This tends to be a versatile dish; the most common variation is baked with bacon, onions, and cheese. This variation, from the cooks at the Hotel Wynegg, one of the most traditional hotels in the region, is light and easy to re-create at home.

Note: The pizokel dough can be made and shaped a day ahead. Grate the dough (yes, with a grater) onto a baking sheet lightly dusted with semolina flour, then refrigerate until ready to use, or freeze for 4 hours before transferring to a ziptop bag. These will keep frozen for up to 2 months.

Bring a large pot of water to a boil over high heat, add a generous amount of salt, turn the heat to medium, and cover; you want the water to just simmer throughout the cooking process.

In a large bowl, combine the flour, milk, quark, eggs, 1 teaspoon salt, ½ teaspoon pepper, and nutmeg. Using a whisk at first, followed by a spatula, work the mixture thoroughly until the ingredients are well combined. (You can also make the dough in a stand mixer fitted with the paddle attachment.) The dough should be just pliable enough to pass through the holes in a spaetzle maker.

Work the dough quickly through the spaetzle maker! (If you don't have a spaetzle maker, the traditional—and dextrous—way of making the pizokel is, working in batches, place a small amount of dough on a wet wooden chopping board and scrape the dough flat on the board with a flexible pastry scraper, forming strands that then careen off the edge of the board into the simmering water.) Give the strands a good stir and, when the pizokel float to the surface, less than 3 minutes after the water returns to a simmer, remove those noodles with a skimmer into a colander, then give them a good rinse under cold water to stop them from overcooking. Repeat until all of the pizokel have been shaped and cooked.

In a large frying pan over medium-high heat, warm the grapeseed oil. Add the onion and sauté until it starts to color, 5 minutes. Add the grapes and walnuts and stir well. Pour in the balsamic vinegar and deglaze the pan, stirring up the browned bits with a wooden spoon. Stir in the honey, followed by the

continued

vegetable broth, then toss in 2 table-spoons of the butter and simmer until the sauce becomes creamy, 2 to 3 minutes.

In a second frying pan over medium-high heat, melt the remaining 2 tablespoons butter. Add the pizokel and fry until golden brown, 1 to 2 minutes.

Stir the pizokel into the walnut-grape sauce, turn the heat to medium, add the Taleggio cubes, and stir for a min-ute or two to make sure the cheese is fully starting to melt. Stir in the minced parsley and season with salt and pepper.

Divide the pizokel and sauce among shallow bowls and garnish with the parsley leaves. Serve immediately.

Ricola Ice Cream

■■■■ MEDIUM
MAKES 1 QUART (950ML)

YOU WILL NEED

Mortar and pestle

Digital instant-read thermometer

Large bowl half-filled with ice, water, and salt, for an ice bath

Ice-cream maker or stand mixer (preferably a KitchenAid) fitted with the ice-cream maker attachment

1-quart (950ml) airtight container with a lid

8 Ricola Mountain Herb lozenges

2 teaspoons confectioners' sugar

1½ cups (360ml) heavy cream

¾ cup (175ml) whole milk

½ cup (120ml) evaporated milk

¼ cup (60ml) light corn syrup

⅓ cup (65g) granulated sugar

½ cup (50g) milk powder

3 egg yolks

Fresh mint leaves for garnish

The closest some people ever get to the Alps is the iconic TV commercial for Ricola cough drops—the one that shows two mountain villagers planted in front of the Matterhorn, one calling out "Ri-co-la," while the other blows on a massive alphorn.

Though Ricola is a Swiss brand and the herbs in the drops are actually from the Valais and Ticino cantons, I admit the idea for this ice-cream flavor didn't come to me while driving through the Swiss Alps, but rather while I was waiting for a prescription at a drugstore back in Montreal. I promise you this ice cream is more than simply soothing for your sore throat—it's now one of my favorites to make in the summer: creamy, but herbal and refreshing. Ricola lists its herbs as sage, linden, mallow, thyme, hyssop, elder, and peppermint. So if you're having trouble imagining this ice cream, those are the flavors we're working with.

You can adjust the intensity of the flavor according to your preference by increasing or decreasing the number of lozenges used. Stick with the recipe for your first attempt, and if you want a stronger herbal hit for the second batch, up the ante.

Note: Even without the lozenges, this is still a delicious, creamy ice cream.

Using a mortar and pestle, crush 5 of the lozenges with the confectioners' sugar until finely ground.

In a heavy saucepan, combine the cream, whole milk, evaporated milk, corn syrup, granulated sugar, milk powder, crushed lozenges, and egg yolks and mix well. Set over medium heat and cook, stirring constantly with a wooden spoon or spatula—including into the corners of the pan—until the mixture reaches 180°F (82°C). A thermometer is key here, because the egg will start to curdle if you go beyond that temperature.

Immediately pour the custard mixture through a fine-mesh sieve into a metal bowl sitting in an ice bath. Let cool, stirring occasionally, for 10 to 15 minutes. Cover with plastic wrap and refrigerate overnight.

The following day, crush the remaining 3 lozenges into very small pieces using the mortar and pestle.

Pour the custard into your ice-cream maker and begin the churning process, according to manufacturer's instructions. At the 15-minute mark, add the crushed lozenges to the ice cream. Continue to churn until the ice cream has the consistency of soft-serve, between 25 and 30 minutes. (I found that 26 minutes was ideal in my machine.) Transfer the ice cream to an airtight container and freeze for at least 3 hours or up to 6 weeks.

When ready to serve, spoon into individual bowls and garnish with fresh mint.

FRANCE

The French Alps: An Overview

Of all the Alpine regions I have explored, the French Alps shine the most for me in the summertime. Those of you who have been taking annual ski trips to France for the past twenty years might be thinking, *Meredith, are you crazy*? Yes, yes I am.

It is true that France holds in its skinny couture pockets some of the most glamorous ski resorts in all of the Alps: Val d'Isère, Chamonix, Megève, Les Trois Vallées (including Courchevel, Val Thorens, Méribel, and Les Menuires). It's also true that skiing made its Olympic debut in the 1924 Winter Games in Chamonix. However, the first Tour de France was held in 1903. And in 1911, the famous Col du Galibier mountain climb was added to the route. Every year since then, the French Alps have been an intrinsic part of the Tour. If you want to win the race, you must perform well in the mountains, whether you are climbing Alpe d'Huez or Le Mont Ventoux, or taking the Pyrenees climbs of Col d'Aubisque and Col du Tourmalet.

The Tour adds an alluring element to summer Alpine travel that the other countries just don't have. (Yes, the Giro d'Italia is fantastic, but it feels secondary to the Tour de France in terms of notoriety.) Cycling through the Alps in the summer feels like a more authentic way to view them than even visiting some of the ski resorts. There is an actual route that anyone can follow on regular or electric bikes, along with intriguing summer chalets, restaurants, roadside vendors, and motels for pit stops (see "Route des Grandes Alpes," page 273).

During my travels in the food and wine world, I've come across the real-life Venn diagram of ex–professional cyclist and wine importer many times. The roads of the wine routes are the same ones traveled during the Tour de France, and they also pass through much of the French Alps. Craig Lewis is an American example of a cyclist turned winemaker. He spent so much time studying local maps and whizzing by vineyards, Alpine pastures, and old monasteries while racing that he developed a not-surprising interest in French and Italian wines.

In the summer, whether on cycle or on foot, there is a direct connection with the terrain that the snow obscures: the pastures teem with vibrant greens, tasty fungi, edible flowers, dairy cows, and goats. I find that my senses become completely elevated. The mountains reveal themselves fully in the summer, and I fall for the seduction every time.

Located in France's Auvergne-Rhone-Alpes region, the French Alps comprise three *départements* (territorial regions): the Haute-Savoie, the Savoie, and Isère. Unlike Italy, Switzerland, and Austria, where the Alps stretch horizontally from east to west, the French Alps are more of a vertical column reaching from the northern border of Switzerland down to the Mediterranean. This is the smallest Alpine region I've covered, but typical of the rest of France, the food and wine—including the noble liqueur of Chartreuse—more than makes up for the size.

I like to step into the French Alps on the sunny side. Just below Lake Geneva (which sits on the border of Switzerland and France) is a small area called the Portes du Soleil (literally, "doors of the sun")

Anna Barrero is a cyclist and sports scientist who hails from Spain. She has cycled the men's Tour de France route several years, running with other amateur female cyclists to promote women's stage racing (why does the Tour not have a female equivalent?). When she's not cycling, she skis in Chamonix or runs in Écrins National Park. She loves two things equally: any sight of the Matterhorn and raclette (see page 240). *Any* raclette will do.

SNAPSHOT

that encompasses Châtel, Avoriaz, Abondance, La Chapelle d'Abondance, Morzine, and other nearby communes of the Haute-Savoie. Unfamiliar to many people outside of France, the mountain culture here is rich, esoteric, and so, so tasty.

One spring, I found a diamond in the rough of a hotel and restaurant called Les Cornettes, and it was here that Savoyard cooking really crystalized for me. Les Cornettes was established in 1894 and is now run by fifth-generation owner and chef Jérémy Trincaz with support of his whole *famille* (family). Typical of the people who run mountain hotels, no one ever seems to sleep. Upon my arrival, Jérémy walked me around the property; it featured a working smokehouse and a back barn that doubled as a wooden puppet theater (which was currently loaded with hanging hams) and a family museum in the basement that included ancient Savoyard cooking tools, about 300 antique coffee grinders, taxidermied animals (and pets), and . . . wax figures, created by a guest who works at the Musée Grévin in Paris, of every family member. Just about the time I started looking for the nearest exit, I was whisked up to the kitchen.

In the comforting *auberge* (hostel) kitchen, sitting in the center of baroque French ovens was a stockpot the size of a Smart car, simmering with beef bones. I sat at a wooden table nearby and the dishes came out: terrines of quail and foie gras, a fondue Savoyarde with morel mushrooms, tartiflette (see page 292), a *croziflette* (like a tartiflette but with *crozets* pasta instead of potatoes), kidneys flambéed with Cognac, frogs' legs from nearby Dombes, and a Berthoud (see page 279), which is cheese made from the town's namesake cattle breed Abondance, baked in the oven with garlic and white wine. For dessert, I had sorbet with Poire (Pear) William and a slice of an impressively gigantic *omelette Norvégienne* (page 280). I have always felt that the heart of France is in its kitchens, and that warmth, generosity, and *L'art Culinaire Français* is definitely still alive at Les Cornettes.

Only 40 minutes south of the Portes du Soleil is the town of Morzine, which has its own mountain resort, the village of Avoriaz, a fully skiable, no-car village that was built up by former downhill champion and sportswear namesake/guru Jean Vuarnet. Back in the 1970s, Avoriaz was considered the Saint Tropez *de neiges* ("of the snow") because of its discotheques and restaurants. Along with the resorts of Flaine and Les Arcs (in Bourg Saint Maurice), Avoriaz is worth the trek if only to see its striking brutalist architecture. In France in the 1960s and 1970s, there was a push to make skiing and summer mountain activities more democratic. Like Swiss French architect and urban planner Le Corbusier's *plan voisin*, the idea was to build concrete hotels, homes, and ski stations where form follows function and the space accommodates the masses. I agree that the mountains are for everyone. Or at least they should be. With these philosophies in pocket, visiting these locations—especially Flaine, where you'll find works by famed architect Marcel Breuer—is a different sort of Alpine exercise. For me, there's a perfect harmony between the bold structures and the dramatic Alpine landscape.

THE FRENCH ALPINE CHEESE HIT LIST

This list is nowhere near exhaustive, but here are some must-try cheeses of the French Alps, from cow's-milk to blue to goat's-milk.

Abondance • Beaufort • Comté • Mont d'Or • Raclette • Tomme de Savoie • Reblochon • Bleu de Bonneval • Bleu du Vercors-Sassenage • Persillé des Aravis • Persillé de Tignes

Miscellaneous regional goat cheeses: There are many small goat farms and independent cheesemakers throughout the French Alps. If you see any of the cheeses for sale, I recommend you buy it, as it's an aromatic and direct, fresh sample of the terroir. Stéphane Pliot from Chèvrerie de la Closette is a great example of an independent cheesemaker to look out for.

Only an hour to the southeast, past the pretty town of Servoz (I recommend staying here), is the definitely-not-brutalist village of Chamonix. Now called Chamonix-Mont-Blanc (even the new name says "in case you are confused, we're at the pinnacle"), this is truly the best mountain resort for skiers in France. If you're a ropes, *piolet* (ice ax), and crampons kind of person, you have the mostly accessible Mont-Blanc massif at your feet. If you're a heli-ski kind of person, this Alpine world is your oyster. If you're a train traveler, bookshop nerd, and good eater (here's where I raise my hand), you're also in luck.

I filled my days in Chamonix with trips on the Montenvers railway (which takes you to 1,913 meters [6,276 feet], where you can sleep at the refuge), take a (scary) trip on the cable car to the top of the Aiguille du Midi, and ski down the Tête de Balme to indulge in the feat that is a *Farçon savoyard* (see page 296) at the on-piste restaurant Ecuries de Charamillon.

Chamonix is deeply steeped in Alpine history. This is where nineteenth-century travel agent Thomas Cook brought his first Alpine travelers (by mule and train). You can see old photographs of these days—ladies in long skirts and coats heaving ladders up mountains to pass from Chamonix to Switzerland—at either the Alpine Museum or the souvenir shops that line the village's main vein. An important outpost for British explorers, Chamonix is also where mountaineer Edward Whymper (the first to ascend the Matterhorn) is buried.

If you are the sort to make pilgrimages to restaurants rather than mountains, your two musts are Flocons de Sel in Megève and La Bouitte farther south in Saint-Martin-de-Belleville. These are serious restaurants, top among all in France, that use the best local Alpine ingredients and cook with traditional French technique.

Passing south through the Savoie, past the Olympic city of Albertville and the great ski area of Les Trois Vallées, is the region of Isère. On its doorstep is the most mythical of mountains (at least in the food and wine world): Chartreuse. It is here you'll find the Carthusian monks, who have been respecting a vow of silence since the first recluse, Saint Bruno, founded the monastery in 1084. Chartreuse, the noble liqueur, is an elixir made with 130 herbs, plants, and flowers; the surrounding hills match its vibrant green. I think it tastes of peppermint, arnica, citrus, génépy, and angelica—in other words, it tastes like the Alps. I bought bottles of both green and yellow Chartreuse and stowed them away in the car for further use (see Chartreuse Soufflé, page 320).

Past Chambéry to the west (and another noble liquor, Vermouth de Chambéry), there are *so, so* many great restaurants and cafés in the mountains down toward the city of Grenoble. Grenoble is a quintessential Alpine city. If you put yourself in the center of town and look up, you will see the Téléphérique de Grenoble-Bastille (the Grenoble cable car) that is affectionately called *les bulles*, or "the bubbles," and takes you from the city to the Vercors mountains. If you look west, you will see the mountains of Chartreuse. To the north is Mont-Blanc and to the east, Mongenèvre and the Via Lattea of Piedmont. In the city, the food is heavily influenced by Lyonnaise cookery—think gingham tablecloths, crayfish and *poulet* (chicken), deep cuts of charcuterie and terrine, and creamy vegetable soups. Grenoble is a melting pot for all sorts of cuisines and has a big student population (many of whom work in Alpine-based studies such as engineering and geology). It also stakes claim to the best wine shop in the Alps, the aptly named Le Vin des Alpes, where the wine merchant, Eric Esnault, will school you on the best winemakers of the Savoie (and beyond) and, of course, what to pair with your tartiflette (see page 292).

It is not far from Grenoble to Alpe d'Huez, where I spent a couple of days before the Tour de France raced through (on the same day that France won the World Cup—a double French whammy!). The roads had been lined with Dutch, German, and Belgian fans, who camp out for weeks, grilling outside of their campers and waiting for the racers to whiz by. The action happens on the journey up the mountain, both in the race and off the course on the side of the road along the twenty-one turns to the top. At the peak, it is quite desolate, rugged, and still relatively wild, despite there being a ski station there.

My journey through the French Alps reminded me how singular French cooking is. The Alpine regions have their own dishes and traditions, but you feel the national embrace of a French *maman* (mother) no matter where in France you travel. I've tried to capture that feeling in the recipes that follow, including a mix of both the eclectic and the classics.

ALPINE COOKING

ROUTE DES GRANDES ALPES

The Touring Club of France developed this summer cycling route in 1909. It runs from north to south through the main Haute-Savoie and Savoie mountain ranges and is like a Tour de France for civilians. Fast-forward more than a century, and the route has changed very little, except it now has charging stations for electric bikes every 40 kilometers (25 miles). By following this route, you can taste the best of the French Alps at local stops along the way. Here is a brief synopsis of the route with highlighted stages.

The first link of the Alps between Lake Geneva and the Mont-Blanc massif, here the Route des Grandes Alpes crosses the Chablais mountain chain with a glimpse of the famous Dents du Midi ("teeth of the south").

After passing the Col de la Colombière, the route plunges into the Aravais and the famous villages of Le Grand-Bornand and La Clusaz (land of chef Marc Veyrat; see snapshot on page 318) and, of course, the Col des Aravis, a mountain pass that has starred in forty Tour de France races.

Next is the Beaufortain. I would be satisfied to enjoy the namesake floral cheese, Beaufort, and a local Savoyard wine, but you might have another plan, like running the Ultra Tour du Beaufortain, a nonstop trail-running race of 105 kilometers (65 miles) and more than 6,400 meters (2,100 feet) of elevation. The surface of Beaufortain is craggy, and from a food, wine, and village standpoint, there isn't a whole lot going on. But for adventure cyclists and trail runners, it seemingly has everything.

La Plagne, Les Arcs, Tignes, Val d'Isère, and Courchevel are all in the Tarentaise Valley, which for cyclists is relatively calm compared to the final Maurienne Valley, known for the summits of Croix de Fer, Col du Galibier, and the Col du Madeleine Mont-Cenis. The route then passes through Écrins National Park in the Briançon region before crossing the Montgenèvre Pass into Via Lattea and Italy. For my purposes, the Alps tour ends here, but for cyclists, the route continues all the way to Nice and the Côte d'Azur in the South of France.

CHEESEMAKING IN THE ALPAGE DU MOUET

The quintessential warm-weather Alpine outing is a hike to the local dairy, or, in the case of France, the *alpage*. Transhumance—nomadic and seasonal movement of livestock from one pasture to another—is a thread running throughout the Alps, and ringing cowbells signal spring and summer.

The Alpage du Mouet, just north of Châtel, is home to Abondance cattle. These girls munch on grass at high altitude and are well-suited for cheesemaking, providing us with Reblochon, Abondance, Tome des Bauges and Beaufort, Tomme de Savoie, and Emmental de Savoie. I arrived at 5 a.m. and the milking was already complete and the cheesemaking had begun. As the sun rose, the cows grazed, the milk was churned, and the massive pucks of cheese rested in the cellar. By 8 a.m., with the cheesemakers' work already behind them, we were enjoying Abondance omelettes and coffee.

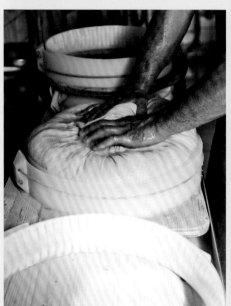

Abondance Salad

SALADE D'ABONDANCE

■■■■ MEDIUM
SERVES 1

YOU WILL NEED

Small ramekin or clay dish for the Berthoud (the kind you see in tapas bars)

Handful of mixed lettuce leaves and greens (arugula or lamb's lettuce work well)

1 teaspoon extra-virgin olive oil

1 teaspoon apple cider vinegar

Fine sea salt and freshly ground black pepper

2 slices cured ham

2 slices best-quality cooked ham

4 slices cured beef

1 slice smoked duck breast

2-ounce (60g) puck fresh goat cheese

2 tablespoons Pickled Mushrooms (page 279)

Berthoud (page 279), hot, for serving

Reblochon Baked Potato (page 279) for serving

CHEESEMAKER STÉPHANE PLIOT WITH HIS GOATS

If you weren't already convinced that the Savoyards (or *Savoisiens*) are hardcore, let me tell you about this "salad" you'll find all over the Abondance Valley and the Chablais region. Like any good salad, the ingredients should be local. In this case, it's homemade charcuterie, a baked potato, pickled mushrooms, and a handful of lettuce leaves, which justify the "salad" in the name, or perhaps to ease digestion of the accompanying Berthoud, a mini fondue made with Abondance cheese (a cheese so good, you will never look at baked Brie again) and vin de Savoie.

Shortly after crossing into France from Switzerland, I landed at Les Cornettes, a roadside hotel in La Chapelle d'Abondance, and was immediately served one of these plates with a glass of Mondeuse, an Alpine red wine varietal.

The serving size is for one person, which calls attention to the abundance of the *Abondance*. Don't be afraid to have friends over and make an Abondance platter, multiplying quantities accordingly.

Notes: The pickled mushrooms need 3 months to ferment to perfection— make them in the fall in anticipation of a winter salad.

I love the goat cheeses that Stéphane Pliot makes in the nearby Alps of Thônes but you should choose your own favorite little tower of fresh goat cheese. Abondance may prove hard to source. Ask your cheesemonger to substitute any other nutty Alpine cheese that melts well.

In the photograph of this salad, which is from Les Cornettes, you'll note a Reblochon baked potato, a breadstick, a nasturtium flower, and a cherry tomato—all are possible, but not necessary.

When you have all the components at hand, toss the salad greens with the olive oil and vinegar and season with salt and pepper. Arrange the greens on a large plate alongside the cured ham, cooked ham, beef, duck, goat cheese, pickled mushrooms, hot Berthoud, and baked potato.

Don't worry if you can't finish your plate; leftovers will keep in an airtight container in the refrigerator, for up to 1 week.

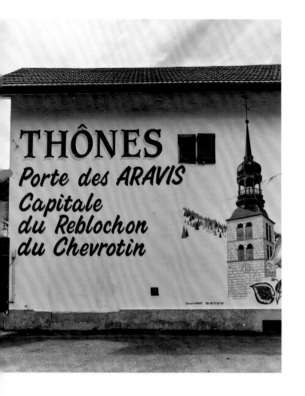

Pickled Mushrooms

MAKES TWO 1-QUART
(950ML) JARS

1 quart (950ml) white vinegar

½ cup (100g) sugar

1 bunch (30g) fresh tarragon

1 tablespoon black peppercorns

2½ pounds (1.1kg) fresh
chanterelles, trimmed

A French Alpine pantry without a stash of pickled mushrooms is no Alpine pantry indeed.

In a large saucepan over high heat, bring the vinegar to a boil. Stir in the sugar, tarragon, and peppercorns; turn the heat to medium; and simmer until the sugar has dissolved, about 2 minutes. Remove from the heat and divide equally among two 1-quart (950ml) jars, letting the vinegar cool, and infuse for 24 hours.

The next day, bring a large pot of water to a boil. Brush and rinse the chanterelles thoroughly, drop them into the boiling water, and blanch for 30 seconds. Drain and set aside on paper towels.

Divide the chanterelles between the jars of aromatic vinegar, then let them infuse for 3 months in a cool, dark place before serving. The mushrooms will keep for up to 1 year.

Berthoud

MAKES 1 SMALL PUCK

4 ounces (115g) Abondance
cheese or other nutty Alpine
cheese, thinly shaved

1 garlic clove, minced

1 tablespoon Madeira

1 tablespoon dry white
Savoie wine

¼ teaspoon freshly
ground black pepper

When served as a stand-alone dish, Berthoud is traditionally accompanied by boiled potatoes in their skins. Serve with a crisp Savoie white, like a Crépy or a Ripaille.

Preheat the oven to 350°F (175°C).

In a medium bowl, stir together the cheese, garlic, Madeira, wine, and pepper.

Transfer to a small ramekin, place on a baking sheet, and bake for 10 to 12 minutes, until browned around the edges. Let cool for 2 minutes before serving.

Reblochon Baked Potato

MAKES 1 POTATO

1 russet potato, scrubbed

¼ cup (40g) diced Reblochon
cheese

½ green onion, white and
green parts, finely chopped

Kosher salt and freshly
ground black pepper

Grating of nutmeg

The only way a baked potato could get any better is to replace the usual cheddar cheese with a tasty Reblochon.

Bring a pot of heavily salted water to a boil over high heat. Add the potato, turn the heat to medium, and simmer until the potato is tender when poked with a fork, 15 to 20 minutes. Set aside.

Preheat the oven to 350°F (175°C).

When the potato is cool enough to handle, slice open the top lengthwise and scoop out the pulp with a spoon, keeping the skin intact.

In a bowl, combine the potato pulp with the cheese and green onion and season with salt, pepper, and nutmeg. Transfer the enriched potato pulp back into its jacket, and bake until the cheese is fully melted and starting to brown, 7 to 10 minutes. Serve piping hot!

Norwegian Omelet

OMELETTE NORVÉGIENNE

■■■■ MEDIUM (IF YOU BUY
THE ICE CREAM), DIFFICULT
(IF YOU DON'T)

SERVES 4 TO 6

YOU WILL NEED

Offset spatula

**Piping bag fitted with
a ¼-inch (6mm) plain tip**

**Piping bag fitted with a ½-inch
(12mm) closed-star tip**

1 Savoie Cake (page 295), baked
in a 9 by 13-inch (23 by 33cm)
baking pan

Grand Marnier to moisten the cake
base, plus 6 tablespoons (90ml)

¾ cup (175ml) strawberry sorbet,
softened

¾ cup (175ml) blackcurrant
sorbet, softened

¾ cup (175ml) raspberry sorbet,
softened

1 cup (240ml) vanilla ice cream,
softened

1½ cups (355ml) egg whites,
at room temperature

1¾ cups (350g) sugar

In Savoie, everything is about as light as André the Giant (who was also French!), so this dessert—a booze-flaming layered ice-cream cake—should be likewise. But why am I including it in an Alpine book? Let's dissect. I made this cake with Jérémy Trincaz (see page 268), whose restaurant, Les Cornettes, is surrounded by the ski *domaine* known as the Portes du Soleil ("doors of the sun") because of its annual sunshine hours. In the summer, it's a popular biking and hiking area, and it can get *hot*. So, what better treat after your Alpine hike than a pound of ice cream wrapped in a flaming meringue?

The base is a Savoie cake, which is spongy and light and works perfectly with ice cream because it has a bit of chew but is somewhat dense, so it doesn't get soggy quickly. Why the ice cream? Because we're in the French Alpine heartland here, with the most famous Abondance cows and their dairy. American friends will recognize this as a more bombastic version of their baked Alaska.

Notes: The omelet pictured on page 283 serves 15 to 20 people. My version is much smaller, but no less delightful!

The texture and temperature of the sorbets and ice cream must be soft enough to spread into layers with an offset spatula. The ideal time for spreading is after homemade sorbet is finished churning in the ice-cream maker, but before freezing. If you buy sorbets to make this dessert, simply leave them out at room temperature to soften for 10 to 20 minutes, then stir each well to achieve a homogenous and spreadable consistency. You may find it easier to stagger the thaw of each sorbet. Apply the first layer of sorbet, then freeze until it sets a little, 5 to 10 minutes, then apply the next layer of softened sorbet.

This recipe calls for a lot of egg whites; but do not be tempted to use liquid egg whites in a carton from your local grocery store—they won't whip up as well as the whites from fresh.

Line a baking sheet with parchment paper.

Place the Savoie cake base on a cutting board and cut into a 4 by 8-inch (10 by 20cm) rectangle. Transfer to the prepared baking sheet and splash some Grand Marnier all over it to moisten slightly.

Using an offset spatula, spread the strawberry sorbet over the cake base. Next, spread on the blackcurrant sorbet, followed by the raspberry sorbet. Spread the vanilla ice cream on top of the raspberry sorbet as well as around all of the sides, mounding a little more vanilla ice cream on top to create a dome down the length of the cake. Use your spatula to finesse the final oblong shape—it should look like a rugby ball. Freeze for 4 hours.

In a stand mixer fitted with the whisk attachment, begin whipping the egg whites on medium-low speed until they are foamy. Increase the speed to medium and very gradually add 1 cup (200g) of the sugar, in a very slow-running stream, until the whites begin to form soft peaks, about 2 minutes. Increase the speed to medium-high, and, still working gradually, add another ½ cup (100g) sugar, whisking until the whites

continued

ALPINE COOKING

CHEF JÉRÉMY TRINCAZ (LEFT) AT LES CORNETTES, THE NIGHT FRANCE WON THE WORLD CUP.

hold firm peaks and look glossy and smooth, and their texture is silky, another 1 to 2 minutes. Finish at high speed for 1 minute longer to "tighten" the meringue.

Transfer half of the meringue to a bowl. Fill a piping bag fitted with a plain tip with two-thirds of the remaining meringue, and fill a piping bag fitted with a closed-star tip with the remaining third.

Preheat the oven to 475°F (245°C). Line an ovenproof platter with parchment paper.

Transfer the frozen cake to the prepared platter. Using an offset spatula, spread the meringue left in the bowl evenly all over the frozen layers of ice cream.

Using the bag with the star tip, pipe little swirls of meringue all around the base of the cake.

To finish, use the bag with the plain tip to pipe little "mountains" of meringue all over the rest of the sides and the top of the cake: pipe a mini dome, then pull up on the bag to create its peak and repeat!

Sprinkle the meringue all over with the remaining ¼ cup (50g) sugar. Place in the hot oven and bake just until the peaks take on a golden brown hue, 6 to 8 minutes.

Before serving, gently heat the remaining 6 tablespoons (90ml) Grand Marnier in a small saucepan until warm.

Bring the cake to the table. Transfer the Grand Marnier to a ladle, then set the alcohol alight with a match (watch your face!) and pour the flames all over the cake. When the fire has burned out, cut into slices and serve.

Crayfish with Tarragon Mayonnaise

ÉCREVISSES À LA MAYONNAISE

■■■ EASY

SERVES 4

CRAYFISH

¼ cup (50g) sugar

¼ cup (65g) fine sea salt

5 fresh tarragon stems (leaves reserved for the mayonnaise)

32 live freshwater crayfish

TARRAGON MAYONNAISE

1 egg yolk

1 teaspoon Dijon mustard

2 teaspoons brown sugar

¼ cup (60ml) freshly squeezed lemon juice

Fine sea salt

1¼ cups (300ml) grapeseed oil

Leaves from 5 tarragon stems, minced

1 cup (50g) wood sorrel

After wining and dining all over the mountains, I wanted to get my hands on some picnic ideas and recipes for the kind of food you could enjoy by an Alpine lake in the summer. Chef-owner Jérôme Bigot at Kamouraska, a restaurant and natural-wine cave in *the* Alpine lake town of Annecy, answered my prayers with this cold-cooked crayfish from Lac d'Annecy that you drag through a tarragon mayonnaise before topping with freshly foraged wood sorrel (known as the poetic *oseille des bois* in French). As Escoffier would surely agree, this tarragon-mayo recipe works with whitefish as well as shellfish.

To cook the crayfish: Fill a large pot with 6½ quarts (6L) water and bring to a boil over high heat. Set up a large bowl of ice water.

Stir the sugar, salt, and tarragon stems into the boiling water. Add the crayfish and cover the pot. As soon as the crayfish are submerged, start your timer: cook the crayfish for 35 seconds. Immediately drain and plunge the crayfish into the ice water.

When the crayfish are cool enough to handle, twist and pull on the middle section to separate the tail from the head and pincers. Remove the intestines and rinse off. Peel the top part of the shell off the tail, leaving some tail exposed, but most of the tail still tucked in. Set aside

in the refrigerator. (The pincers can be reserved for another use or discarded; they tend to be too small and finicky to crack into.)

To make the mayonnaise: In a medium bowl, whisk together the egg yolk, mustard, brown sugar, lemon juice, and 1 teaspoon salt. While whisking continuously, pour in the grapeseed oil, in a thin stream, continuing to whisk until an emulsion forms and all of the oil has been incorporated. Stir in the minced tarragon, and adjust the seasoning.

Transfer the mayonnaise to a dipping bowl and the crayfish to a platter (with a bowl for discarded bits). Top with or serve alongside the wood sorrel. Don't forget to give sucking on the crayfish heads a try!

OTHER SAVOIE TREATS

A bottle of Côtillon des Dames from Jean-Yves Péron or maybe a beer from La Brasserie des Voirons (the Spéciale Belluard beer is macerated on the same lees as Domaine Belluard, a Savoie wine producer

A small puck of chèvre made by Stéphane Pliot at Chèvrerie de la Closette in Thônes

A disk of le Tamié cheese, from the Abbaye de Tamié, not far from Lac d'Annecy

Fresh walnuts picked from trees along the way

A fresh loaf of bread from Pan & Gatô, a wonderful boulangerie-patisserie in Annecy

A *patte d'ours* ("bear paw")—puff pastry shaped like a paw, filled with crème pâtissière

Cabbage Tart with Smoked Whitefish

TARTE AU CHOU ET AU FÉRA FUMÉ

■■■■ DIFFICULT

SERVES 2

YOU WILL NEED

4¾-inch (12cm) tart pan with removable bottom or a tart ring

Baking weights or beans

Offset spatula

Kitchen blowtorch

5 ounces (150g) puff pastry dough, cold

SMOKED FISH CREAM

1 cup (240ml) water

9 ounces (250g) smoked fera or whitefish, finely diced

⅓ cup (40g) minced lemongrass

¼ cup (30g) minced fresh ginger

½ cup (50g) finely chopped green onions, white and green parts

½ cup (110g) unsalted butter

¼ cup (40g) minced shallots

Juice of 1 lemon

Fine sea salt and freshly ground black pepper

2 ounces (55g) salmon or trout roe

1 small savoy cabbage

⅓ cup (60g) kosher salt

¼ cup (60ml) extra-virgin olive oil

Freshly ground black pepper

Two 9-ounce (250g) fera or whitefish fillets, skin and bones removed

BEURRE BLANC SAUCE

1 shallot, minced

⅓ cup (80ml) white wine

2 tablespoons white wine vinegar

¼ cup (60ml) heavy cream

4 tablespoons (55g) unsalted butter, cubed

2 ounces (55g) salmon or trout roe

This recipe is from Laurent Petit, chef at Michelin-starred restaurant Le Clos des Sens. Translated, the name of the restaurant evokes a walled garden that excites the senses. And indeed, next to the restaurant is a wild herb garden with horsemint, Szechuan peppers, lemongrass, arugula, fennel, and much more. Petit prides himself on having a vegetable-forward menu that reads like poetry and features local fish, an ode to three lakes of the Savoie: Léman, Annecy, and Bourget. Le Clos des Sens also has *the best* natural Alpine wine list—period. And Thomas Lorival, the restaurant's in-house wine guy, is full of information about the Alps, if you need help navigating the Alpine Arch (see page 8). For this tart, he suggests a bottle of Crépy.

This delicate dish is for lovers and is meant to be shared between two people.

Note: Fera is a type of Alpine fish that has thrived in the area's great lakes, but is difficult to find outside of its native habitat. Substitute any white-fleshed freshwater fish that's been gently smoked. Alternatively, you could also make this tart with salmon or trout.

Preheat the oven to 425°F (220°C).

Roll out the puff pastry dough to a thickness of ¼ inch (6mm). Cut out a 6-inch (15cm) circle. Lay the pastry in a tart pan, trim the edges, and prick the dough evenly with a fork. Cover the circle with parchment paper and baking weights and blind bake for 10 minutes. Remove the parchment and weights and continue to bake until golden, another 5 to 7 minutes. Set aside. Turn the oven temperature to 140°F (60°C) or your lowest setting.

To make the smoked fish cream: In a medium saucepan over high heat, combine the water, smoked fish, lemongrass, and ginger and bring to boil. Remove from the heat, skim off any impurities, and stir in the green onions. Cover and let infuse for 30 minutes, then strain through a fine-mesh sieve.

In a saucepan over medium heat, melt the butter. Stir in the shallots, lemon juice, and strained fish stock. Turn the heat to medium-low and simmer, reducing the liquid slowly until the mixture thickens and coats the back of a spoon, about 8 minutes. Season with just a pinch of sea salt and some pepper and then mix to emulsify. Stir in the fish roe and remove from the heat.

Tear off the cabbage leaves one by one down to the heart. Bring 4 quarts (3.8L) water to a boil, then stir in the kosher salt. Fill a large bowl with water and ice cubes.

Working in batches, blanch the cabbage leaves for a minute or two, until softened, then plunge them into the ice water. Pat the leaves dry between two clean kitchen towels. Lay the leaves out on a tray and brush with the olive oil and season with pepper.

continued

Using a very sharp knife, cut the fish (on the diagonal) into ¾-inch (2cm) wide slices. You should have approximately fifteen slices. Using an offset spatula, spread the fish cream evenly inside the bottom of the cooked puff pastry shell.

Starting with the smallest cabbage leaves, begin layering the leaves tightly inside the shell, slowly building a dome of cabbage. Use the offset spatula and your hands to make sure the leaves stay tucked inside the pastry shell.

Layer the fish slices over the cabbage dome until it's completely covered, making sure to tuck the bottom slices into the pastry case. Wrap the tart tightly in plastic. Lay the wrapped tart on a small baking sheet and bake until gently heated through, about 1 hour.

To make the beurre blanc sauce: Shortly before the tart is heated through, in a small saucepan over medium heat, combine the shallot, wine, and vinegar and cook, stirring, until the wine and vinegar have reduced to about 2 tablespoons, about 10 minutes. Stir in the cream and bring to a vigorous simmer, then add the butter, whisking well until all of the butter has melted and the sauce is emulsified.

Remove the tart from the oven and carefully remove the plastic wrap. Cut into two halves, then color the exposed cabbage with a blowtorch.

Transfer the tart halves to two plates. Stir the fish roe into the beurre blanc, then spoon over the top of each tart. Serve immediately.

LAURENT PETIT (RIGHT) AND TEAM DURING SERVICE

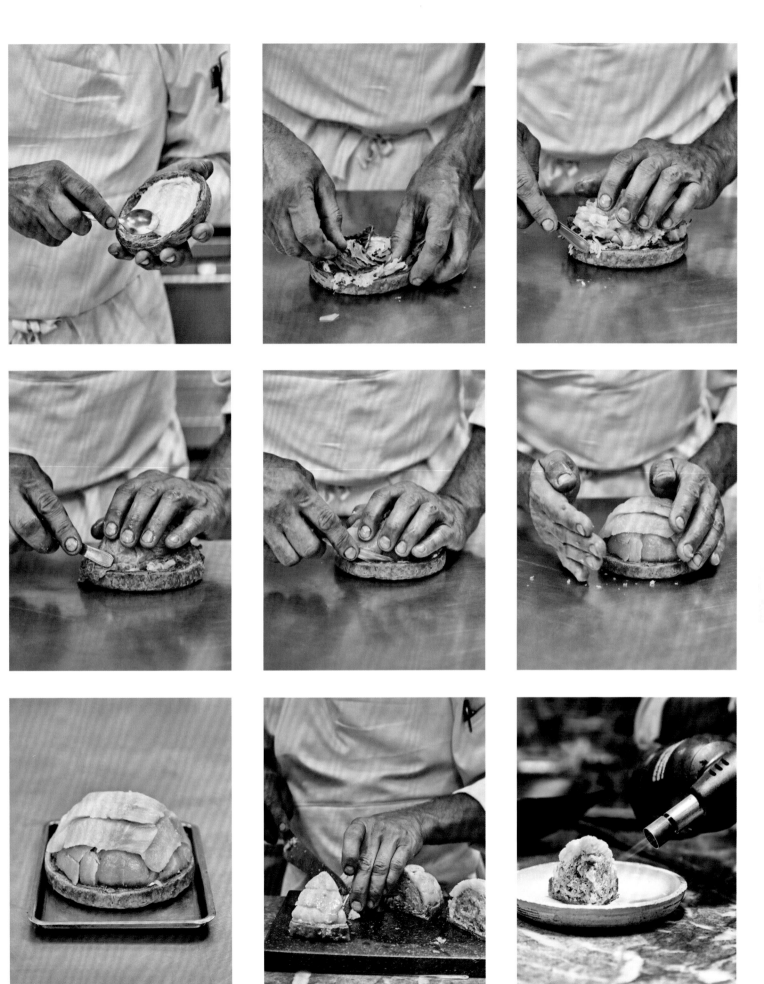

Cured Beef with Génépy

BŒUF SÉCHÉ AU GÉNÉPI

MEDIUM

SERVES 2 OVER A 2-DAY HIKE

1 cup (180g) kosher salt

1 cup (200g) sugar

1 pound (450g) eye round of beef or loin, trimmed of fat and silverskin

⅔ cup (160ml) génépy

20 juniper berries, crushed

1 teaspoon freshly ground black pepper

30 fresh blackcurrants

The idea for this recipe of beef cured with génépy, juniper berries, and fresh cassis or currants was to make a tastier version of jerky that you can wrap up in your knapsack and eat while climbing a mountain. Génépy, the iconic wormwood liqueur of the French Alps, is the curing liquid, of course. Jérôme Bigot (see page 284) and I played with the curing time to get it just right.

Note: The meat takes 5 days to cure. Use a spice grinder to grind the juniper berries and black peppercorns coarsely.

In a medium jar, combine the salt and sugar and shake well to mix.

Using your hands, liberally rub ½ cup (95g) of the salt-sugar mixture all over the meat. Moisten two sheets of paper towel with the génépy and wrap it around the meat. Roll tightly in plastic wrap, place on a small plate or tray, and refrigerate for 48 hours.

After 48 hours, remove and discard the plastic and paper towel. Rub another ½ cup (95g) of the salt-sugar mixture over the meat, then wrap in paper towels (without the génépy), followed by plastic. Return to the fridge. Repeat every 24 hours, changing to fresh paper towels and plastic daily, another two times, for a total curing period of 5 days.

If it looks like there's an excess of salt-sugar still coating the meat, rinse it off under cold water, then pat completely dry with a clean kitchen towel. (Because this is not a long curing process, the finished product, when not in your backpack, will keep in an airtight container, in the refrigerator, for up to 1 week.)

When you're ready to eat, cut the beef into very thin slices (preferably with an Opinel pocket knife). Sprinkle with the crushed juniper berries and the pepper. Serve alongside the blackcurrants.

Catherine Destivelle is France's "Rock Queen." In 1992, she became the first woman to solo climb the Eiger's north face. A mountaineer by trade, she had her first taste of climbing at the age of twelve, when she became a member of the French Alpine Club. She has been included in no less than ten documentaries about climbing and has since become a writer as well as a publisher, focusing on books for Alpinists. She has written seven books of her own about the sport.

SNAPSHOT

Tartiflette

■■■■ EASY

SERVES 4 TO 6

YOU WILL NEED

Oval baking dish that measures 13½ by 7¼ by 2½ inches (34 by 19 by 6.5cm)

8 ounces (225g) thick-sliced bacon, cut into lardons or diced

2 yellow onions, finely chopped

3 tablespoons unsalted butter

2 pounds (900g) Yukon gold potatoes, peeled and cut into medium dice

1 teaspoon fine sea salt

1 teaspoon freshly ground black pepper

1 cup (240ml) Savoie white wine, such as Apremont, Chignin-Bergeron, or Roussette de Savoie

½ cup (120ml) crème fraîche

1 wheel Reblochon cheese

1 garlic clove, smashed

Cornichons and/or Pickled Mushrooms (page 279) to serve (optional)

Baguette or other crusty bread to serve (optional)

This dish is potato gratin turned up to eleven: potatoes, crème fraîche, bacon, wine, and an entire wheel of cheese. You cannot travel through the Savoie without running into tartiflette—named after the old Savoyard word for potato, *tartifle*. *Reblochon* comes from the verb *reblocher*, which means "to milk a second time" (resulting in more cream in the milk). Only three breeds of cow produce the milk used to make AOC (*Appellation d'origine contrôlée*) Reblochon: the Abondance—you're well acquainted with these girls—the Montbéliarde, and the Tarine. All of these cows can happily navigate mountainous terrain, which is crucial in the summer when they are moved up to Alpine meadows and milked at higher altitude for the season.

Notes: Many people cook the potatoes for tartiflette in oil, but Savoie royalty and chef Marc Veyrat (see snapshot, page 318) told me to fry them in a bit of butter before baking, so who am I to argue? The guy has Reblochon running through his veins.

By definition, tartiflette can be made only with Reblochon: the type of cheese is nonnegotiable. However, because commercially importing Reblochon, a raw-milk cheese, into the United States is illegal (thanks to the FDA mandate on pasteurization), and because border agents tend to view the smuggling of stinky cheeses as nonnegotiable also, American readers can substitute a Reblochon-style tomme called Le Délice du Jura, which is available at any good cheese shop. Ask your cheesemonger for one whole tomme. Most weigh around 1 pound (450g) and are about 5½ inches (14cm) in diameter.

Preheat the oven to 400°F (200°C).

In a large sauté pan over medium-low heat, cook the bacon until it starts to render its fat and crisp slightly around the edges, about 5 minutes. Stir in the onions and cook until translucent, 5 to 7 minutes. Stir in the butter, followed by the diced potatoes.

Turn the heat to medium and continue to cook, stirring occasionally, until the potatoes begin to soften, about 5 minutes. Season with the salt and pepper and pour in the wine. Continue to cook until the wine has been absorbed, 5 to 7 minutes. Remove from the heat and stir in the crème fraîche.

Scrape any white mold off the skin of the Reblochon to reveal its saffron-orange rind. Take the cheese wheel and cut it across the center into two "full moon" halves. Then cut each moon into two half-moons.

Rub the inside of a baking dish all over with the smashed garlic. Spoon in half of the potato-bacon mixture. Top with two of the Reblochon half-moons, rind-side down. Add the rest of the potato-bacon mixture and top with the remaining cheese half-moons, rind-side up.

Bake until the cheese is melted and the potatoes are fork-tender, about 20 minutes.

Serve the tartiflette with cornichons and/or pickled mushrooms and a nice loaf of crusty bread, if desired.

Savoie Cake

GÂTEAU DE SAVOIE

MEDIUM
SERVES 6

YOU WILL NEED
9- or 10-inch (23 or 25cm) fluted tube pan, or six 1-cup (240ml) mini-Bundt or mini-fluted pans

CAKE
6 eggs, separated

¾ cup plus 2 tablespoons (175g) granulated sugar

1 teaspoon vanilla extract (optional)

Pinch of fine sea salt

1¼ cups (150g) cornstarch, sifted

½ cup (60g) confectioners' sugar

CHANTILLY CREAM
⅔ cup (160ml) heavy cream

1 tablespoon granulated sugar

2 cups (350g) wild blueberries

This is an extremely old French recipe that was a joy to discover as I drove through the Haute-Savoie region. I first spied the cake cooling on the windowsill of Les Cornettes's kitchen, where it was later used as the cake base for a Norwegian Omelet (see page 280). Next, I was able to sample it, pure and simple, at Kamouraska restaurant in Annecy, where chef-owner Jérome Bigot made it into individual mini cakes served with local blueberries (pictured on the facing page). I like this cake for its plain, airy texture, similar to a sponge cake or *Gugelhupf*; it's not too sweet, which makes it the perfect foil to whipped cream and berries, or served alongside a cheese plate. It has a chew to it, and this is why I prefer it in smaller portions, like the mini Bundt option given here.

To make the cake: Preheat the oven to 425°F (220°C). Grease and flour the cake pan(s).

Using a stand mixer fitted with the whisk attachment, on medium-high speed, whisk the egg yolks, granulated sugar, and vanilla (if using) until thickened and very pale, about 3 minutes, stopping the mixer as needed to scrape down the sides and bottom with a spatula. The mixing is done when you can lift the whisk and the batter holds a ribbon shape for about 5 seconds before "melting" back into the mixture. Transfer to a large bowl.

Clean and dry the mixer bowl—it needs to be spotless before beating the egg whites. Starting with the mixer on medium speed, whip the egg whites with the salt for 4 minutes, until soft peaks form. Turn the speed to medium-high and continue to whip another 2 minutes, or until stiff peaks form.

Place the cornstarch in a medium bowl and set beside the egg yolks and egg whites. Using a spatula, gently incorporate a large spoonful of cornstarch into the yolk-sugar mixture, then fold in a spoonful of egg whites. Repeat in this pattern, one spoonful at a time, finishing with the last of the egg whites. Transfer the batter to the prepared pan(s), filling the cavity only two-thirds of the way up.

If you are making one large cake, bake for 6 minutes, then lower the oven temperature to 275°F (135°C) and bake for an additional 25 to 30 minutes, until puffed and golden. If you are making mini cakes, bake for 4 minutes before lowering the temperature to 265°F (130°C) and baking for an additional 10 to 12 minutes. (If you are baking the cake in a 9 by 13-inch [23 by 33cm] baking sheet for the Norwegian Omelet, bake for 15 minutes.) A toothpick inserted into the center of the cake(s) should come out clean. Let the cake(s) cool slightly before unmolding onto a cooling rack. Let cool completely and then dust with the confectioners' sugar.

To make the Chantilly cream: In the stand mixer or by hand, whip the cream and granulated sugar until medium-firm peaks form, 2 to 3 minutes.

Serve the cake with the whipped cream and fresh blueberries.

Farçon Savoyard

YOU WILL NEED

Rabolire mold (aka *moule à farcement*), or a large tube pan

Ovenproof saucepan large enough to hold the mold in a water bath

1 cup (140g) raisins

2½ cups (400g) pitted prunes

1 cup (240ml) marc de Savoie

1¼ pounds (550g) smoked bacon slices

5 pounds (2.25kg) Yukon gold potatoes, peeled

4 eggs, beaten

¾ cup plus 2 tablespoons (200ml) heavy cream

1 pound (450g) lardons (slab bacon cut into matchsticks), or thick-cut bacon sliced into lardons

⅓ cup (40g) all-purpose flour

2 teaspoons freshly grated nutmeg

1 teaspoon fine sea salt

½ teaspoon freshly ground black pepper

TRAVEL HACK

To get to Les Écuries de Charamillon in the Domaine de Balme ski area, take the Tour-Charamillon *télécabine*, then switch to the chairlift to Les Autannes. At the top, enjoy the view: Switzerland is just a few hundred meters away (as the crow flies). Ski down the Le Col piste toward Charamillon and Les Écuries is there. After lunch, you can quickly ski down Les Caisets (a red run) or take the télécabine—which one you decide to do will depend on how much farçon you've had.

If you want to get medieval on someone's ass, make them this beast of a dish: a gigantic potato cake stuffed with raisins, brandy, and lardons with a "frosting" of sliced bacon—it's a (very) dramatic riff on potato gratin. Farçon is quintessentially Alpine. Which is to say, it's adapted to and from the mountain way of life. It cooks low and slow (about 5 hours at 120°C [250°F]), ensuring that cattle herders have time to move up the hillside to check on their animals without worrying about overcooking something back in the hut. Very little kitchen supervision is needed here. This also (apparently) worked well for making Sunday lunch (Savoyards had time to go to church and back). And the mold for farçon is so big, you can use it to toboggan down a snowy hillside, legs in the air, if need be. (I made this last one up, but the rest is all true.)

I found my favorite farçon in the least expected place: Les Écuries de Charamillon (see Travel Hack), an old stable that has been converted into a small restaurant just a couple of sidesteps from the Le Col de Balme downhill run in very snowy Chamonix. The kitchen is very small and rustic, which works because farçon is not difficult to make, but it takes time and the kind of grocer a French *maman* (mother) might favor. I should mention that a farçon is traditionally served with *diots de Savoie*, small pork sausage links. However, I forgo the links in favor of a small glass of génépy, the Savoie liqueur.

Notes: Marc de Savoie is brandy made from the pressed skin, pulps, seeds, and stems left over from winemaking. Substitute grappa as needed.

If you want to serve with diots de Savoie, ask your butcher for plain pork sausage and poach them in white wine.

Bring 1 cup (240ml) water to a boil.

In two separate bowls, soak the raisins and the prunes in a mix of ½ cup (120ml) boiling water and ½ cup (120ml) marc de Savoie.

Generously butter a farçon mold and line the mold with overlapping slices of smoked bacon. If you're using a mold with a tube, lay the slices starting at the base of the central post and running up the sides of the mold (don't try to line the tube). If you're using a Charlotte-type mold, line the bottom of the mold first, followed by the sides.

Grate the potatoes into a large bowl.

Drain the raisins. Add the raisins, eggs, cream, lardons, flour, nutmeg, salt, and pepper to the grated potatoes and stir until well mixed.

Drain the prunes.

Lay one-fourth of the potato mixture into the mold. Next, layer one-third of the soaked prunes over the potatoes, followed by another fourth of the potato mixture, another layer of the prunes, and so on, finishing with the potatoes. Fold the bacon slices that are lining the mold over the top of the final potato layer, closing any gaps with any remaining slices of bacon, trimmed. If you are using a mold with a cover, cover the farçon now. Alternatively, wrap the entire mold tightly in several layers of plastic wrap.

Preheat the oven to 250°F (120°C).

continued

Bring a kettle of water to a boil. Place the farçon in a large ovenproof saucepan, then place that onto the oven rack. Pour the boiling water into the saucepan to fill it at least half-way up the side of the mold. Bake for 4 to 5 hours—test the internal temperature with a sharp knife. If the blade feels hot to the touch, it's ready.

Unmold the farçon onto a cutting board. Cut into slices and serve.

Mont-Blanc Tart

■■■ DIFFICULT

SERVES 6

YOU WILL NEED

2-inch (5cm) ring mold or
cookie cutter

3-inch (7.5cm) ring mold or
cookie cutter

Six 2½ by ¾-inch (6.5 by 2cm)
perforated tart rings

Disposable piping bags

⅛-inch (4mm) plain piping tip

⅜-inch (1cm) plain piping tip

Mont-Blanc (multi-opening)
piping tip

Pizza wheel (optional)

Ruler

Offset spatula

CHESTNUT CREAM

1 cup (240ml) heavy cream

1 cup (240g) mascarpone

5 egg yolks

¼ cup (50g) granulated sugar

14 ounces (400g) chestnut purée

2½ sheets leaf gelatin

MERINGUE CAPS

4 egg whites, at room temperature

Pinch of fine sea salt

1 cup (200g) granulated sugar

PASTRY SHELLS

¾ cup plus 1 tablespoon (100g)
all-purpose flour

Scant ½ cup (50g) confectioners'
sugar

¼ teaspoon fine sea salt

½ vanilla bean, split and seeded

7 tablespoons (100g) cold
unsalted butter, diced

1 egg yolk

Unlike its annoyingly conspicuous Swiss Italian neighbor, the Matterhorn (aka Monte Cervino), Mont-Blanc's stature reveals itself slowly, crowded as it is by the Dôme du Goûter, the Aiguille de Goûter, the Aiguille du Midi, Mont Maudit ("cursed mountain"!), and the aptly named Les Bosses ("the bumps").

In my experience, the best view from which to appreciate the Mont-Blanc massif is from the Skyway, only a five-minute walk from Auberge de la Maison (see page 84). A system of cable cars, the Skyway starts off near the Mont-Blanc Tunnel (which takes cars from Italy to France, or in ski-speak, from Courmayeur to Chamonix). Not to sound like a brochure, but the Skyway truly is an incredible feat of engineering, ascending all the way up to Punta Helbronner at 3,466 meters (11,371 feet), from which you can really study each and every crevasse, bowl, and glacier of the Mont-Blanc massif. It's like a puzzle of rock face.

Mont-Blanc the dessert, with its finely piped sky-high chestnut cream on a bed of meringue, is perhaps more easily recognizable than the mountain. Outside of Paris and the Instagrams of trendy pastry chefs such as Cédric Grolet, the local bakeries of the Grandes Jorasses mountain (on the border between Haute-Savoie and Aosta) do it best. Alpine pastry wizard Paolo Griffa from the Petit Royal restaurant in Courmayeur showed me how to make his version. This dessert—another feat of engineering!—may look ambitious, but it is totally possible for the home cook.

Note: Canned chestnut purée and candied chestnuts can be purchased online or found in fine European-style delis.

To make the chestnut cream: The day before you want to serve the tart, in a saucepan over medium heat, combine the heavy cream and mascarpone and warm, stirring frequently, until just below the boiling point. In a bowl, whisk together the egg yolks and granulated sugar. When the cream mixture is just about to boil, remove the saucepan from the heat and, whisking constantly, slowly add ½ cup (120ml) of the hot liquid to the yolk-sugar mixture, until smooth.

Return the egg-cream mixture to the saucepan over medium heat and cook, whisking nonstop, until the custard begins to thicken, 4 to 5 minutes. Remove from the heat and whisk in the chestnut purée.

Submerge the gelatin sheets in a bowl of cold water for 10 minutes. Squeeze the excess water from the

softened gelatin and whisk the gelatin into the chestnut mixture. Let cool to room temperature—stirring from time to time to stop a skin from forming, or laying plastic wrap directly on the surface. Refrigerate overnight.

To make the meringue caps: Preheat the oven to 200°F (95°C). Line a baking sheet with parchment paper, then mark the paper with twelve 2-inch (5cm) circles, using a ring mold as your guide.

Using a stand mixer fitted with the whisk attachment, at medium-low speed, beat the egg whites until foamy. Add the salt, increase the speed to medium, and continue to whip until the egg whites form soft peaks—they should have the consistency of shaving cream. Add the granulated sugar

continued

MASCARPONE CREAM

½ cup (120ml) heavy cream

½ cup (120g) mascarpone, at room temperature

5¼ ounces (150g) chestnut purée

½ vanilla bean, split and seeded

8 ounces (220g) chestnut purée

6 whole candied chestnuts (*marrons glacés*)

Confectioners' sugar for dusting

TRAVEL HACK

If you take the panoramic Skyway cable-car ride between Courmayeur and Punta Hellbronner to admire Mont-Blanc, be sure to also walk through the tunnel, which leads to Rifugio Torino, a very fun bar that makes a great bombardino (see page 65) at 3,462 meters (11,358 feet).

one-third at a time and then beat at medium speed for 1 minute more. Increase the speed to medium-high, whisking until long stiff peaks form when you lift the whisk.

Transfer this meringue to a pastry bag fitted with a ⅛-inch (4mm) plain tip and pipe as many 2-inch (5cm) rounds as you can onto the prepared baking sheet—once cooked, you'll be picking the nicest six meringues.

Bake until meringue is firm to the touch, 1½ to 2 hours (if the meringues start to color during baking, lower the heat). Transfer the meringues to a rack and let cool completely.

To make the pastry shells: Sift the flour, confectioners' sugar, and salt into a large bowl. Add the vanilla bean seeds. Add the butter and rub the mixture in with your fingertips until it resembles fine bread crumbs. Add the egg yolk and, using a spatula, stir it into the mixture until a firm dough forms (you may need to add a splash of cold water if the dough feels crumbly). Knead the dough briefly and gently on a floured surface. Wrap in plastic and refrigerate for 30 minutes.

Preheat the oven to 325°F (160°C). Line a baking sheet with parchment paper.

On a lightly floured work surface, roll out the dough to a thickness of ⅛ inch (3mm). Using a sharp knife or a pizza wheel and a ruler, cut six strips each measuring about ¾ by 8½ inches (2 by 21cm). Arrange each strip around the inside of the perforated tart rings, applying gentle pressure where the dough overlaps to secure the seal. Place each lined ring onto the prepared baking sheet.

Using a 3-inch (7.5cm) ring cutter, cut out six circles of dough (you may have to collect the dough scraps and roll them to get all six circles). Gently lay each circle inside a lined tart ring, pressing gently around the inside edges to create a seal between the walls and the base.

Bake until golden, about 12 minutes. Transfer the ringed pastry shells to a rack to cool.

To make the mascarpone cream: In a medium bowl, whip the heavy cream until soft peaks form. In a separate bowl, whisk the mascarpone, chestnut purée, and vanilla bean seeds until combined and smooth. Fold in the whipped cream. Transfer to a piping bag fitted with a ⅜-inch (1cm) plain tip.

Fill each pastry shell with mascarpone cream right to the top edge of the pastry. Smooth the top with an offset spatula. Top each with a meringue cap (you have the option of using two meringue caps on each tart, if you want to build taller Mont-Blancs) and transfer each to a separate plate (or something you can rotate during piping). Using a disposable pastry bag with a small corner cut off, pipe a central "mountain" of pure chestnut purée, about 1½ inches (4cm) tall, inside the edges of the meringue cap.

Give the cold chestnut cream a good stir to loosen it up, then transfer it to a pastry bag fitted with the Mont-Blanc tip. Starting at the base of the chestnut purée "mountain," pipe the cream around the base, working your way up the mountain, rotating the plate as needed. Repeat with the remaining tarts.

Top each peak with a candied chestnut, dust with confectioners' sugar, and serve.

Duck Magret with Pont-Neuf Polenta

MAGRET DE CANARD AVEC POLENTA PONT-NEUF

■■■■ MEDIUM

SERVES 4

YOU WILL NEED

Offset spatula

Digital instant-read thermometer

Four 6-ounce (170g) or two 12-ounce (340g) boneless duck breast halves

Fine sea salt and freshly ground black pepper

1 recipe Polenta (page 86)

2 shallots, minced

1 cup (240ml) full-bodied red wine

1 sprig thyme

3 tablespoons honey

3 tablespoons redcurrant jelly

¼ cup (25g) redcurrants

4 jumbo asparagus stalks, cut in half horizontally

4 sprigs flat-leaf parsley

Now it's time to come back down to the valley and have a simple piece of game with polenta molded into Pont-Neuf (the thick rectangular french fries named after the Paris bridge). This dish is as if polenta snuck into France from Italy via the Col du Petit Saint-Bernard and arrived on our elevated plate in Chamonix, directly on a sun-soaked terrace. I recommend that you use a Mondeuse red from Nicholas Gonin in the Isère as your cooking wine—it's a terrific table wine that will neither be wasted in the sauce nor—more important—in the glass. If you can't find Mondeuse, a red Rhône will do.

Note: Cook the polenta as directed. When it's ready, transfer to a wooden board or small baking sheet and smooth it with an offset spatula to a thickness of about ½ inch (12mm). Set aside to cool and set.

Using a sharp knife, score the duck skin in a crisscross pattern—this will help render the fat under the skin. Season the duck breasts with salt and pepper.

Warm a large frying pan over medium heat until it is hot, about 2 minutes. Place the duck breasts, skin-side down, in the pan and turn the heat to medium-low. The fat will start to render in 4 to 5 minutes. Continue to cook until the fat has melted and the skin is golden brown, another 20 minutes or so.

Turn the breasts and cook another 3 to 5 minutes, until an instant-read thermometer registers 125°F (52°C). Transfer the duck to a wooden board and cover loosely with aluminum foil, letting it rest. Pour off most of the melted fat from the pan into a heat-resistant jar or Pyrex pitcher and return the pan to the stove top.

Position the top rack of the oven about 4 inches (10cm) from the broiler and preheat the broiler. Line a baking sheet with foil and brush with the reserved duck fat.

Cut the polenta into Pont-Neuf sticks (1 inch by 2¾ inches/2.5 by 7cm). Lay the polenta sticks on the prepared baking sheet and brush the tops with more of the duck fat. Broil on the top rack until golden, 15 to 20 minutes, turning them over at the 7 minute mark.

While the polenta is broiling, add the shallots to the pan in which you cooked the duck and sauté over medium-high heat until softened, 2 to 3 minutes. Pour in the wine, add the thyme, and cook until the liquid has reduced by half, 5 to 7 minutes. Stir in the honey and jelly. Remove from the heat, stir in the redcurrants, and season with salt and pepper. Set aside and keep warm.

In a saucepan over medium-high heat, bring 1 inch (2.5cm) of water to boil. Place a steamer basket with the asparagus over the saucepan, cover, and steam until the spears bend easily, 4 to 6 minutes.

Slice the duck breasts in half (if you used 2 larger breasts, cut those in half, then in half again), and place both halves of one breast on each plate. Lay a few polenta fries onto each plate, followed by two asparagus halves and a few parsley leaves. Spoon the sauce around the duck. Enjoy!

Roussette-Poached Trout

TRUITE POCHÉE À LA ROUSSETTE DE SAVOIE

MEDIUM
SERVES 4

Four 1-inch (2.5cm) slices cotechino

1½ cups (360ml) Roussette de Savoie or a good-quality Sauvignon Blanc wine

1 cup (250ml) chicken stock or low-sodium chicken broth

Sprigs of flat-leaf parsley, thyme, and 1 bay leaf, tied together into a small bouquet garni

Fine sea salt and freshly ground white pepper

4 cippolini or pearl onions

2 small Yukon gold potatoes, peeled and quartered

4 small white turnips, scrubbed

Four 7-ounce (200g) trout fillets

2 tablespoons unsalted butter

1 small bunch fresh red or green sorrel, finely chopped

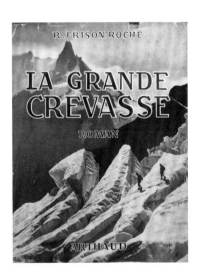

Picture, if you will, Zian, the mountain guide and main character of Roger Frison-Roche's adventure book *La Grande Crevasse*, striding across a melting glacier full of jumping Alpine trout (they don't actually jump, but it doesn't matter, it's fiction). He would net and fillet a few trout with his trusty, rusty pocket knife, or worse, his *piolet* (climbing axe). Just 100 meters (330 feet) or so downhill, the terrain turns from rock to green pasture, so rich in soil that the terraced vines of Roussette grapes grow in abundance, creating natural pergolas to shade the glacier's waterfall from the heat. Being the resourceful man that he is, Zian carries a small Dutch oven in his rucksack, big enough to simmer a few fillets of fish, along with the wine and whatever dried sausage he looped through his belt along with his trusty climbing *cordes* (ropes). A turnip here, an Alpine herb there, perhaps a few sorrel leaves, all collected with a light broth in mind, the reward and the fuel for another day in the mountains. . . .

Though I've traveled thousands of miles and experienced so many real Alpine moments, it is sometimes a childhood memory, or a pleasant fantasy, or even an idyllic misconception that inspires a recipe as satisfying as reality. My good friend Fred Morin has never been to the French Alps, but his unrealized urge to visit was ignited long ago by nights in a sleeping bag reading by flashlight of adventurer and novelist Roger Frison-Roche. And so, this dish is inspired by Frison-Roche's great writing.

Notes: I love the wines of Florian and Marie Curtet, and their flagship Roussette is excuse enough to make this recipe. In line with classic French and Italian cooking, use half the bottle in your cooking and drink the other half. Even if you don't go the Roussette route, choose a wine rewarding of your effort.

The Savoyard longeole sausage is what you're after, but any cotechino you can get your hands on works here.

In a heavy saucepan over low heat, combine the cotechino slices and 2 cups water, cover, and simmer until very tender and moist, 2½ hours.

In a Dutch oven over medium-high heat, bring the wine to a simmer and reduce by half, until approximately ⅔ cup (160ml), about 8 minutes, then add the chicken stock and bouquet garni and return to a simmer. Reduce by a third, until you are left with 1¼ cups (300ml) stock, about 5 minutes. Season lightly with salt and white pepper.

Add the onions (in their skins), potatoes, and turnips to the stock and cook, covered, for 5 to 15 minutes to keep each vegetable on the still-firm side. Transfer to a large bowl as each comes to doneness (onions first, followed by potatoes, then turnips). Peel the onions with a sharp paring knife. Cover with plastic wrap.

Add the fish and sausages to the stock and cover. Turn the heat to low and simmer gently for about 5 minutes, then carefully transfer to the bowl with the vegetables.

Bring the stock to a boil, reduce for 2 minutes, add the butter, and swirl until well emulsified. Check and adjust the seasoning as needed, then gently pour over the fish and vegetables. Sprinkle the sorrel atop each portion of fish.

Serve immediately.

Fondue Brioche

BRIOCHE À LA FONDUE SAVOYARDE

MEDIUM
MAKES 12 BRIOCHES

YOU WILL NEED
12 individual brioche molds
(I used a tall popover pan,
which works too)

BRIOCHE DOUGH
2¾ cups (345g) bread flour

⅓ cup (80ml) condensed milk,
at room temperature

1 tablespoon milk powder

2 tablespoons sugar

1¼ teaspoons fine sea salt

¼ ounce (7g) active dry yeast

3 eggs, at room temperature

14 tablespoons (200g)
unsalted butter, cubed,
at room temperature

FONDUE FILLING
¾ cup (175ml) dry white wine

2 tablespoons unsalted butter

¼ cup (30g) all-purpose flour

2 cups (230g) grated Gruyère,
Emmental, and/or Beaufort
cheese

1 egg yolk

3 tablespoons cold milk whisked
with 1 egg yolk, for egg wash

Some people come to the Alps for the mountains, *not for the food.* (Can you believe it?) They eat for sustenance, hurrying to get back on the hills while there is time in the day. If this rings a cowbell, this recipe is for you: a fondue Savoyarde in brioche form—no utensils, no fondue set, no sitting down. Bake it, wrap it up, stuff it in your pocket, and go.

Note: The dough and filling need to chill for 8 hours. Start the recipe before bedtime for brioche by lunch, or early in the morning, if you're going to enjoy it for dinner.

To make the brioche dough: In a stand mixer fitted with the dough hook, combine the bread flour, condensed milk, milk powder, sugar, salt, yeast, eggs, and butter. Mix for 5 minutes on medium speed, then increase the speed to medium-high and continue to beat until the dough becomes very smooth and satiny looking, another 5 to 7 minutes.

Gather the dough up into a ball (it will be very soft), knead a handful of times on the counter, then transfer to an oiled bowl and cover tightly with plastic wrap. Let it rise for 1 hour, then punch it down, re-cover it, and refrigerate for 8 hours.

To make the fondue filling: In a small saucepan over medium-low heat, combine the wine and butter and bring to a gentle simmer.

In a medium bowl, stir the flour into the cheese. Add the flour-coated cheese to the simmering wine-butter mixture and mix well with a wooden spoon until thoroughly melted. Remove from the heat and stir in the egg yolk. Line a small plate with plastic wrap, pour the cheese mixture on the plate, and refrigerate overnight.

When it's go-time, preheat the oven to 375°F (190°C) and set a pot of water on the stove to boil—this will help create a nice proofing environment for the dough.

Lightly butter twelve brioche molds or a popover pan.

Divide the dough into four equal pieces. Set one piece aside. Cut each of the three remaining pieces of dough into two, then each of those six pieces into two. You should have twelve more-or-less even pieces of dough. These are the buns. Divide the remaining large piece of dough into twelve even pieces to form the top knots. Roll these twelve small pieces into balls.

Remove the fondue filling from the fridge. Use your hands to shape twelve chunks of fondue into balls— approximately 2 tablespoons each.

Working on a clean, lightly oiled surface, shape each of the larger pieces of dough by hand into 8-inch (20cm) wide disks. Place a fondue ball into the center of each disk. Then fold up the dough around the cheese, pinching the top shut to create a seam. Transfer each ball of dough to its mold, seam-side down. Use your thumb to make an indent in the top of each brioche ball and lay a top knot into each. Set the brioche molds on a baking sheet. Butter a large piece of plastic wrap, then lay it, buttered-side down, on top of the brioches. Move the tray to a warm and humid location, and let the dough proof until doubled in size, and puffy, 2 to 2½ hours. Brush the brioches gently with the egg wash.

Bake until golden, 18 to 20 minutes. Let cool for 10 minutes before eating. Be careful, as the inside will be molten-rock hot! These brioches can be kept wrapped in plastic, at room temperature, for up to 3 days.

Popcorn Bread

PAIN DE MAÏS SOUFFLÉ

■■■ DIFFICULT
MAKES 1 LOAF

YOU WILL NEED

Baking stone or cast-iron pan

Baking peel

2 large handfuls of ice

2 teaspoons active dry yeast

1 cup plus 2 tablespoons (275ml) warm (105° to 110°F/ 40° to 45°C) water

1¼ cups (150g) stone-ground fine yellow cornmeal

3¼ cups (400g) bread flour

½ teaspoon fine sea salt

⅓ cup (60g) raw corn kernels

2 tablespoons coarse-ground yellow grits, or popcorn ground in a high-speed blender

¼ cup (40g) coarse semolina flour

Run by father and son René and Maxime Meilleur, La Bouitte is known as one of the best restaurants in France. Regardless of how you feel about the Michelin star system (La Bouitte has three), the experience of eating here feels authentically Alpine.

A highlight: the bread service. After the amuse-bouche, one of the servers wheels a large cart to the table to offer a choice of ten breads. One of them was this offering made with local corn. The next day, I returned to the restaurant to beg them to give me another loaf. They kindly obliged, and included an incredible Alpine butter ball (see page 312). I ate it all en route from La Bouitte to the Grande Chartreuse monastery.

This bread depends on the best cornmeal and grits you can find. Bob's Red Mill has dependable options; order the grits online from Anson Mills.

In a small bowl, combine the yeast with 5 tablespoons (75ml) of the water and let stand until bubbles form, about 5 minutes.

In a stand mixer fitted with the dough hook, combine the remaining 13 tablespoons (200ml) water, yeast mixture, cornmeal, bread flour, and salt. Mix at the lowest speed (2 on a KitchenAid stand mixer) for 4 minutes. Increase the speed by one notch (4) and knead for 6 minutes. Lower the speed back to 2 and add the kernels. Continue to knead for another 4 minutes; the dough should look smooth and feel slightly tacky.

Cover the bowl and let the dough sit at room temperature until doubled in size, about 1 hour (it will proof even better if you place the bowl alongside a glass of steaming hot water in the microwave).

Line a baking sheet with parchment paper and lightly oil a work surface.

Turn the dough out onto the work surface and knead it a few times. Form the dough into a pear-shaped oval loaf and transfer to the prepared baking sheet. Transfer to a warm, humid place (this could be your kitchen with a large pot of water boiling away) to proof for 30 minutes or so, until nice and puffed.

In the meantime, preheat the oven to 475°F (245°C) with a baking stone or cast-iron pan on the middle rack.

Using sharp scissors, make strategic and fairly deep cuts into the dough. Start by cutting one *épi* (ear) at the top of the bread, followed by two, then three, then four, as the pear shape widens. Spray or brush the dough lightly all over with water, then sprinkle the tips of each épi with the coarse corn grits.

Pour two handfuls of ice into a drip tray (or a rectangular metal cake pan).

Sprinkle a baking peel with the semolina, and gently move the bread onto the peel. Transfer the bread to the hot baking stone or cast-iron pan, then quickly and carefully place the drip tray on the bottom of the oven (the evaporation approximates the steam in an industrial oven, and helps the formation of a crisp crust!). Close the oven door.

Bake for 15 minutes, then lower the temperature to 400°F (200°C) and continue baking for 10 minutes.

Let the bread cool completely before serving. This bread is best eaten on the day of baking.

Alpine Butter Ball

MAKES ONE 2-INCH
(5CM) BALL

½ cup (110g) high-quality
cultured butter, at room
temperature

2 tablespoons sérac cheese
or fresh ricotta

Fleur de sel for sprinkling

This "surprise" butter ball is made from cultured butter wrapped around a core of sérac, which is a fresh cheese traditionally made in the French and Swiss Alps from the whey by-product of making a pressed cheese such as Comté or Emmental; fresh ricotta is a great substitute. Cultured butter is a higher-fat butter, which has been "cultured" with active bacteria, resulting in silkier texture and tangier, richer flavor.

Using a small spatula or wooden spoon, paddle the butter in a small bowl until soft and spreadable.

Lay a square of plastic wrap over the counter. Using an offset spatula, and a ruler as a guide, spread the butter into an even disk shape about 4 inches (10cm) diameter.

Using your hands, roll the sérac into a ball and set it in the center of the butter disk.

Pick up the plastic wrap and, working with your hands (but with the plastic protecting the butter), gently draw the edges together, tightening while shaping the ball with one hand to help the butter wrap around the fresh cheese. Wrap tightly and refrigerate for 2 hours.

When ready to serve, unwrap and sprinkle with fleur de sel.

MAXIME (LEFT) AND
RENÉ (RIGHT) MEILLEUR

Tomme Tartine

GROSSE TARTINE À LA TOMME DE SAVOIE

■■■■ EASY
SERVES 4

Large head of lettuce (preferably with hefty ribs)

2 shallots, minced

2 tablespoons unsalted butter

2 garlic cloves; 1 minced, 1 whole

⅔ cup (160ml) heavy cream

¼ cup (40g) finely diced cooked ham, such as jambon blanc

Fine sea salt and freshly ground black pepper

Pinch of freshly grated nutmeg

2 thick slices country bread, sliced on the diagonal

2 tablespoons extra-virgin olive oil

Ten ⅛-inch (3mm) thick slices Tomme de Savoie cheese

Here, I'm treating a head of lettuce almost like a tertiary cut of meat . . . *et voilà!*

My inspiration was a tartine I had at Chalet Forestier de Rochebrune in Megève, a stop-worthy lunch location. It consisted of toasted bread topped with lettuce ribs braised in a cream and lardons sauce, covered with the local cheese, Tomme de Savoie, melted abundantly on top.

Note: Serve with a simple green salad made from the leftover lettuce leaves, dressed with a good old vinegar and a generous pour of walnut oil.

Separate the ribs from the lettuce leaves, keeping the tender leaves for the salad you should make to accompany this dish.

Bring a pot of salted water to a boil and fill a bowl with water and ice. Blanch the lettuce ribs in the boiling water for a few seconds and plunge them into the bowl of ice water to stop the cooking. Drain on paper towels, then chop coarsely. Set aside.

In a sauté pan over medium heat, sweat the shallots in the butter until translucent, about 4 minutes. Stir in the minced garlic, lower the heat slightly, and cook for another 1 minute.

Stir the chopped lettuce ribs, cream, and diced ham into the pan. Cover and cook gently until the ribs are tender, 4 to 5 minutes. Uncover, return the heat to medium, and simmer to reduce the cream until it thickens and coats the lettuce, 4 to 5 minutes more. Season with salt and pepper and the nutmeg. Set aside.

Preheat the broiler.

Put the bread on a baking sheet and place in the top third of the oven. Toast on both sides, keeping a close eye to prevent burning. Rub each slice with the whole garlic clove, then brush each with the olive oil.

In an ovenproof pan or on a baking sheet lined with parchment paper, lay out the slices of bread. Spoon the creamed lettuce mix evenly over each piece of bread. Cover with the slices of Tomme and broil until adequately browned, 5 to 6 minutes (depending on the strength of your broil setting; it's best to keep an eye on it). Cut each slice into two and transfer to four plates.

Serve immediately.

THE GARDEN OF LE CLOS DE SENS

A LITTLE POETIC ALPINE SALAD

This hyperspecific salad of herbs and flowers foraged in local Alpine meadows and gardens, a gift from Emmanuel Renaut at Flocons de Sel (see snapshot, page 315), is a pure mountain salad that expresses itself with wood sorrel, lovage, and yarrow. It also includes plants that can be grown almost anywhere: chives, nasturtium, tarragon, marigolds. *The Sound of Music* in salad form. The good news is that the salad is intended to be adapted to where you are living in the world: look for herbs and seasonal flowers at your local farmers' market, or even better, grow your own!

- Lettuces to choose from include romaine, frisée, red oak leaf, green oak leaf, red butterhead

- Herbs to choose from can be sorrel, tarragon, chervil, flat-leaf parsley, oregano, nasturtium leaves, mint, lovage, fennel, wood sorrel

- Edible flowers to choose from are golden marigold, bee balm, caraway, scented geranium, nasturtium, elfin thyme, daylily, elderberry, ground elder (bishop's weed)

In a large bowl, combine your choice of lettuces and top with as many herbs and edible flowers as your heart desires.

For a dressing, combine 2 teaspoons lime juice, 2 teaspoons elderberry cordial, and 2 teaspoons savory-infused wine vinegar with a splash of extra-virgin olive oil. Season with salt and freshly ground black pepper.

Dress the salad, toss, and serve.

Savoie-Style Mushrooms

CHAMPIGNONS À LA SAVOYARDE

■■■ EASY

SERVES 4

6 tablespoons (85g) unsalted butter

4 ounces (115g) salt pork, rinsed, patted dry, and cut into ½-inch (12mm) cubes

1 pound (450g) chanterelle or morel mushrooms, trimmed and cleaned

2 yellow onions, minced

½ cup (120ml) sour cream

1 cup (115g) grated Gruyère cheese

4 slices country loaf or pumpernickel bread, toasted (optional)

4 eggs

¼ cup (10g) minced fresh flat-leaf parsley

Freshly ground black pepper

Having grown up in Canada, I'm fluent in the language of eating a hot, buttered slice of country loaf drenched in mushroom soup from my frostbitten hands. Still today, when I'm starving, I'll open a can of soup and add toast with whatever roots or fungi are in the fridge and some ends of cheese. This recipe is a pimped-out version of that instinct . . . without the canned soup.

I made this soul-warming mushroom tartine while staying in a nightmare rental apartment (it had red-eyed dolls piled on a glass shelf directly across from my bed) near Flumet between La Clusaz and Megève, almost directly on the Route des Grandes Alpes (see page 273). I had enjoyed a wonderful farçon in La Clusaz and some delicious blueberry éclairs from Le Four à Bois des Aravis in Aravis, but missing home, I gathered ingredients at a small mountain grocer and turned this out in a Dutch oven. Had the butcher shop been open, I would have over-the-topped it with sweetbreads or a little can of truffles or foie gras.

In a large sauté pan or Dutch oven over medium-low heat, melt 4 tablespoons (55g) of the butter. Add the salt pork and the mushrooms and cook until the mushrooms start to release their water, 3 to 4 minutes. Stir in the onions, turn the heat to very low, cover, and sweat for 25 minutes.

Spoon the sour cream into the pan, then add the grated cheese and stir well. (If you're planning to serve with toasted bread, toast the bread now.) Turn the heat to medium, and keep stirring until the sour cream has warmed through and the cheese is melted, about 2 minutes. Turn off the heat.

In a large frying pan over medium heat, melt the remaining 2 tablespoons butter. Crack the eggs into the pan and fry sunny-side up.

Spoon the mushroom mixture onto the four toast slices or plates. Top each with a fried egg, then sprinkle with the parsley and a good grind of black pepper. Serve immediately.

Seemingly never without his signature black hat, chef **Marc Veyrat** wins the farçon for the most psychedelic cover on his cookbook *Forkful of Magic*. He is perhaps the most well-known Savoie chef of all time and can be spotted in many a documentary, gathering herbs and flowers from Alpine meadows. At the helm of Maison des Bois ("House of the Woods") for decades, he is considered a mentor to many chefs in the Alps and beyond. His favorite Alpine food is *pormonier*, a pork sausage ground with leeks, Swiss chard, and spinach. A good day for Marc is a morning of skiing at nearby La Clusaz, followed by lunch at Châlet Savoyard on the Col des Aravis.

SNAPSHOT

HOW DO YOU LIKE YOUR EGGS?

When people ask me about my favorite dish, they're invariably surprised or disappointed because my favorite thing to eat is eggs—specifically two barely cooked scrambled eggs on toast with good butter and a couple of slices of Gruyère or Fontina. I could add some maple-smoked bacon cut into small lardons, along with fried leek fronds, which isn't so different from an *omelette à la savoyarde* (slivers of ham, some Gruyère, and a splash of heavy cream, *bien sûr*). I might also include about one-fourth of the mushrooms from the previous Savoie-Style Mushrooms recipe. Or skip the bacon and leek and top the eggs with some sturgeon eggs instead. Not fancy caviar, but good-quality farmed sturgeon eggs, or really any kind of fish egg.

These barely, creamy eggs with a hit of fat from the cheese require something equally lush to drink—the silk pajamas' wine equivalent is Chardonnay from Austria's Georgium, or an Alsatian Riesling, like the one produced by Florian and Mathilde Beck-Hartweg.

Chartreuse Soufflé

SERVES 4

YOU WILL NEED
Four 1-cup (240ml) ramekins

3 tablespoons unsalted butter, at room temperature

2 to 3 tablespoons superfine sugar

⅓ cup (80ml) milk

2 teaspoons cornstarch

½ teaspoon granulated sugar, plus 3 tablespoons

4 eggs, separated

2 tablespoons green Chartreuse

Candied angelica for garnish

In her book *Honey from a Weed*, rustic dweller-writer-survivalist Patience Gray noted that *Angelica archangelica* grows wild "near abandoned ruins and damp places." And history tells us of the legend that an angel appeared to a monk in a dream, revealing to him that this plant—that the monks chewed to help with stomach ailments—would cure a plague. Angelica was one of the original herbs macerated in the 1605 Chartreuse elixir recipe. And so, a piece of candied angelica is an appropriate garnish for this dish, not only because of its mythical goodness but also because that sliver of green gives us a hint of what's inside. Chartreuse is polarizing; it's too herbal and medicinal tasting for some. This soufflé softens the edges of the liqueur and so there is a hint but it's not overbearing. It's quite a sophisticated, nuanced taste.

Jean Sulpice was born in the Alps. An avid skier and serious cyclist, his days are spent passionately working with mountain foragers and fisherman in the morning, prepping with his kitchen team in the afternoon, and perfecting service at his two-Michelin-starred restaurant at the Auberge du Père Bise in Talloires on Lac d'Annecy. This recipe is his.

Notes: Although the recipe calls for green Chartreuse, yellow will also do. If you have bottles of both types, then use 1 tablespoon of each.

The soufflé batter can be made, portioned, and refrigerated up to 2 hours before baking.

CHEF JEAN SULPICE

With a pastry brush, brush the butter onto the bottom and sides of four ramekins, using vertical strokes along the wall. Sprinkle with the superfine sugar to coat, shaking off any excess. Set aside in the refrigerator.

In a small saucepan over medium heat, combine the milk, cornstarch, and ½ teaspoon granulated sugar. Bring to a simmer, whisking frequently to dissolve the sugar and cornstarch, then set this custard aside to cool for a few minutes.

In a stand mixer fitted with the whisk attachment, beat the egg whites on medium speed until they form soft peaks. With the machine running, gradually add the remaining 3 tablespoons granulated sugar and beat until the egg whites become glossy and just start to form stiff peaks.

In a medium bowl, whisk together the egg yolks and Chartreuse. Slowly pour the milk-cornstarch mixture into the egg yolks, whisking constantly.

Using a spatula, boldly stir a fourth of the egg whites into the custard base until well incorporated, then gently fold in the remainder of the egg whites.

Preheat the oven to 375°F (190°C).

Place the ramekins on a baking sheet. Gently divide the mixture among the ramekins, leaving ¾ inch (2cm) free at the top to allow the soufflé some support in its rise. Transfer to the oven and bake until the soufflés have risen fully and dramatically above the rim of the ramekins, 17 to 20 minutes.

Garnish the ramekins with candied angelica and serve immediately.

THE BENDS OF ALPE D'HUEZ

Polka Dot Paris-Brest

LA ROUE DES GRANDES ALPES

■■■ DIFFICULT
SERVES 8

YOU WILL NEED
Pastry bag fitted with a ¾-inch (2cm) plain tip

Pastry bag fitted with a ½-inch (12mm) star tip

Mortar and pestle

CHOUX PASTE
1 cup (240ml) milk

3 tablespoons unsalted butter

⅛ teaspoon fine sea salt

¼ teaspoon granulated sugar

1 cup (120g) all-purpose flour

5 eggs, beaten

1 egg yolk whisked with 1 tablespoon heavy cream, for egg wash

PISTACHIO PRALINE
½ cup (100g) granulated sugar

¾ cup (90g) shelled pistachios

BUTTERCREAM FILLING
2 egg yolks

5 tablespoons (60g) granulated sugar

1 tablespoon plus 1 teaspoon potato starch

¾ cup (175ml) whole milk

½ cup (110g) unsalted butter, at room temperature

2 cups (480ml) heavy cream

2 tablespoons kirsch

A handful of small strawberries, sliced horizontally

Confectioners' sugar for dusting

We made it to the top of Alpe d'Huez, our last stop through the Alps! How fitting that my last days in the Alps researching this book fell during the Tour de France, atop cycling's most grueling mountain. First included in the race in 1952, with twenty-one sharp bends, the Alpe d'Huez is an absolute killer to which pros and amateurs alike make annual pilgrimages to climb. When I was there, the sides of the road were lined with Belgian and German fans; some camped out for weeks (not days) to secure a spot along the route to the top.

This dessert, made of choux pastry and a rich cream filling, was first created in honor of the endurance bicycle ride from Paris to Brest (in Brittany) and back—its circular shape meant to represent the wheel of a bicycle.

I've modified my version to represent the iconic white and red-polka-dot jersey (*maillot à pois rouges*), with strawberries for polka dots and a little pistachio praline as our summer greenery. The jersey is awarded at the end of each mountain stage of the Tour de France to signal the best climber/rider of the *étape* (stage), that is, the King of the Mountain. So, harness your inner Bernard Hinault or Alberto Contador and make this last recipe count.

To prepare the choux paste: In a saucepan over medium heat, combine the milk, butter, salt, and granulated sugar. Bring to a boil, then remove from the heat and add the flour in one go. Using a wooden spoon, stir the mixture quickly to gather it together. Return the saucepan to medium heat and cook, while still stirring vigorously, until the dough looks like modeling clay and a floury residue starts sticking to the bottom of the saucepan, another 1 to 2 minutes.

Transfer the dough to the bowl of a stand mixer. Add one-fifth of the beaten egg and stir at low speed until the egg is incorporated and any lumps have subsided. Add another one-fifth of the egg and stir until the dough comes together again. Repeat adding the egg another two to three times—the dough should look very smooth but still hold its shape (you may not need all of the egg). Transfer the choux paste to a pastry bag fitted with a plain tip.

Preheat the oven to 375°F (190°C). Line a baking sheet with parchment paper. With a pencil and using a tart ring or pot lid as a guide, draw a 12-inch (30cm) circle. Flip the parchment over so the pencil mark is on the underside.

Pipe out a circle of choux paste (the paste will slip out gently from the bag, without much squeezing) along the pencil circle. Starting at a different point in the circle, pipe another ring of choux paste inside the circle, followed by a third circle of paste on top of them, along the line between them—again, starting it at a different point (this increases the structural integrity of the finished pastry circle).

Brush the dough with the egg wash (it's okay if the circles of paste start to merge into each other). Drag the tines of a fork through the egg wash, along the circle, to create lines all around the top of the choux batter.

continued

Bake for 25 minutes, then lower the oven temperature to 350°F (175°C) and bake until nicely browned and puffed, another 30 minutes. Turn off the oven and open the oven door—propping a wooden spoon between the door and the stove to keep the door ajar. Let the Paris-Brest cool for 30 minutes.

To make the pistachio praline: Meanwhile, lightly oil a baking sheet and set aside.

In a small, heavy saucepan over medium-high heat, cook the granulated sugar, stirring occasionally to incorporate the melting sugar into the still-dry sugar. Keep cooking the sugar until it is light amber in color and then stir in the pistachios. Don't worry if things look very clumpy. Keep cooking the caramel-nut mixture until it turns a deep caramel color. Pour the mixture onto the prepared baking sheet, spreading it out with a spatula to cool. Let set at room temperature.

When the praline has set, break into pieces and, using a mortar and pestle (or a few pulses in a food processor), pound until it has turned to coarsely ground bits.

To make the buttercream filling: In a large bowl, combine the egg yolks, 3 tablespoons of the granulated sugar, and the potato starch and whisk until pale and combined.

In a medium saucepan over medium heat, bring the milk to a boil and then pour slowly into the bowl, whisking continuously. Return this mixture to the saucepan and bring to a boil, whisking all the time, especially around the edges. Boil for a few seconds only, then remove from the heat and cover the surface of this cooked custard with plastic wrap. Set aside to cool.

When the custard has cooled to room temperature, put the butter in the bowl of a stand mixer fitted with the whisk attachment. Whisk until the butter is fluffy and similar in texture to the cream, 2 minutes or so. Add the cream to the butter and beat on high speed until well combined, 45 seconds or so. Transfer to a large bowl.

In the cleaned stand mixer bowl fitted with the paddle attachment, combine the cream mixture, kirsch, and remaining 2 tablespoons granulated sugar. Mix at medium-high speed until stiff peaks form.

Using a whisk, incorporate one-third of the whipped cream into the large bowl, mixing well. Use a spatula to fold the rest of the whipped cream into the buttercream mixture. Transfer to a pastry bag fitted with a star tip.

Using a sharp knife, remove the top third of the Paris-Brest, cutting horizontally all the way around. Sprinkle the crushed pistachio praline into the pastry circle. Fill the pastry ring with the buttercream, covering all the pistachio praline. Scatter the strawberries throughout to resemble red polka dots.

Arrange the lid on top of the buttercream, then dust with confectioners' sugar. Chill for 1 hour or up to 3 days. When ready to serve, use a sharp knife to slice into eight equal portions.

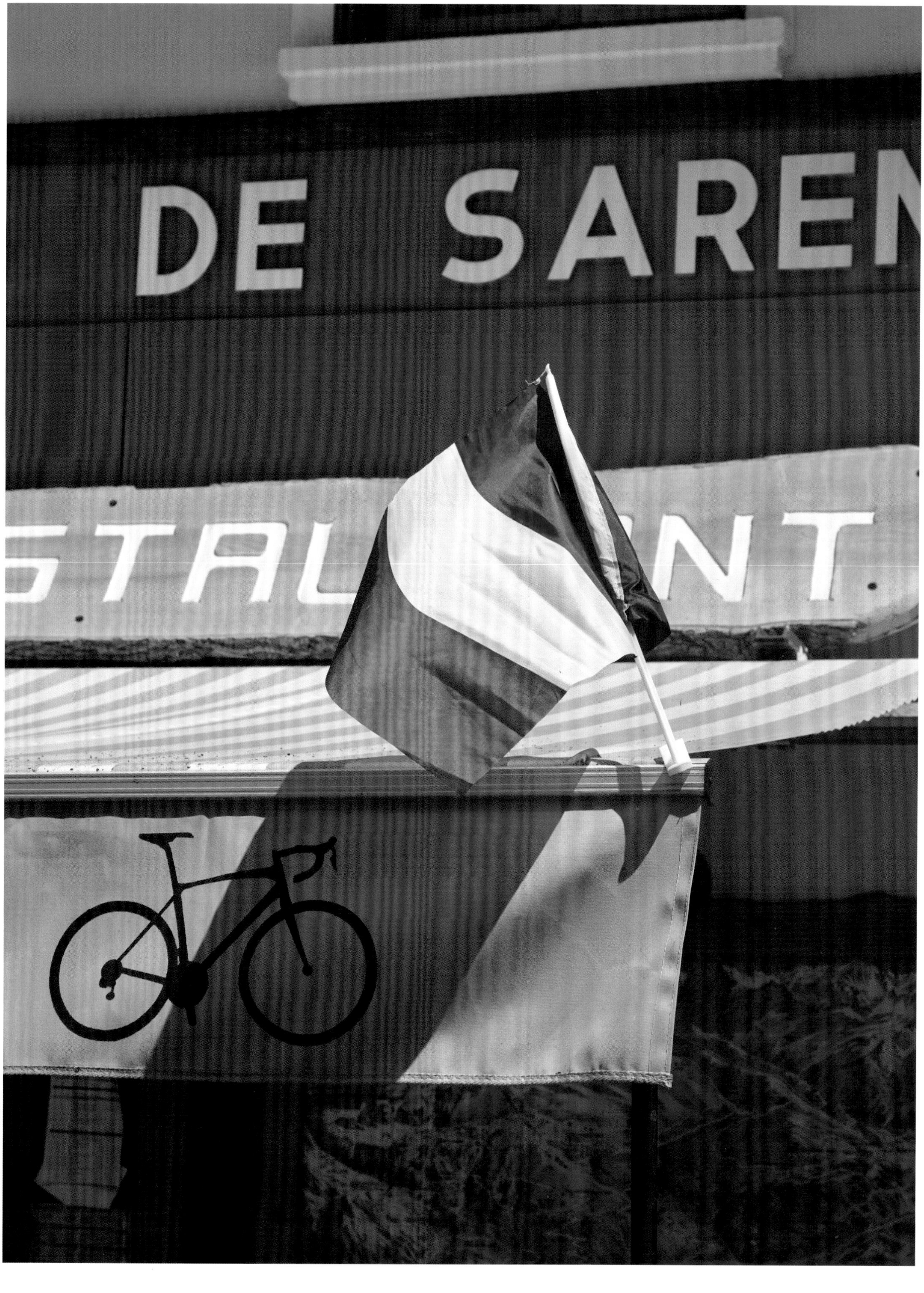
DE SAREN

MAPS

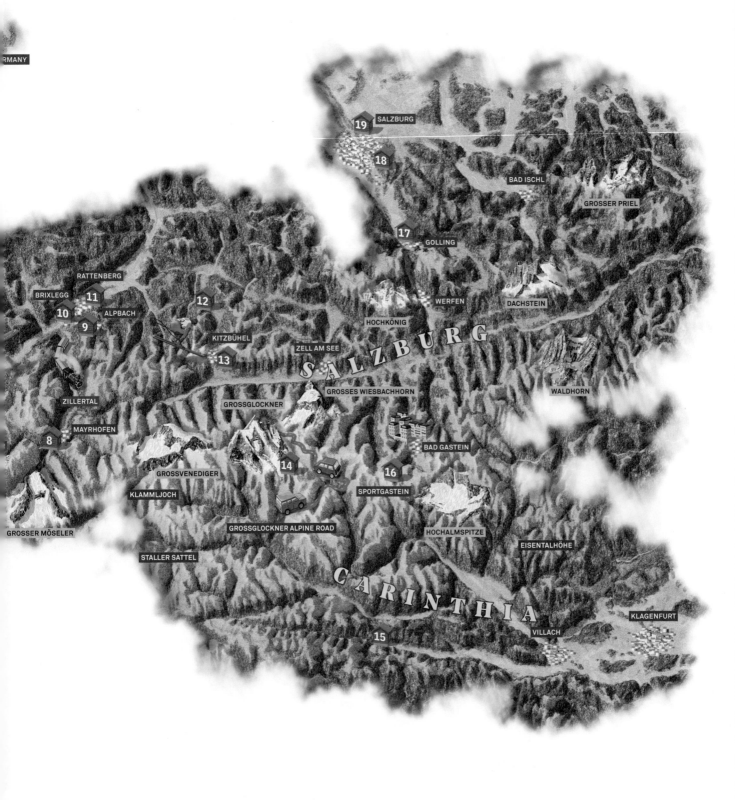

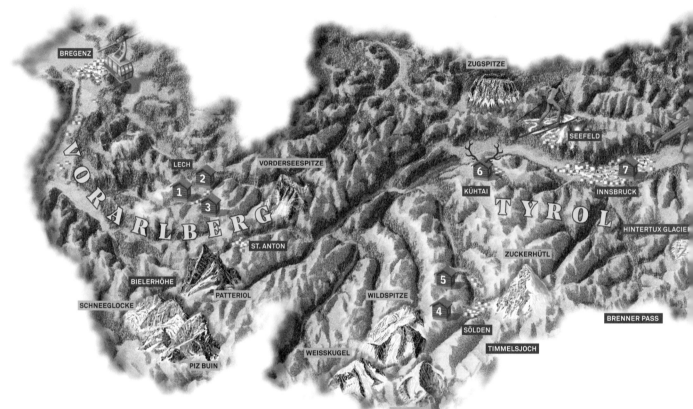

MUNICH, GE

Austria

1 Klösterle, Zug 175

2 Alter Goldener Berg, Lech 171

3 Almhof Schneider, Lech 166

4 Ice Q, Sölden 155

5 Gampe Thaya, Sölden 161

6 Jagdschloss, Kühtai 151

7 Weisses Rössl, Innsbruck 148

8 Mayrhofen 143

9 Alpbach 129

10 Sigwart's Tiroler Weinstuben, Brixlegg 126

11 Café Hacker, Rattenberg 135

12 Kitzbühel 140

13 Resterhöhe & Lodge Berggasthaus, Kitzbühel Alps 139

14 Grossglockner 144

15 Kötschach-Mauthen, Carinthia 125

16 Valeriehaus, Sportgastein 122

17 Döllerer, Golling 114

18 Bärenwirt Tavern, Salzburg 118

19 Hotel Sacher, Salzburg 115

20 Munich, Germany 108

Italy

1 Auberge de La Maison, Entrèves 84

2 Chateau Branlant, Courmayeur 87

3 Les Neiges d'Antan, Cervinia 95

4 Hotel Monterosa, Alagna Valsesia 66

5 Lou Ressignon, Cogne 91

6 Hotel Bellevue, Cogne 92

7 Chalet Il Capricorno, Sauze d'Oulx 71

8 Hotel La Torre, Sauze d'Oulx 80

9 Torino 75

10 Del Cambio, Torino 76

11 Livigno 65

12 Merano 36

13 San Luis, Avelengo 35

14 Fichtenhof, Cauria 45

15 Sofie Hütte, Ortisei 41

16 Rifugio Col Alt, Corvara 46

17 Hotel & Spa Rosa Alpina, San Cassiano 48

18 Ciasa Salares, San Cassiano 52

19 El Brite de Larieto, Cortina d'Ampezzo 57

20 Sesto 60

21 Laite, Sappada 64

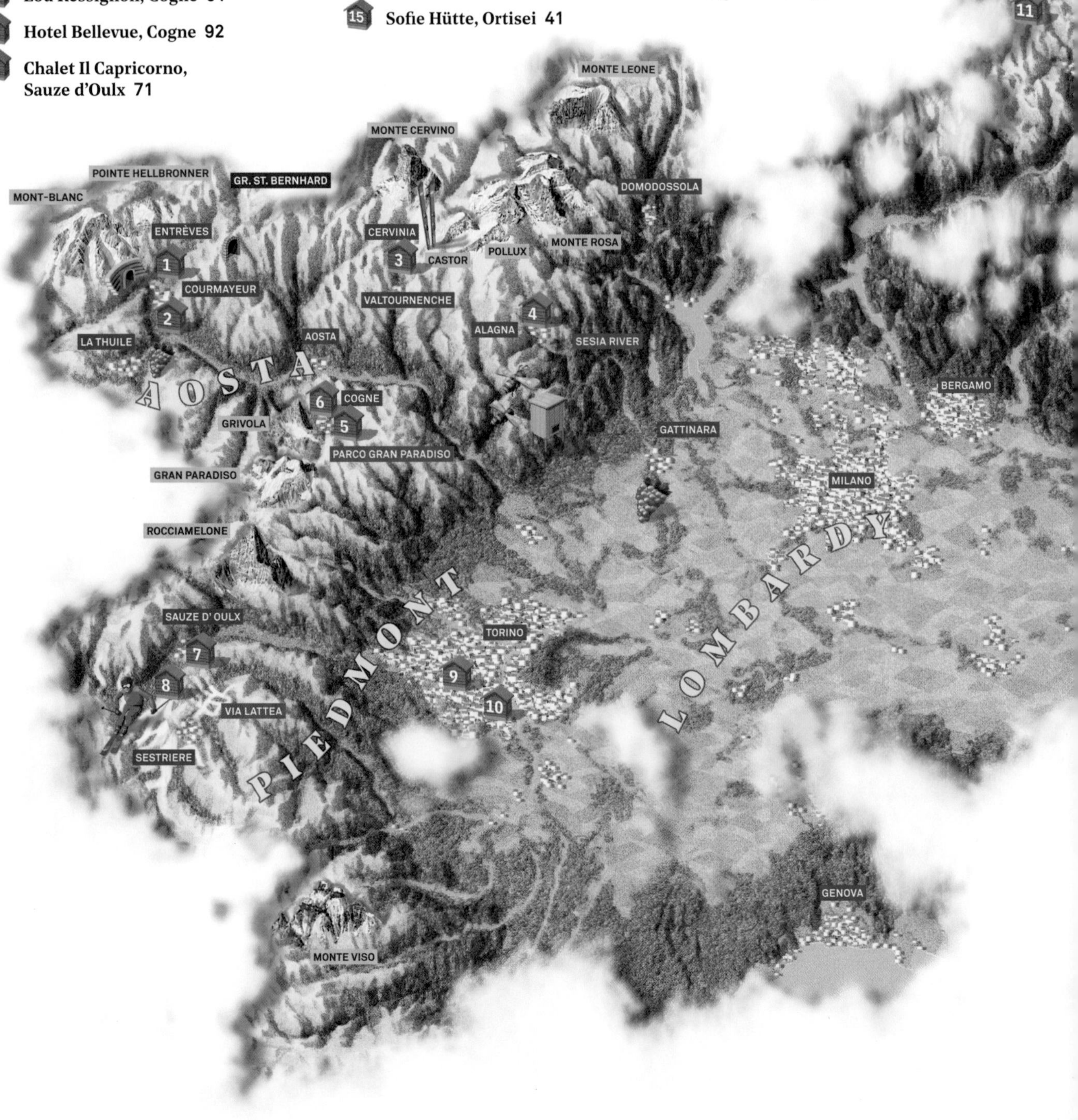

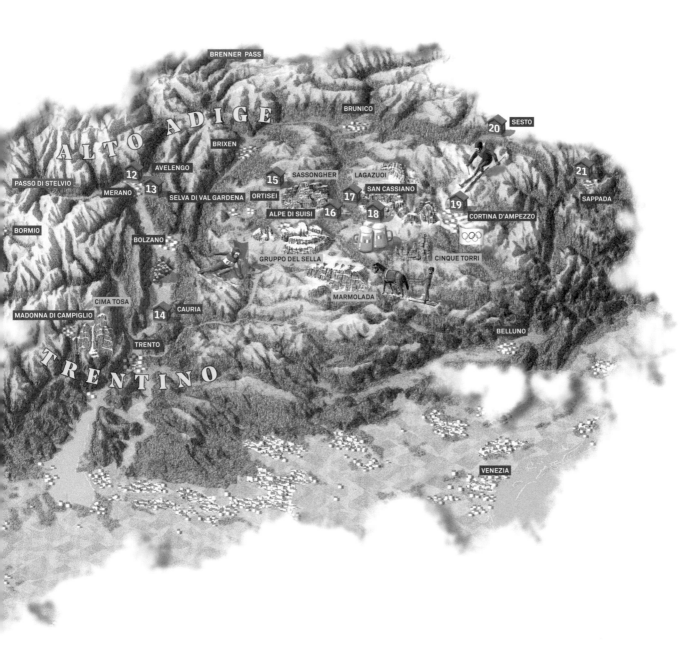

BRENNER PASS

ALTO ADIGE

BRUNICO

20 SESTO

BRIXEN

AVELENGO

12 SASSONGHER LAGAZUOI 21

PASSO DI STELVIO 13 MERANO SELVA DI VAL GARDENA ORTISEI 15 SAN CASSIANO SAPPADA

17

BORMIO ALPE DI SUISI 16 18 19 CORTINA D'AMPEZZO

BOLZANO

CINQUE TORRI

GRUPPO DEL SELLA

CIMA TOSA MARMOLADA

MADONNA DI CAMPIGLIO 14 CAURIA BELLUNO

TRENTO

TRENTINO

VENEZIA

Map Key

RECIPE INSPIRATIONS

TOWNS

NATURAL PLACES

MOUNTAIN PASSES

MOUNTAIN PEAKS

REGIONS

ST. GALLEN

13

APPENZELLER

14 **15**

SÄNTIS

16

ZÜRICH

12

A P P E N Z E L L

BAD RAGAZ

KLOSTERS

PIZ LINARD

ENGELBERG

TITLIS

17

TÖDI

DAMMASTOCK

AROSA

DAVOS

ANDERMATT

G R A U B Ü N D E N

PIZ KESCH

10 **11**

ST. GOTTHARD PASS

ST. MORITZ

UMBREIL PASS

FURKA PASS

19

ORN

18

BERNINA PASS

T I C I N O

PIZ CORBET

PIZ BERNINA

LOCARNO

BELLINZONA

LUGANO

Switzerland

1   Neuchâtel 207

2   Hotel Alpenland, Lauenen 228

3   Gstaad Palace, Gstaad 215

4   Chesery, Gstaad 227

5   Les Diablerets 211

6   Château de Villa, Sierre 240

7   Zum See, Zermatt 239

8   Salzano, Interlaken 235

9   Gässli-Beck, Habkern 231

10 Furka Pass 220

11 Andermatt 261

12 Zurich 212

13 Wildhaus, St. Gallen 254

14 Berggasthaus Aescher-
    Wildkirchli, Appenzeller 253

15 Gasthaus Ebenalp,
    Toggenburg 250

16 Berggasthaus Forelle
    am Seealpsee 256

17 Hotel Wynegg, Klosters 259

18 St. Moritz Tobogganing Club,
    Cresta Run 245

19 Da Vittorio,
    St. Moritz 248

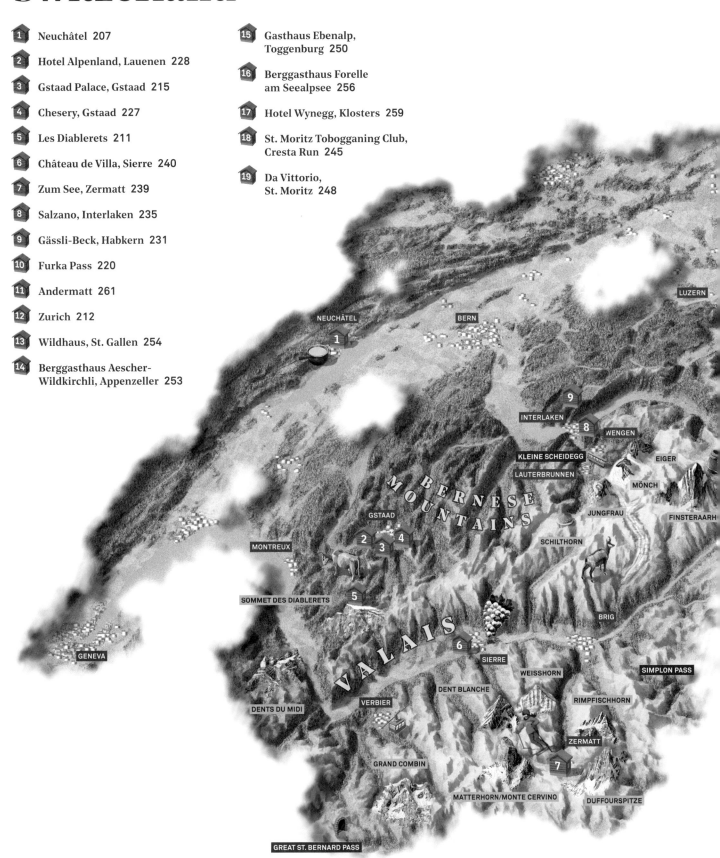

France

1   **Les Cornettes de Bise, Abondance** 280

2   **Les Cornettes, La Chapelle d'Abondance** 276

3   **Avoriaz** 295

4   **Les Écuries de Charamillon, Chamonix** 296

5   **Chamonix** 304

6   **Mont-Blanc Massif** 300

7   **Chalet Forestier de Rochebrune, Megève** 315

8   **Flumet** 318

9   **Thônes** 292

10   **Le Clos des Sens, Annecy-le-Vieux** 287

11   **Kamouraska, Annecy** 284

12   **Chartreuse Mountains** 321

13   **Grenoble** 291

14   **Alpe d'Huez** 323

15   **La Bouitte, Saint-Martin-de-Belleville** 311

16   **Courchevel** 307

17   **Val d'Isère** 308

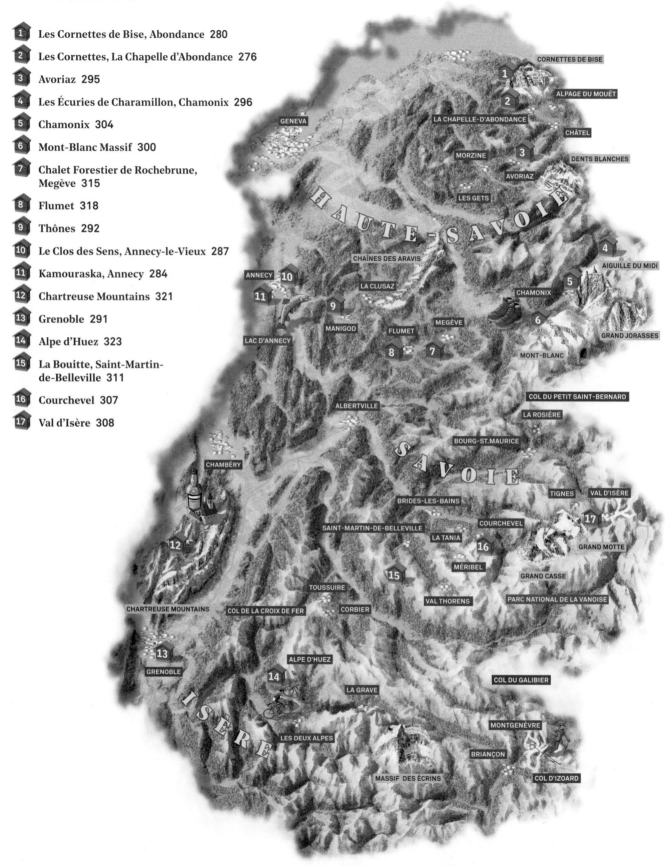

FURTHER ALPINE READING

Following are some of my favorite Alpine books (excluding guidebooks) across genres.

The Alps: A Cultural History by Andrew Beattie (SIGNAL BOOKS, 2006)

The Auberge of the Flowering Hearth by Roy Andries de Groot (ECCO, 1996)

Byron and the Romantics in Switzerland by Elma Dangerfield (ASCENT BOOKS, 1978)

Cuisine Alpine by Andreas Döllerer (D + R HOLDING GMBH, 2015)

The Dolomites and Their Legends by Karl Felix Wolff (VOGELWEIDER BOLZANO, 1930)

A Farewell to Arms by Ernest Hemingway (SCRIBNER, 1929)

Frankenstein by Mary Shelley (LACKINGTON, HUGHES, HARDING, MAVOR & JONES, 1818)

Heidi by Johanna Spyri (ORIGINALLY PUBLISHED IN 1881; NUMEROUS EDITIONS)

Killing Dragons: The Conquest of the Alps by Fergus Fleming (ATLANTIC MONTHLY PRESS, 2002)

Das Kulinarische Erbe der Alpen by Dominik Flammer (GERMAN VERSION ONLY; VERLAG, 2012)

Manfred: A Dramatic Poem by Lord Byron (JOHN MURRAY, 1817)

Premier de Cordée: Suivi de la Grande Crevasse, et de Retour à la Montagne, a trilogy by Roger Frison-Roche (FRENCH VERSION ONLY; ARTHAUD, 1942, 1948, 1957)

Scrambles Amongst the Alps by Edward Whymper (JOHN MURRAY, 1871)

Slow Train to Switzerland by Diccon Bewes (NICHOLAS BREALEY PUBLISHING, 2014)

Swiss Cheese: Origins, Traditional Cheese Varieties and New Creations by Dominik Flammer and Fabian Scheffold (SHOPPENKOCHEN, 2010)

Voyage au Coeur des Alpes by Jean Blanchard and Léo Garin (FRENCH VERSION ONLY; GLÉNAT, 2007)

White Spider by Heinrich Harrer (RUPER HART-DAVIS, 1959)

ADDRESS BOOK

These listings, organized by region, are a mix of family-run inns, rifugios, and hotels where I stayed during the six years of traveling I did for this book. The list is by no means exhaustive. I have stayed at places in all rating categories (from 2 to 5 stars), including shared rooms at 2,000 meters (6,550 feet) with no running water as well as Princess-treatment suites. My only requirement is that the accommodation be unique (not generic) and have a sense of place.

If survivalism and adventure (for example, an isolated rifugio at altitude with a kitchen and little running water) is more your speed, this website is a good resource for shelters: www.refuges.info/nav.

An asterisk [*] denotes that the property is accessible by foot or train only (not by car). Please see an accommodation's website for detailed arrival information.

ITALY

Parkhotel Laurin
Via Laurino 4, 39100 Bolzano BZ, Italy

Ottmanngut
Via Giuseppe Verdi 18,
39012 Merano BZ, Italy

Hotel Bavaria
Via Salita Alla Chiesa 15,
39012 Merano BZ, Italy

San Luis Lodge
Vöranerstraße 5,
39010 Avelengo Bozen, Italy

Fichtenhof
Cauria 23, 39040 Cauria,
Salorno BZ, Italy

Albergo Briol
Via Briol 1, 39040 Barbiano BZ, Italy

da Aurelio Ristorante
Passo Giau, 5
32020 Colle Santa Lucia, BL, Italy

Hotel Splendid
Via Clotes 71, 10050 Sauze d'Oulx
TO, Italy

Hotel Ciao Pais
Via Case Sparse 17,
10050 Sauze d'Oulx TO, Italy

Hotel la Torre
Via della Torre 4,
10050 Sauze d'Oulx TO, Italy

Hotel Monterosa
Piazza degli Alberghi,12,
13021 Alagna Valsesia VC, Italy

Bellevue Hotel & Spa—Cogne
Rue Grand Paradis, 22,
11012 Cogne AO

Hotel Gran Baita
Strada Castello Savoia 26,
11025 Gressoney-Saint-Jean AO, Italy

Auberge de La Maison
Frazione, 11013 Entreves AO, Italy

l'Hotel Ristorante Lavachey
Localita' Lavachey, 1 Val Ferret,
11013 Courmayeur AO, Italy

Hotel Courmayeur
Via Roma 158,
11013 Courmayeur, Italy

Hotel Hermitage
Via Piolet 1,
11021 Cervinia AO, Italy

Les Neiges D'Antan
Fraz Cret De Perreres 10,
11021 Cervinia AO, Italy

Hotel Baita Cretaz*
Loc. Campetto 1,
11021 Breuil-Cervinia,
Valtournenche AO, Italy

Franceschi Park Hotel
Via Cesare Battisti 86,
32043 Cortina d'Ampezzo BL, Italy

Hotel & Spa Rosa Alpina
Strada Micurà de Rü 20,
39030 San Cassiano in Badia BZ, Italy

Rifugio Fuciade
Localita Fuciade,
38030 Passo San Pellegrino,
Soraga TN, Italy

Ciasa Salares
Strada Prè de Vì 31,
39030 San Cassiano BZ, Italy

Berghotel Ladinia
Strada Pé de Corvara 10,
39033 Corvara In Badia BZ, Italy

Alpenroyal Grand Hotel
Strada Meisules 43,
39048 Selva di Val Gardena BZ, Italy

La Fiorida
Via Lungo Adda, 12,
23016 Mantello SO

AUSTRIA

Almhof Schneider
Tannberg 59, 6764 Lech, Austria

Hotel Lech
Dorf 263, 6764 Lech, Austria

Hotel Tannenhof
Nassereinerstraße 98,
6580 St. Anton am Arlberg, Austria

Hospiz Alm
St. Christoph 18, 6580 St. Anton am
Arlberg, Austria

Après Post Hotel Stuben
Stuben 17, 6762 Stuben am Arlberg,
Austria

Hotel Zur Post
Alpbach 184, 6236 Alpbach, Austria

Resterhöhe Berggasthas & Lodge
Passthurn 19, 5730 Mittersill, Austria

Hotel Rasmushof
Hermann Reisch Weg 15, 6370
Kitzbühel, Austria

Hotel Resch
Alfons-Petzold-Weg 2, 6370
Kitzbühel, Austria

Das Central
Auweg 3, 6450 Sölden, Austria

Hinterkaiserhof
Kaisertal 10, Ebbs, Tirol, Austria 6341

Naturhotel Forsthofgut
Hütten 2, 5771 Leogang, Austria

Angerer Alm
Berglehen 53, 6380 St. Johann in
Tirol, Austria

Jagdschloss Kuhtai
Kühtai 1, 6183 Kühtai, Austria

Restaurant-Hotel Obauer
Markt 46, 5450 Werfen, Austria

Gasthof Weisses Rössl
Kiebachgasse 8, 6020 Innsbruck,
Austria

Wedelhütte, Katelbach*
Hochzillertal Piste 13 / Wedelexpress
oder, 6272 Kaltenbach, Austria

Döllerer Hotel
Markt 56, 5440 Golling an der
Salzach, Austria

Hotel Sacher Salzburg
Schwarzstraße 5-7, 5020 Salzburg,
Austria

SWITZERLAND

Berggasthaus Rotsteinpass
CH-9057 Weissbad, Switzerland

Alpenblick Hotel
Oberdorfstrasse 106, 3920 Zermatt,
Switzerland

Riffelalp Hotel*
2,222 m, 3920 Zermatt, Switzerland

Piz Linard
Plazza Gronda 2, 7543 Zernez,
Switzerland

Hotel Wynegg
Landstrasse 205, 7250 Klosters-
Serneus, Switzerland

Hotel Bellevue Des Alpes*
3801 Kleine Scheidegg, Switzerland

Hotel Jungfrau Wengernalp*
3823 Wengernalp, Switzerland

Hotel Belvedere Wengen
Galliweidli 1440A, 3823 Wengen,
Switzerland

Berghof Hotel Amaranth
Oberdorfstrasse 23, 3812 Wilderswil,
Switzerland

Aspen Alpin
Aspen 1, 3818 Grindelwald,
Switzerland

Hotel Central Unterseen
Bahnhofstrasse 43, 3800 Interlaken,
Switzerland

Salzano Hotel
Seestrasse 108, 3800 Interlaken,
Switzerland

Hotel Chetzeron*
Rue de Chetzeron 2112, 3963
Crans-Montana, Switzerland

Hotel Alpina Grimentz
Route des Amis de la Nature 14, 3961
Grimentz, Switzerland

Hamilton Lodge*
3914 Belalp, Switzerland

Hotel Alpenland
Hinterseestrasse 5, 3782 Lauenen,
Gstaad, Switzerland

Le Grand Bellevue Gstaad
Untergstaadstrasse 17, 3780 Gstaad,
Switzerland

Gstaad Palace
Palacestrasse 28, 3780 Gstaad,
Switzerland

Hotel du Pillon
Les Bovets
CH—1865 Les Diablerets,
Switzerland

Experimental Chalet
Route de Verbier Station 55, 1936
Bagnes, Switzerland

Hotel Crans Montana La Prairie
Route de la Prairie 34, 3963
Crans-Montana, Switzerland

Carlton St. Moritz
Via Johannes Badrutt 11, 7500
St. Moritz, Switzerland

Hotel Villa Flor
Villa Flor, Somvih 19, 7525 S-chanf,
Switzerland

Badrutt's Palace
Via Serlas 27, 7500 St. Moritz,
Switzerland

Cabane Mont-Fort*
Tortin, 1936 Bagnes, Switzerland
(near the village of Verbier)

Chalet de Flore
Rue de Médran 20, 1936 Verbier,
Switzerland

Albergo Ospizio Bernina
Via Dal Bernina 2371, 7710 Poschiavo,
Switzerland

Refuge Diavolezza
Talstation Diavolezza, 7504 Pontresina,
Switzerland

Grand Hotel Villa Castagnola
Viale Castagnola 31, 6900 Lugano,
Switzerland

Best Western Hotel du Lac
Riva Antonio Caccia 10, 6900 Lugano,
Switzerland

FRANCE

Les Cornettes
18-D22
74360 La Chapelle-d'Abondance,
France

Le Clos des Sens
Rue Jean Mermoz,
74940 Annecy-le-Vieux, France

L'Auberge de Père Bise
303 Crêt Road, 74290
Talloires-Montmin, France

Flocons de Sel
1775 Route du Leutaz, 74120
Megève, France

Alpaga
66 Allée des Marmousets, 74120
Megève, France

Refuge du Plan de l'Aiguille
Unnamed Road
(see refuge-plan-aiguille.com) 74400,
Chamonix-Mont-Blanc, France

Hotel Hameau Albert 1er
38 Route du Bouchet, 74400
Chamonix-Mont-Blanc, France

Hotel Le Fitz Roy
Place de l'Eglise, 73440 Val Thorens,
France

La Ferme des Vonezins
Le Planet route de Glapigny, 74230
Thônes, France

Chalet Hotel de L'Adray Telebar
73550 Les Allues (Meribel), France

La Bouitte
3440 Hameau de St Marcel, 73440
Saint-Martin-de-Belleville, France

Hôtel les Bruyères
Quartier Les Bruyères, 73440
Les Menuires,
Saint-Martin-de-Belleville, France

Marc Veyrat Maison de Bois
Col de la Croix-Fry, 74230 Manigod,
France

Hôtel des Dromonts
40 Place des Dromonts, 74110
Avoriaz, France

Hôtel Le Sporting
34 Route des Nants, 74110
Morzine, France

Chalet Hôtel Alpen Valley
2843 Route de la Cry Cuchet, 74920
Combloux, France

Hôtel Restaurant Relais du Petit
Saint Bernard La Rosière 1850, 73700
Montvalezan, France

Le Portetta
234 Rue de la Rosière, 73120
Saint-Bon-Tarentaise, France

Aman Le Melezin
310 Rue de Bellecôte, 73120
Saint-Bon-Tarentaise, France

Les Monts Charvin
Impasse des Verdons, 73120
Saint-Bon-Tarentaise, France

Le Grand Hôtel Grenoble
5 rue de la République, Grenoble,
France

Hotel Le Chamois
164 Chemin de la Chapelle, 38750
Huez, France

ACKNOWLEDGMENTS

Thank you to all the chefs and *maîtres de maisons* (hosts) who opened their hearths and hearts to me.

Thank you to Christina Holmes for bringing this book to life. You immediately understood the tone and energy of this project, and your images stand out beautifully. My sidekick over the course of two years, thank you for your dedication over thousands of miles and across many mountains high.

Thank you to Kendra McKnight for your sharp eyes, tireless recipe testing, and support—both emotional and professional—over the last six years of this project.

To Kristian Kahn, thank you for your deep research, your organizing of dozens of trips, and your support while I was "on the ground" . . . and your irreplaceable sense of humor. I really could not have done this project without you.

Thank you to Renato Ferola for your kindness, generosity, and being my ride-or-die. You made this book fun during a time when it could have been otherwise. Undying gratitude for getting me down the metaphysical mountain.

Thank you to my three parents, Irwin Erickson and Mary and Paul McArthur, for guiding me since, well, birth, and supporting this project in the moments when it seemed like a very bad idea indeed.

To my close friends, Joe and Erin Battat, for morning coffee club and all the love.

Thank you to my good pal Fred Morin for your collaboration on the France chapter. Your cooking and long phone calls were well appreciated during this solo journey.

Thank you to Dagmar Wollmann for your translation of a handful of Austrian recipes.

Thank you to Julie Bennett for your patience and understanding.

And thank you to Aaron Wehner and Kimberly Witherspoon for believing.

Thank you to Melis Bischofberger and the Bischofberger Gallery for allowing the use of the beautiful photos.

Thank you to Betsy Stromberg for design and Sam Bucheli for your gorgeous map illustrations.

Thank you to Doug Ogan for your editorial work and to Jane Chinn for production. Also to Andrea Chesman for your copyedit.

Thank you to the following tourism boards for your support: Alpbach, Alto Adige (specifically, Deborah Carlin), Aosta (Elizabeth and Claudine David), Cervinia, Chamonix, Gstaad (Antje Buchs), Kitzbühel, Klösters, Lech (Fabienne Kienreich), Salzburg, Sauze d'Oulx, Tyrol (Barbara Wurzer), Valais, Werfen Tourism, and Zermatt.

INDEX

A

Abbaye de Tamié, 284
Abondance Salad, 276–79
advice, 15
Aescher-Wildkirchli, Berggasthaus, 253, 257
Agnelli, Giovanni, 80
Agnolotti, Piedmontese-Style, 76–79
airports, 268
Alagna, 66, 69
Aletsch Glacier, 196
Allera, David and Elisabeth, 91
Almabtrieb cattle procession, 133
Almhof Schneider, 101, 166, 168, 175
Alpage du Mouet, 274
Alpe d'Huez, 267, 272, 322, 323
Alpenblick, 200
Alpenland, Hotel, 200, 228
Alpina, Hotel, 199
Alpine Arch, 8, 9
Alpine clubs, 15
AlpiNN, 49
Alps
    accessibility of, 7
    altitudinal zones of, 8
    cuisine of, 9
    formation of, 7
    geography of, 9, 21, 24, 105–6, 195, 267–68
Alter Goldener Berg, 106, 108, 171, 172
Anderson, Wes, 103
angelica, 320
Aosta Preserves Trolley, 95
apples
    Apple Horseradish, 115
    Apple Strudel, 175–76
    Toggi-Schnitzel with Apple-Chive Slaw, 250–51
Après Post Hotel, 106
Apricot Dumplings, 166
arctic char
    Smoked Char, Col Alt–Style, 46
Aspingerhof Farm, 63
Auberge de La Maison, 84, 88–89
Auberge du Père Bise, 320
Autoverlad, 197
Avoriaz, 268

B

Bäckerei Konditorei Vincenz, 196
bacon
    Farçon Savoyard, 296–99
    Herdsman Macaroni, 228
    Tartiflette, 292
    Valpelline Soup, 87
    Veal Carbonnade with Polenta, 84–86
Bad Gastein, 103, 105
Bakery Hanselmann, 203
Bärenwirt, 103
Baronetto, Matteo, 76, 79
Barrero, Anna, 267
Bavaria, Hotel, 28
beans
    Aosta Preserves Trolley, 95
    Ditalini with Fava Beans, 92
Beck-Hartweg, Florian and Mathilde, 319
beef
    Abondance Salad, 276–79
    Aosta Preserves Trolley, 95
    Cured Beef with Génépy, 291
    Gobbi in Broth, 71–72
    Hangover Soup with Cheese Dumplings, 139
    Meranerwürstel, 36–39
    Raclette, 240–43
    Sofie's Goulash with Speck Dumplings, 41–42
    Tafelspitz, 115–16
    Tyrolean Hash, 148
beets
    Beet and Arugula Slaw, 255
    Beet and Poppy-Seed Casunziei, 64
    Beet Gnocchi, 48–49
    Salsify Soup, 215
    Smoked Trout with Cabbage and Beet Tagliatelle, 235–36
Bellevue des Alpes, Hotel de (Kleine Scheidegg), 194, 196
Bellevue Hotel & Spa (Cogne), 24, 54–55, 92
Bellevue Hotel (Gstaad), 212
Berggasthaus Aescher-Wildkirchli, 253, 257
Berggasthaus Ebenalp, 257
Berggasthaus Forelle, 256, 257
Berggasthaus Rotsteinpass, 220
Berggasthof Sonnbühel, 179

Berthoud, 279
Beurre Blanc Sauce, 287–88
Bich, Ludo, 95
Bich, Maurizio, 95
Bigot, Jérôme, 284, 291, 295
Billia, Rino, 54, 92
Bioch Hütte, 24
Bischofberger, Bruno, 246
blueberries
    Rosettes with Berries, 227
    Savoie Cake, 295
Blue Trout, 256
Bogner, Willy, Jr., 155
Bolzano, 23, 28, 32
Bombardino, 65
Bond films, 159
Bonèt, Torinese, 80–83
La Bouitte, 271, 311
brandy
    Bombardino, 65
    Monaco Bombardino, 65
    Pirata Bombardino, 65
bread
    Bread Soup with Chicory and Egg, 57–58
    Cogne-Style Soup, 91
    Croutons, 58
    Ditalini with Fava Beans, 92
    Fondue Brioche, 308–9
    Popcorn Bread, 311
    Puccia Bread, 58
    Radicchio Dumplings, 45
    Speck Dumplings, 42
    Tomme Tartine, 315
    Valpelline Soup, 87
    Wine Cave Fonduta, 52
    See also rolls
Breuer, Marcel, 268
El Brite de Larieto, 21, 57, 59, 64
Bullshot, A Proper, 245
butter
    Alpine Butter Ball, 312
    clarifying, 146
Byron, Lord, 220

C

Cabane des Violettes, 186
cabbage
    Cabbage Tart with Smoked Whitefish, 287–88

Smoked Trout with Cabbage and
Beet Tagliatelle, 235–36
Valpelline Soup, 87
Café des Alpes, 236
Café Hacker, 135
Cairo, Eli, 108, 200
cakes
Farçon Savoyard, 296–99
Norwegian Omelet, 280–83
Quark Cake with Peaches, 151–52
Savoie Cake, 295
Torinese Bonèt, 80–83
Tyrolean Cake on a Spit, 135–36
Caloz, Sandrine, 186, 240
Camineto, El, 57
Il Capricorno, Chalet, 27, 71, 75
Carestia, Antonio, 24
Carezzana family, 71
Carrel, Jean-Antoine, 96
car rentals, 15
Carrot Rémoulade, 254
Casunziei, Beet and Poppy-Seed, 64
Chalet Etoile, 200
Chalet Forestier de Rochebrune, 315
Chalet Il Capricorno, 27, 71, 75
Châlet Savoyard, 318
Chamois Pie, 220–23
Chamonix, 16, 271
Champagne Fondue, 208
Chantilly Cream, 295
Chartreuse, 271
Chartreuse Soufflé, 320
Chateau Branlant, 87
Château de Villa, 240
cheese
Abondance Salad, 276–79
Alpine Butter Ball, 312
Aosta Preserves Trolley, 95
Apricot Dumplings, 166
Beet and Poppy-Seed Casunziei, 64
Berthoud, 279
Cheese Spaetzle, 171–72
Cogne-Style Soup, 91
Ditalini with Fava Beans, 92
Fondue, 207–9
Fondue Brioche, 308–9
French varieties of, 269
Gobbi in Broth, 71–72
Grape and Walnut Pizokel, 259–60
Hangover Soup with Cheese
Dumplings, 139
Herdsman Macaroni, 228
Mont-Blanc Tart, 300–303
Piedmontese-Style Agnolotti,
76–79
Pinzgauer Kasnochen, 172
Quark Cake with Peaches, 151–52
Raclette, 240–43
Radicchio Dumplings, 45

Reblochon Baked Potato, 279
Savoie-Style Mushrooms, 318
Spiced Cheese Spread, 140
Spinach and Cheese Mezzaluna,
60–63
Swiss varieties of, 202
Tartiflette, 292
Toggi-Schnitzel with Apple-Chive
Slaw, 250–51
Tomme Tartine, 315
Valpelline Soup, 87
Vittorio's Paccheri, 248
Wine Cave Fonduta, 52
Chesery, 200, 207, 220
chestnuts
Chamois Pie, 220–23
Mont-Blanc Tart, 300–303
Chez Vrony, 198, 238
Chicory, Bread Soup with Egg and,
57–58
chocolate
Hot Chocolate with Alpine
Herbs, 211
Torinese Bonèt, 80–83
Ciasa Salares, 52, 92
Clems and Fabs, 199
Le Clos des Sens, 287, 316
Cogne, 24
Cogne-Style Soup, 91
Col Alt, 26, 30, 31, 46
Cook, Thomas, 271
corn
Popcorn Bread, 311
Les Cornettes, 268, 276, 280, 282,
283, 295
Les Cosmos, 200
Crayfish with Tarragon
Mayonnaise, 284
Croissants, Hazelnut, 231–32
Croutons, 58
Cucumber Salad, 255
currants
Cured Beef with Génépy, 291
Duck Magret with Pont-Neuf
Polenta, 304
Poppy-Seed and Currant Roll,
155–56
Curtet, Florian and Marie, 307

D
Daikon, Marinated, 254
Dallmayr, 108
Da Vittorio, 203, 248
Del Cambio, 27, 76
Demel, 107
Derout, Franck, 286
desserts
Apple Strudel, 175–76
Apricot Dumplings, 166

Chartreuse Soufflé, 320
Honey Semifreddo with Bee
Pollen, 66
Kaiserschmarrn, 161
Mont-Blanc Tart, 300–303
Norwegian Omelet, 280–83
Polka Dot Paris-Brest, 323–24
Pumpkin Seed Oil Sundae, 50
Quark Cake with Peaches, 151–52
Ricola Ice Cream, 261
Rosettes with Berries, 227
Salzburger Nockerl, 118
Savoie Cake, 295
Torinese Bonèt, 80–83
Tyrolean Cake on a Spit, 135–36
Destivelle, Catherine, 291
Les Diablerets, 200
Dimo, Salvatore, 66
Ditalini with Fava Beans, 92
Döllerer, 103, 114, 120
Döllerer, Andreas, 48, 114, 120
Dolomieu, Déodat de, 28
Dolomites, 9, 28–30
drinks
Bombardino, 65
Hot Chocolate with Alpine
Herbs, 211
Monaco Bombardino, 65
Pine Schnapps, 125
Pirata Bombardino, 65
A Proper Bullshot, 245
Spring Rhubarb Cocktail, 129
duck
Abondance Salad, 276–79
Aosta Preserves Trolley, 95
Duck Magret with Pont-Neuf
Polenta, 304
dumplings
Apricot Dumplings, 166
Hangover Soup with Cheese
Dumplings, 139
Huckleberry Dumplings, 114
Radicchio Dumplings, 45
Speck Dumplings, 42

E
Ebenalp, Berggasthaus, 257
Les Écuries de Charamillon, 271, 296
eggs, 319
Bread Soup with Chicory and Egg,
57–58
Chartreuse Soufflé, 320
Norwegian Omelet, 280–83
Tyrolean Hash, 148
Eisriesenwelt, 136
Esnault, Eric, 272
Etoile, Chalet, 200

F

Faeh, Franz, 215
Farçon Savoyard, 296–99
Farmerhaus, 238
Feinkost Egger, 28
Fenoglio, Andrea, 28
Fichtenhof, 27–28, 45, 95
fish
    Aosta Preserves Trolley, 95
    Blue Trout, 256
    Cabbage Tart with Smoked
        Whitefish, 287–88
    Roussette-Poached Trout, 307
    Smoked Char, Col Alt–Style, 46
    Smoked Trout with Cabbage and
        Beet Tagliatelle, 235–36
    Vitello Tonnato, 75
Fitness Salad, 254–55
Fleming, Ian, 159
Flocons de Sel, 271, 315, 317
Fluhalp, 238
Fondue, 207–9
    Champagne Fondue, 208
    Fondue Brioche, 308–9
Fonduta, Wine Cave, 52
Foradori, Elisabetta, 95, 186, 187
Forelle, Berggasthaus, 256, 257
Forestier de Rochebrune, Chalet, 315
Le Four à Bois des Aravis, 318
Foyer des Guides, 96
Frison-Roche, Roger, 307

G

Gahleitner, Michael, 115, 116
Galerie Bruno Bischofberger, 246
Gampe Thaya, 161, 165
Garin, Léo and Alessandra, 84, 88
Gaspari, Riccardo and Ludovica,
    57, 58
Gasser, Harald, 63
Gässli-Beck, 231
Génépy, Cured Beef with, 291
gin
    Spring Rhubarb Cocktail, 129
Gnocchi, Beet, 48–49
Gobbi in Broth, 71–72
Gonin, Nicholas, 304
Gostner Schwaige, 30, 103
Goulash with Speck Dumplings,
    Sofie's, 41–42
Grape and Walnut Pizokel, 259–60
grappa
    Pine Schnapps, 125
Gray, Patience, 320
Grenoble, 270, 271–72
Griffa, Paolo, 80, 300
Grolet, Cédric, 300
Gros, Piero, 11, 72
Gstaad Palace, 208, 215, 217

H

Habeler, Peter, 35
Hacker, Reihard, 135
Hahnenkamm, 105
ham
    Abondance Salad, 276–79
    Toggi-Schnitzel with Apple-Chive
        Slaw, 250–51
    Tomme Tartine, 315
    Wine Cave Fonduta, 52
    See also pancetta; speck
Hangover Soup with Cheese
    Dumplings, 139
Hash, Tyrolean, 148
hazelnuts
    Hazelnut Croissants, 231–32
    Honey Semifreddo with Bee
        Pollen, 66
Herb Sauce, Mixed, 239
Herdsman Macaroni, 228
Hermitage, Hotel, 63
Hoch, Christoph, 208
Honey Semifreddo with Bee Pollen, 66
horseradish
    Apple Horseradish, 115
    Beet Gnocchi, 48–49
hotels, lodges, and inns
    address book for, 335–37
    Almhof Schneider, 101, 166,
        168, 175
    Alpenblick, 200
    Après Post Hotel, 106
    Auberge de La Maison, 84, 88–89
    Auberge du Père Bise, 320
    Bellevue Hotel (Cogne), 24,
        54–55, 92
    Bellevue Hotel (Gstaad), 212
    Berggasthaus Forelle, 256, 257
    Berggasthaus Rotsteinpass, 220
    Berggasthof Sonnbühel, 179
    Chalet Il Capricorno, 27, 71, 75
    Les Cornettes, 268, 276, 280, 282,
        283, 295
    as family businesses, 10–11
    Gampe Thaya, 161
    Gstaad Palace, 208, 215, 217, 218
    Hotel Alpenland, 200, 228
    Hotel Alpina, 199
    Hotel Bavaria, 28
    Hotel de Bellevue des Alpes,
        194, 196
    Hotel Hermitage, 63
    Hotel Jungfrau Wengernalp, 196
    Hotel La Torre, 27, 80
    Hotel Monterosa, 66
    Hotel Piz Linard, 197, 200, 201
    Hotel Sacher, 103, 115, 116
    Hotel Splendid, 27
    Hotel Wynegg, 259
    Klösterle, 106, 175
    Krone, 95
    Kulm Hotel, 203, 245
    Lou Ressignon, 24, 91
    Miramonti Majestic, 159
    Ottmanngut Merano, 35
    Palace Henri Chenot, 28
    La Perla Hotel, 92
    Resterhöhe Berggasthaus & Lodge,
        139, 143
    Rosa Alpina, 35, 48, 49, 50, 106,
        120, 136
    Salzano, 199, 235
    San Luis Hotel, 34, 35
    Sonnleitner, 125
    Therme Vals, 251
Huckleberry Dumplings, 114

I

ice cream
    Norwegian Omelet, 280–83
    Pumpkin Seed Oil Sundae, 50
    Ricola Ice Cream, 261
Ice Q, 155, 159
inns. See hotels, lodges, and inns

J

Jancou, Pierre, 236
Jungfrau Wengernalp, Hotel, 196

K

Kaiserschmarrn, 161
Kamouraska, 284, 295
Kasnochen, Pinzgauer, 172
Kirchlechner, Martin, 35
Kitzbühel, 105, 140, 159, 179
Klaffenböck, Otto, 122
Kleine Scheidegg, 195–96
Klösterle, 106, 175
Krone, 95
Kronenhalle, 212
Kulm Hotel, 203, 245

L

Lageder, Alois, 186
Laite, 64
Landhaus-Kellerwand, 125
Lauberhorn, 105, 195
Lavertezzo, 7
lettuce
    Abondance Salad, 276–79
    for salads, 317
    Tomme Tartine, 315
Linse, Joakim and Tine Guth, 66

liver
  Pan-Fried Calf Liver, 239
  Tyrolean Liver Salad, 126
lodges. *See* hotels, lodges, and inns
Lorival, Thomas, 287
Lou Ressignon, 24, 91
Lumen Museum of Mountain Photography, 49

M

Maison des Bois, 318
maps, 15, 329–32
Marchand-Arvier, Marie, 299
Marchesi, Gualtiero, 76
Marsala
  Bombardino, 65
  Monaco Bombardino, 65
  Pirata Bombardino, 65
Mateo, 28
Mayonnaise, Tarragon, 284
Meilleur, René and Maxime, 311, 312
Meranerwürstel, 36–39
Merano, 28, 36, 39
Messner, Reinhold, 11, 35
Messner Mountain Museum, 35
Metullio, Matteo, 52
Mezzaluna, Spinach and Cheese, 60–63
Miramonti Majestic, 159
Monaco Bombardino, 65
Mont-Blanc Tart, 300–303
Monterosa, Hotel, 66
Morin, Fred, 135, 307
Moroder, Giorgio, 38
Muesli, 35
Mulser, Franz, 30, 103
museums
  Lumen Museum of Mountain Photography, 49
  Messner Mountain Museum, 35
mushrooms
  Chamois Pie, 220–23
  Pickled Mushrooms, 279
  Savoie-Style Mushrooms, 318
  Veal Strips in Cream Sauce, Zürich Style, 212

N

Les Neiges d'Antan, 95
Niederkofler, Norbert, 48, 49, 51, 120, 136
Norwegian Omelet, 280–83
Nussbaumer, Hans, 203

O

oats
  Muesli, 35
Obauer, Karl and Rudolf, 30, 103, 136
Olympia Provisions, 108, 200
Omelet, Norwegian, 280–83
Ottmanngut Merano, 35

P

Paccheri, Vittorio's, 248
Palace Henri Chenot, 28
pancetta
  Bread Soup with Chicory and Egg, 57–58
Pan & Gatô, 284
Paradies, 238
Pardatscher, Ingrid, 45
Paris-Brest, Polka Dot, 323–24
pasta and noodles
  Beet and Poppy-Seed Casunziei, 64
  Cheese Spaetzle, 171–72
  Ditalini with Fava Beans, 92
  Gobbi in Broth, 71–72
  Grape and Walnut Pizokel, 259–60
  Herdsman Macaroni, 228
  Piedmontese-Style Agnolotti, 76–79
  Pinzgauer Kasnochen, 172
  Smoked Trout with Cabbage and Beet Tagliatelle, 235–36
  Spinach and Cheese Mezzaluna, 60–63
  Vittorio's Paccheri, 248
Pastry Dough, Sour-Cream, 223
Pavese, Ermes, 95, 181, 184
Peaches, Quark Cake with, 151–52
La Perla Hotel, 92
Péron, Jean-Yves, 184, 186, 284
Petit, Laurent, 287, 288
Le Petit Restaurant, 54
Petit Royal, 300
Piedmontese-Style Agnolotti, 76–79
Pine Schnapps, 125
Pinzgauer Kasnochen, 172
Pirata Bombardino, 65
pistachios
  Polka Dot Paris-Brest, 323–24
pistes, classification system for, 11
Piz Gloria, 159
Piz Linard, Hotel, 197, 200, 201
Pizokel, Grape and Walnut, 259–60
Pizzinini, Hugo, 35, 48, 49
Plank, Klaus, 148
Pliot, Stéphane, 276
Polenta, 86
  Duck Magret with Pont-Neuf Polenta, 304

Veal Carbonnade with Polenta, 84–86
Polka Dot Paris-Brest, 323–24
Popcorn Bread, 311
Poppy-Seed and Currant Roll, 155–56
pork
  Gobbi in Broth, 71–72
  Meranerwürstel, 36
  Piedmontese-Style Agnolotti, 76–79
  Toggi-Schnitzel with Apple-Chive Slaw, 250–51
  Weisswurst, aka The Münchener, 108–11
  See also bacon; ham; pancetta; speck
potatoes
  Beet and Poppy-Seed Casunziei, 64
  Beet Gnocchi, 48–49
  Farçon Savoyard, 296–99
  Hangover Soup with Cheese Dumplings, 139
  Herdsman Macaroni, 228
  Potatoes and Chives, 255
  Raclette, 240–43
  Reblochon Baked Potato, 279
  Rösti, 253
  Roussette-Poached Trout, 307
  Tartiflette, 292
  Tyrolean Hash, 148
Prantl, Jakob, 161
Prinoth, Markus, 41
Prinoth, Sofie, 41, 42
A Proper Bullshot, 245
prunes
  Farçon Savoyard, 296–99
Puccia Bread, 58
puff pastry
  Cabbage Tart with Smoked Whitefish, 287–88
  Hazelnut Croissants, 231–32
Pumpkin Seed Oil Sundae, 50

Q

Quark Cake with Peaches, 151–52

R

Raclette, 240–43
Radicchio Dumplings, 45
railway routes, 197, 204
raisins
  Farçon Savoyard, 296–99
  Poppy-Seed and Currant Roll, 155–56
Rauscher, Philipp, 139
Reblochon Baked Potato, 279
Renaut, Emmanuel, 315, 317

restaurants
  AlpiNN, 49
  Alter Goldener Berg, 106, 108,
    171, 172
  Auberge de La Maison, 84, 88–89
  Auberge du Père Bise, 320
  Bärenwirt, 103
  Berggasthaus Aescher-Wildkirchli,
    253, 257
  Berggasthaus Ebenalp, 257
  Berggasthaus Forelle, 256, 257
  La Bouitte, 271, 311
  Branlant, Chateau, 87
  El Brite de Larieto, 21, 57, 59
  Cabane des Violettes, 186
  Café des Alpes, 236
  El Camineto, 57
  Chalet Etoile, 200
  Chalet Forestier de
    Rochebrune, 315
  Chalet Il Capricorno, 27, 71, 75
  Châlet Savoyard, 318
  Chateau Branlant, 87
  Château de Villa, 240
  Chesery, 200, 207, 220
  Chez Vrony, 198, 238
  Clems and Fabs, 199
  Le Clos des Sens, 287, 316
  Les Cornettes, 268, 276, 280, 282,
    283, 295
  Les Cosmos, 200
  Dallmayr, 108
  Da Vittorio, 203, 248
  Del Cambio, 27, 76
  Döllerer, 114, 120
  Les Écuries de Charamillon,
    271, 296
  as family businesses, 10–11
  Farmerhaus, 238
  Fichtenhof, 27–28, 45, 95
  Flocons de Sel, 271, 315, 317
  Fluhalp, 238
  Foyer des Guides, 96
  Gostner Schwaige, 30, 103
  Ice Q, 155, 159
  Kamouraska, 284, 295
  Kronenhalle, 212
  Laite, 64
  Lou Ressignon, 24, 91
  Maison des Bois, 318
  Mateo, 28
  Les Neiges d'Antan, 95
  Paradies, 238
  Le Petit Restaurant, 54
  Petit Royal, 300
  Piz Gloria, 159
  Restaurant Obauer, 103, 136
  Restaurant Sissi, 28
  Salzano, 199, 235
  Sigwart's Tiroler Weinstuben, 126
  La Siriola, 52
  Skihütte Schneggarei, 168
  Sofie Hütte, 41, 43
  Sonnleitner, 125
  St. Hubertus, 48
  Stump's Alpenrose, 200
  Valeriehaus, 122
  Whymper Stube, 200
  Zum See, 200, 238, 239
  Zum Weissen Kreuz, 212
  Zur Rose, 125
Resterhöhe Berggasthaus & Lodge,
  139, 143
rhubarb
  Rhubarb Syrup, 129
  Spring Rhubarb Cocktail, 129
rice
  Cogne-Style Soup, 91
Ricola Ice Cream, 261
Riente, Guido, 87
rifugios
  address book for, 335–37
  Bioch Hütte, 24
  Carestia, 24
  Col Alt, 26, 30, 31, 46
  Gabiet, 24
  Margherita, 24
  navigational website for, 15, 335
  Pastore, 27
  Scotoni Hütte, 30, 49
  Torino, 303
Ringgenberg, Christina, 196, 231
rolls
  Hazelnut Croissants, 231–32
  Poppy-Seed and Currant Roll,
    155–56
  Sweet Bread Rolls with Jam, 143
Rosa Alpina, Hotel & Spa, 35, 48, 49,
  50, 106, 120, 136
Rosettes with Berries, 227
Rösti, 253
Rotsteinpass, Berggasthaus, 220
Roullet, Laura, 92
Roussette-Poached Trout, 307
Route des Grandes Alpes, 273
rum
  Pirata Bombardino, 65

S

Sacher, Hotel, 103, 115, 116
salads
  Abondance Salad, 276–79
  Cucumber Salad, 255
  Fitness Salad, 254–55
  of herbs and flowers, 317
  Tyrolean Liver Salad, 126
  See also slaws
Salsify Soup, 215
Salzano, 199, 235
Salzburg, 103, 108, 118
Salzburger Nockerl, 118
Salzburger Würstelkönigin cart, 108
San Luis Hotel, 34, 35
sauces
  Beurre Blanc Sauce, 287–88
  Mixed Herb Sauce, 239
  Vanilla Sauce, 156
  Venison Glaze, 224
sausages
  Meranerwürstel, 36–39
  Piedmontese-Style Agnolotti,
    76–79
  types of, 113
  Weisswurst, aka The Münchener,
    108–11
Savoie Cake, 295
Savoie-Style Mushrooms, 318
Savoyard, Châlet, 318
Schnapps, Pine, 125
Schneider, Andi, 168
Schneider, Gerold and Katia, 168
Schneider, Hannelore, 175
schnitzel
  history of, 144
  Toggi-Schnitzel with Apple-Chive
    Slaw, 250–51
  variations of, 145
  Wiener Schnitzel, 144–46
Scotoni Hütte, 30, 49
Semifreddo, Honey, with Bee Pollen, 66
Sigwart, Anton, 104, 126
Sigwart, Traudi, 126
Sigwart's Tiroler Weinstuben, 126
La Siriola, 52
Sissi, Restaurant, 28
Skihütte Schneggarei, 168
slaws
  Apple-Chive Slaw, 250
  Beet and Arugula Slaw, 255
Sofie Hütte, 41, 43
Sofie's Goulash with Speck
  Dumplings, 41–42
Sonnbühel, Berggasthof, 179
Sonnleitner, 103, 125
Sonnleitner, Sissy, 103, 125
sorbet
  Norwegian Omelet, 280–83
Soufflé, Chartreuse, 320
soups
  Bread Soup with Chicory and Egg,
    57–58
  Cogne-Style Soup, 91
  Hangover Soup with Cheese
    Dumplings, 139
  Salsify Soup, 215
  Valpelline Soup, 87

Sour-Cream Pastry Dough, 223
Spaetzle, Cheese, 171–72
speck
  Radicchio Dumplings, 45
  Speck Dumplings, 42
  Toggi-Schnitzel with Apple-Chive
    Slaw, 250–51
Speth, Robert, 220, 222
spinach
  Creamed Spinach, 115, 116
  Piedmontese-Style Agnolotti,
    76–79
  Spinach and Cheese Mezzaluna,
    60–61
Splendid, Hotel, 27
Sportgastein, 105, 122
Spring Rhubarb Cocktail, 129
squash
  Chamois Pie, 220–23
Stelvio Wines, 267
St. Hubertus, 48
St. Moritz, 200, 203, 245
Stock, Venison, 224
strawberries
  Polka Dot Paris-Brest, 323–24
Strudel, Apple, 175–76
Stump's Alpenrose, 200
Sulpice, Jean, 320
Sutter family, 257
Syrup, Rhubarb, 129

T
Tafelspitz, 115–16
Targhetta, Fabio, 31
Tarragon Mayonnaise, 284
Tartiflette, 292
Tartine, Tomme, 315
tarts
  Cabbage Tart with Smoked
    Whitefish, 287–88
  Mont-Blanc Tart, 300–303
terminology, 16
Therme Vals, 251
tomatoes
  Ditalini with Fava Beans, 92
  Vittorio's Paccheri, 248
Tomme Tartine, 315
Torinese Bonèt, 80–83
Torino, 27, 76
La Torre, Hotel, 27, 80
Tour de France, 267, 272, 273,
    295, 323
trains, 197, 204
Trincaz, Jérémy, 268, 280, 282
trout
  Aosta Preserves Trolley, 95
  Blue Trout, 256

Roussette-Poached Trout, 307
  Smoked Trout with Cabbage and
    Beet Tagliatelle, 235–36
tuna
  Vitello Tonnato, 75
turnips
  Roussette-Poached Trout, 307
  Smoked Char, Col Alt–Style, 46
Tyrolean Cake on a Spit, 135–36
Tyrolean Hash, 148
Tyrolean Liver Salad, 126

V
Valentini, Markus, 24
Valeriehaus, 122
Valpelline Soup, 87
vanilla
  sugar, 118
  Vanilla Sauce, 156
veal
  Gobbi in Broth, 71–72
  Meranerwürstel, 36–39
  Pan-Fried Calf Liver, 239
  Piedmontese-Style Agnolotti,
    76–79
  Tyrolean Liver Salad, 126
  Veal Carbonnade with Polenta,
    84–86
  Veal Strips in Cream Sauce,
    Zürich Style, 212
  Vitello Tonnato, 75
  Wiener Schnitzel, 144–46
venison
  Chamois Pie, 220–23
  Tyrolean Liver Salad, 126
  Venison Glaze, 224
  Venison Ragout, 122
  Venison Stock, 224
Verzasca, 7
Vespani, Enrico, 31, 46
Veyrat, Marc, 273, 292, 318
Vienna, 101, 107
Le Vin des Alpes, 272
Vitello Tonnato, 75
Vittorio's Paccheri, 248
vodka
  A Proper Bullshot, 245
Vuarnet, Jean, 268

W
Walnut Pizokel, Grape and, 259–60
Wechsberg, Joseph, 107
Weisses Rössl, 148
Weisswurst, aka The Münchener,
    108–11
Whitefish, Smoked, Cabbage Tart
    with, 287–88

Whymper, Edward, 96, 200, 271
Whymper Stube, 200
Wiener Schnitzel, 144–46
Wieser, Jan Clemens, 52, 53
Wieser, Stefan, 52
wine, 181, 183–84, 186–87, 189–90
Wine Cave Fonduta, 52
Wynegg, Hotel, 259

Z
Zermatt, 199, 200, 238, 239
Zum See, 200, 238, 239
Zumthor, Peter, 251
Zum Weissen Kreuz, 212
Zur Rose, 125
Zweig, Stefan, 103

Published in the United States by Ten Speed Press, an imprint of
Random House, a division of Penguin Random House LLC, New York.
www.tenspeed.com

Ten Speed Press and the Ten Speed Press colophon are registered
trademarks of Penguin Random House LLC.

Library of Congress Cataloging-in-Publication Data
 Names: Erickson, Meredith, 1980- author. | Holmes, Christina, photographer.
 Title: Alpine cooking : recipes and stories from Europe's grand mountaintops
   / Meredith Erickson ; photographs by Christina Holmes.
 Description: California : Ten Speed Press, [2019] | Includes index.
 Identifiers: LCCN 2019016564 | ISBN 9781607748748 (hardcover) |
   ISBN 9781607748755 (ebook)
 Subjects: LCSH: Cooking—Alps Region. | Cooking, European. | LCGFT: Cookbooks.
 Classification: LCC TX723.5.A37 E75 2019 | DDC 641.59494/7—dc23
 LC record available at https://lccn.loc.gov/2019016564

Hardcover ISBN: 978-1-60774-874-8
eBook ISBN: 978-1-60774-875-5

Printed in China

Design by Betsy Stromberg
Photographs on pages 12–13, 30, 42, 45, and 120 by Meredith Erickson
Photograph on pages 216–217 courtesy of Gstaad Palace
Photographs on pages 309, 311, and 316 by Renato Ferola
Photograph on page 322 courtesy of the Tourism Board of Alpe d'Huez
Snapshot art by Claudio Divizia/Shutterstock.com
Travel Hack art by Yuriy Boyko/Shutterstock.com
Food and prop styling by Christina Holmes and Meredith Erickson
Recipe development and testing by Kendra McKnight
Alpine research assistance by Kristian Kahn

10 9 8 7 6

First Edition